Also by Allen Churchill:

The Incredible Ivar Kreuger
Park Row: Turn of the Century Newspaper Days
The Improper Bohemians: Greenwich Village in Its Heyday
The Year the World Went Mad: 1927
They Never Came Back: Eight People Who Vanished
The Great White Way: Broadway's Golden Era
A Pictorial History of American Crime: 1849–1929
The Roosevelts: American Aristocrats
Remember When: A Loving Look at Days Gone By
Over Here: The Homefront in World War I
The Upper Crust: An Informal History of New York's Highest Society
The Literary Decade: Writers and Writing of the 1920's
The Splendor Seekers: America's Multimillionaire Spenders

Edited by Allen Churchill:

All In Fun: An Anthology of Humor
The *Liberty* Years: An Anthology

THE THEATRICAL 20's

Allen Churchill

McGraw-Hill Book Company

New York   St. Louis   San Francisco

Book design by A Good Thing, Inc.

1 2 3 4 5 6 7 8 9 RABP 7 9 8 7 6 5

Library of Congress Cataloging in Publication Data

Churchill, Allen, date
The theatrical twenties.
Bibliography: p.
Includes index.
1. Theater–United States–History.   I. Title.
PN2266.C57   792'.0973   75-6789
ISBN 0-07-010860-9

The wondrous lovely madness of the night
went out of American life with the Twenties.
You are a lucky man if you got a taste of it.

George Jean Nathan

We all have a girl friend and her name is Nostalgia.

Ernest Hemingway

Contents

THE SCENE

In the entertainment world of the year 1920, the legitimate theatre was king.

The theatre fully dominated the glittering area around Times Square in New York City fondly known as Broadway, Times Square or the Great White Way. It also dominated theatre in the rest of the United States, for shows from Broadway toured profitably and tirelessly over the nationwide web of local theatres known as the Road, stopping in major cities for runs of months or weeks, in smaller towns for one-night stands. In just a few years there would be so many touring companies of the fabulously successful play *Abie's Irish Rose* that the author forbade any more. Even in the days of small-bite income taxes, the shows were bringing the lady too much money.

This, of course, was the era we are now pleased to call the Good Old Days. Few alive at the beginning of the decade dreamed of television or talking pictures, while radio was little more than a whisper in the wind. Yet before the decade ended radio and talking pictures would arrive, to the intense discomfiture of the theatre. In 1920 silent films had just succeeded in tossing off swaddling clothes, allowing the public to grow aware of the existence of a glamorous Hollywood. Vaudeville, which had entertained countless millions, was already sliding into a decline. This left the entertainment field as the major province of what *Variety*, the weekly bible of show biz, tersely called the legit.

On Broadway and in the hinterlands the theatre reigned supreme in the entertainment world. In the Times Square area seventy-six playhouses were available to producer and public; today there are fewer than forty. The Broadway theatre was so active that on some nights as many as five plays opened simultaneously.

In those halcyon days the average number of plays (including musical comedies, revues, and operettas) produced annually on Broadway was 225; in 1927, peak theatre year of the decade, the number was 268. Today we are lucky to have sixty. Because of this happy state of affairs so many eager theatregoers existed that there was a continuing audience for even moderate successes. Unlike the present time, people did not insist on seeing only hits. One writer sees the theatre of the Twenties as a seedbed of talent teeming with plays and players. Critic John Mason Brown has written, "Its aims were high, its costs were low, and happily its offerings were not condemned to being flops just because they were not hits."

But theatre in the Twenties was not entirely a paradise. Even then play production involved hazard and expense, although costs and actors' salaries were low. Of 100 plays offered on Broadway in those days, an average of seventy failed outright or did badly, while 30 percent hit the jackpot or were moderate successes. As for the Road, the memoirs of actors of the time are strewn with anecdotes of being stranded in the sticks.

But counteracting these dismal facts of life was the wonder in the air. Great and surprising things were happening to the theatre. Actresses like Katharine Cornell and actors like Leslie Howard suddenly appeared on the scene, along with striking, trail-blazing plays by Eugene O'Neill, Sidney Howard, and Maxwell Anderson. In the field of musical comedy, jazz burst in the air, while comedy brought forth newcomers like Beatrice Lillie, Fred Allen, and Bert Lahr to add a fresh dimension to lovely laughter.

Marc Connelly, most energetic survivor of the era, cites the singular lack of envy, resentment, or jealousy over the success of others. Everyone seemed united in a desire to brighten the Broadway scene. "We threw our hats in the air when someone like Gershwin came along," Connelly recalls.

Lyricist Irving Caesar, another of the gallant few who remain, leans back in a comfortable chair in his Brill Building office and intones, "It was like spring busting out all over in those days. All that fermentation, all that talent!" Naturally the man who wrote "Swanee" with George Gershwin and "Tea for Two" with Vincent Youmans is most interested in the music of the era. "Its songs were the result of a great mingling of new American ethnic groups," he states.

With so many plays, the competent (or better) thespian usually stepped from one role to another several times in the course of a season; one play closed, another role awaited. Actors like Richard Bennett, Lowell Sherman, and Roland Young, as well as gifted actresses like Ina Claire, Katharine Cornell, and Helen Hayes, could skip from one play to another, accumulating experience, popularity, and dollars.

The year 1920 was an especially heady one for the profession. Only a few months before, in August 1919, the fledgling Actors' Equity union had ordered a strike against the all-powerful Broadway producers, who made actors pay for their own costumes, rehearse without pay, and imposed a variety of other abuses. After only a month the arrogant producers caved in. Actors' Equity did not win its full demands but did gain enough to justify claims of victory.

Having quelled the mighty producers, the actors (especially young ones) were currently in revolt against something else. To them the style of acting prevalent before and during World War I seemed stilted and unnatural. Popular players, or the directors who guided them, believed in letting an audience know that those onstage were really **acting**. Speech and gestures were both exaggerated and a play's dialogue was often so-called "stage English," somewhat more elegant in word and tone than everyday speech.

Many aspiring actors objected to this mannered emoting and affected delivery. As one of them said, "Broadway is awash with bilge from the sinking ship of Thespis." But there was nowhere for them to go except the experimental theatre groups in Greenwich Village. Over the next few years these Village groups—notably the Theatre Guild—would change the contours of American drama.

Broadway of 1920 stood ready. During 1919 the Yanks had returned
from George M. Cohan's "Over There." Now, at the opening
of a new decade, the area Walter Winchell
would christen the "Main Stem" awaited
its most colorful theatrical
decade.

People went to the theatre
in those days; it was the nation's number-one
entertainment medium. This play with two Barrymores, written by John's
latest wife, got bad reviews from critics, but theatregoers flocked to it anyway.

Playwrights of the Teens had specialized in plays in which plot, clever situations, and coincidence counted more than the impulses of characters. Now young dramatists craved to write more human plays but claimed to be held back by hidebound producers whose control over a script was total. Led by Owen Davis and George Middleton, playwrights began to agitate for a Dramatists' Guild which would give an author a hold on his script so that it would not be rewritten without his permission or cast without his approval. The fight for the Guild became as tense, if not as outwardly dramatic, as the actors' strike of 1919 or the battle of composers and lyricists for a protective **ASCAP**.

At the dawn of a new decade the Broadway theatre was a mixture of old and new. John Drew, First Gentleman of the Theatre since the turn of the century, still trod the boards. So did William Faversham, Minnie Maddern Fiske, and Margaret Anglin. Laurette Taylor, of **Peg o' My Heart** fame, was somewhat younger, and Jane Cowl, whose **Smilin' Through** opened on December 31, 1919, younger still. Ethel, Lionel, and John Barrymore—John Drew was their uncle—had been on the stage well over fifteen years and already were considered the Royal Family of the Theatre.

To them add fresh names like Helen Hayes, nineteen, recent child actress; Alfred Lunt, drawing attention to himself in **Clarence**, a play fashioned to his talents by Booth Tarkington; and Lynn Fontanne, about to score a comparable success in **Dulcy**, by the young playwrights George S. Kaufman and Marc Connelly. These were the days when Ruth Chatterton was a sought-after young actress, Peggy Wood an adornment of the operetta stage, and Katharine Cornell visible in tiny parts. By mid-decade such names as Edward G. Robinson and Spencer Tracy would appear in theatre programs.

In days before air conditioning, the heat of summer brought problems, for people were reluctant to sit in sweltering theatres with other perspiring human beings. Most plays closed late in May, with the producers and those performers able to afford it taking long summer vacations. In 1921 a young Englishman named Noël Coward landed on these shores in midsummer and had difficulty finding a single producer on Broadway to impress with his talents.

However, the lavish girl-and-comedy revues were deemed hot-weather entertainment, and these usually opened in the summer months and ran as long as possible into fall or winter. Producer Florenz Ziegfeld, who offered the most tasteful and sumptuous of them all, had opened his first **Follies** on a sweltering July night in 1907, and thereafter the superstitious man insisted on a summer premiere for his annual triumph.

Tickets to Broadway shows were reasonably priced—or so it seems today. The best seats to **Lightnin'**, 1920's longest-running-play-in-town, cost $3.50 on weekdays and $4 on Saturday nights; from there the sum ran backward to $1 for the topmost balcony seats. Some not so successful plays offered top balcony seats for a mere fifty cents.

The first big
musical-comedy hit of the decade was
Sally, with Marilyn Miller and comedian–eccentric
dancer Leon Errol. The Florenz Ziegfeld–Charles Dillingham
production had music by Jerome Kern, book by P. G. Wodehouse and Guy Bolton.

Elaborate shows like the **Ziegfeld Follies** and operettas like **Apple Blossoms**, in which John Charles Thomas sang and youngsters Fred and Adele Astaire danced, might charge $5 for orchestra seats on Saturday nights, but it was still possible to sit in the balcony for $1.50 or $1.

The basement of Gray's Drug Store, on the east side of Times Square, housed the cut-rate ticket agency known as Joe Leblang's. An hour or more before curtain time, box offices began sending batches of unsold tickets over to Leblang's, where they were posted on boards at prices commencing at fifty cents. For some reason the tickets passed along to Leblang's were called "fish." "How many fish do you have out tonight?" the producer of one limping show would ask another.

From our vantage point the Broadway–Times Square area of 1920 seems quiet and backward. The Times Building was still its most conspicuous edifice (the tall Paramount Building with its clock did not arrive until 1926), and most other buildings in the vicinity were no more than four or five stories high. Just a few years before the producer-actor-playwright-composer-dancer George M. Cohan—known as Mr. Broadway—looked out the window of his Times Building office and said to his producing partner, Sam H. Harris, "Look, Sam, there's not a single horse in all of Times Square."

If anything, Times Square was a neighborhood. Situated among the theatres between Sixth and Eighth Avenues (and west of Eighth) were rows of brownstone boardinghouses for members of the theatrical profession. Rooms cost $8 to $10 a week, with a good dinner, including red wine, at a nearby restaurant coming to 85 cents. Many of those who occupied rooms in the brownstones were vaudevillians, and on warm summer nights they clustered on the stoops to regale one another with tales of success in towns like Akron. Not long before, the rope-twirling cowboy Will Rogers had been among those who sat on stoops of a summer night. Now he was a star in Mr. Ziegfeld's **Follies**. No business like show business!

Although there were many other enterprises in the area, Broadway had the unmistakable aura of a theatre district. Beginning at 11:00 A.M. most of those hurrying through the streets were actors and actresses making the job-hunting rounds of producers' offices, as well as visiting the few actors' agents in business at the time. It was the custom of the era for actors to have cards printed up with their names and the plays in which they had appeared. Not only could these be left at casting offices, but they were used to get into theatres, for in those days actors were accorded free admission to most shows. "Do you recognize the profession?" an actor would ask, flashing his card. Then he was allowed inside. "Do you recognize the profession?" someone asked the sardonic Brock Pemberton, who had left the drama desk of **The New York Times** to produce plays. "A mile away," he answered.

It was a time when legitimate theatres actually lined Broadway itself. Among these were the Empire, Wallack's, Knickerbocker, Casino, George M. Cohan, Criterion, Astor, Gaiety, Globe, Central, and Winter

The mannered theatre of the past was fading, but some of its stalwarts
lingered on. John Drew, uncle of the Barrymores, continued as a
light comedian of peerless skill until his death
later in the decade. Caricature by Perriton
Maxwell, from *Theatre Magazine*.

Funnyman
Ed Wynn, known to an adoring public as the Perfect
Fool, was a surprising mover and shaker in the 1919 strike
that established Actors' Equity. Frank Bacon, Ethel Barrymore,
Eddie Cantor, and others also fought for the cause. George M. Cohan opposed it.

Garden. Forty-second was known as the Street of Theatres: the New Amsterdam, Sam H. Harris, Liberty, Eltinge, Frazee, Selwyn, Times Square, Apollo, Lyric, and Republic. Downtown on 39th Street stood the Princess, the Maxine Elliott, and the 39th Street. Uptown on 44th Street east were the Belasco and Hudson; west of Broadway were the Shubert, 44th Street, Broadhurst, Nora Bayes (all owned by the brothers Shubert), and Winthrop Ames's Little Theatre. On 45th were the Booth, Avon, and upcoming Music Box. On 48th were the Vanderbilt, Playhouse, Belmont, and 48th Street. Nearby were the Cort and the Ambassador. Further uptown lay the John Golden on 58th Street, the Cosmopolitan at Columbus Circle, and, two blocks above, the Century on Central Park West. Around the corner on 62nd Street was Daly's, where Mae West would gain immortality in **Sex**.

Competing with legitimate playhouses were the grand new cinema palaces on Broadway. First came the Mark Strand, managed by genial S. L. Rothafel, who urged the world to call him Roxy; soon he had his own cathedral of the cinema bearing that informal name. After the Strand were the Capitol, the Rivoli, and the Rialto. Each of these had a pit orchestra, with a shaggy-haired maestro conducting, and preceded each showing with a rousing classical overture. Then the orchestra played mood music throughout the film.

However, Broadway rated as more than a theatre district; it was an all-around mecca of popular entertainment. Close by the lighted theatres stood the after-theatre pleasure domes known as supper clubs.

In 1911 Irving Berlin's "Alexander's Ragtime Band" swept the land, bringing with it the jazz beat initially called syncopation. This, and the jazz that followed, was music to be danced to. At first people went to the supper clubs to watch the flying feet and intricate skills of professional dancers like Irene and Vernon Castle, Maurice and Florence Walton, Mae Murray and Rudolph Valentino. Then the slower, simpler fox trot emerged, and patrons shoved professionals aside to dance themselves. Between dances they sat down to eat and drink—and everybody was happy!

The curtain of Prohibition fell on Broadway—as well as the rest of the country—on January 17, 1920, and the pleasant era of dining and dancing ended with a whimper. Some café owners, believing the good days gone, closed their establishments forever on this dismal night. One dramatically locked his doors and tossed the key into the nearest gutter. Others set about facing a dubious future by offering only dinners and music to patrons.

Then a tremor ran through Broadway. The majority of Americans might believe that man's God-given right to drink had been plucked away from him, but some hardheaded bar owners and restaurateurs were wiser in human vagaries. A few in New York (and Chicago too) figured the law of the land just might not work. Deciding to defy it, they began serving drinks.

First it was whispered around Broadway that hot spots with names like the Jungle Club served liquor in demitasse or teacups. Then speakeasies began opening, and how their number increased! Both nightclubs and speakeasies were forced to buy from underworld characters who brought the booze into the country illegally, either across the border from Canada or by boats anchored outside the twelve-mile limit. A few manufactured their alcohol and beer in hideaway stills. Men violating the law by so-called rumrunning became the new breed of gangster, and as their wealth increased, so did their power.

Soon gangsters controlled nearly every Broadway night spot, bringing a sinister note to the Great White Way. The best people drank their liquor, and the prettiest showgirls feared to reject their advances. New York's tough guys never became as celebrated as those of Chicago, but as always its night life vastly outshone that of the Windy City or anywhere else. During the Twenties, Gotham's hectic gaiety played a strident obbligato to the theatre and other artistic endeavors.

In 1920 A.D.
Ina Claire, who won raves
as a child impressionist in the *Ziegfeld
Follies*, had gone on to become the brightest of
light comediennes for David Belasco. Helen Hayes,
leaving her child-actress career behind, had scored with veteran
William Gillette in *Dear Brutus*.

Laurette Taylor, famed
as Peg o' My Heart, was at the peak of a notable
career. Ruth Gordon called attention to
herself in Booth Tarkington's
Seventeen.

Irving Berlin wrote "Alexander's Ragtime Band" in 1911, bringing jazz
to Broadway and the world. Later he did words and music for
numerous Broadway shows, including "A Pretty Girl
Is Like a Melody," the theme song of the glamour-
drenched *Ziegfeld Follies*. Now he
planned **Music Box Revue** for
his own Music Box Theatre.

Tallulah Bankhead had arrived in New York the teenage winner of a movie-
magazine beauty contest. By accident her chaperone registered
at the Hotel Algonquin, allowing Tallu's (even then)
vivid personality to be discovered by famous
folk of the Round Table. Though she became a hit with
the intelligentsia, her success as an actress was only moderate.
On the advice of an astrologer she tried London, where fame embraced her.

THE TITAN

Only two weeks and a few days after the pall of Prohibition fell over Broadway, the curtain rose on a milestone in American theatrical history. For a major playwriting talent appeared on the scene. The encomiums tossed at a man destined to dominate the decade were many, but the most succinct of them said, "Before him the United States had theatre; after him it had drama."

The playwright was Eugene O'Neill, and he was thirty-two years old at the time of his first Broadway production. He was the son of James O'Neill, an actor who had abandoned all aspirations in the theatre to tour endlessly in the great success **The Count of Monte Cristo**. O'Neill disliked his father for this compromise with life, though he tried hard to love him as a son. The result was a tormented youth who became a tormented man.

O'Neill also toured with his father as actor and stage manager and came to despise the overblown dramas of the time. He wanted to write realistic plays, interpreting contemporary life as he saw it. At the age of twenty-two he had been expelled from Princeton for drinking. With this, he signed as an ablebodied seaman on a Norwegian barque for a sixty-five-day voyage to Buenos Aires. All through life O'Neill preferred to associate with human misfits and found them a-plenty in the fo'c'sle of this and other ships on which he sailed. He also continued to drink and shout, "Life's a tragedy—hurrah, hurrah!"

After a series of voyages O'Neill contracted tuberculosis, in part from malnutrition but also because of drinking bouts. At his father's expense he went to a Connecticut sanitarium where, out of boredom, he began writing plays about the days at sea. He had several of these under his arm on the day of his release from the sanitarium. Supposed never to touch liquor again, he made his first stop at a bar. There fate interceded resoundingly in his life, for O'Neill struck up a conversation with a Greenwich Villager headed for Provincetown, Massachusetts, where a group of drama-hungry Villagers had established the summertime Wharf Theatre.

O'Neill accompanied his new pal to Provincetown and found himself welcomed by the Wharf group. Indeed, the Wharf and O'Neill were made for one another, and in time each became responsible for the other's fame. The Wharf Players put on O'Neill's short fo'c'sle plays like **Bound East for Cardiff**, then in the winter brought them to the Provincetown Theatre in the Village. Drama critic George Jean Nathan touted O'Neill's genius, and hard-boiled Broadway wondered if he had ever written a full-length play.

He had. Titled **Beyond the Horizon**, it told of two brothers on a farm. One brother—in him a touch of the poet—had the feel of the sea in his bones and determined to ship out from the nearest port. Before this happened, though, he was trapped by a conniving girl, marriage, and fatherhood. So it was his land-loving brother who went to sea, with tragic results all around. "I could curse God," shouted a character in a line shocking at the time.

Producer John D. Williams quickly accepted **Beyond the Horizon** for uptown showing and talked grandly of casting John and Lionel Barrymore as the brothers. When the Barrymores proved unavailable, his enthusiasm lapsed, and the producer began to vacillate and question his own judgment.

While Williams dallied O'Neill wrote other plays, including **The Emperor Jones** and **Chris Christopherson**, which later became **Anna Christie**. He also found time to marry an attractive girl and beget a child. Into the marriage ceremony he inserted the bitter words, "Till love do us part."

An actor propelled **Beyond the Horizon** toward the stage. Richard Bennett was appearing in the John D. Williams' production of Elmer Rice's **For the Defense**. One day in Williams' office this successful performer picked up the script of **Beyond the Horizon** and began reading. To Bennett, it was a play combining naturalism and tragedy with colloquial contemporary dialogue. Employing no melodramatic tricks or coincidences, it depended on development of character alone and avoided plot for plot's sake. At the end, Bennett knew he must act in this play.

Bennett was so enthusiastic that he coralled actors from his own and other plays (one was Edward Arnold, later of the movies) to rehearse **Beyond the Horizon** in their spare time. Because he and the others had their own plays, it was decided to present the O'Neill play in a special matinee at the Morosco Theatre on the afternoon of February 3, 1920. If the matinee proved a success, producer Williams promised to shut **For the Defense** and run **Beyond the Horizon** at night.

A show-wise audience, full of actors and critics, filed into the Morosco Theatre on that February afternoon. O'Neill's father and mother were there, as were many Provincetown Players. O'Neill, sick with nerves, tried to hide. When the curtain rose he felt that the actors were giving dragging performances, and his anguish increased. At the end of the first act the audience clapped politely and went outside to smoke. O'Neill's old-school father said, "It's all right, Gene, if that's what you want to do, but people come to the theatre to forget their troubles, not to be reminded of them. What are you trying to do—send the audience home to commit suicide?"

Beyond the Horizon had been trimmed down but still ran until ten minutes of six in the evening. The weary audience clapped again and quit the theatre, leaving the playwright to his misery. Next morning's reviews were excellent. In **The New York Times** Alexander Woollcott called the play, "absorbing, significant, and memorable tragedy, so full of meat that it makes most [Broadway] fare seem like the merest

Broadway hailed Eugene O'Neill as America's finest playwright
after ***Beyond the Horizon*** was presented in the first days of 1920. Perhaps the
greatest tribute to his genius was that no one in the Twenties tried to imitate him.

Richard Bennett is usually
recalled as the father of Constance and Joan
Bennett, beautiful screen stars. Yet Bennett was one
of the most impressive actors of the 1920s, the fellow whose sharp eye
first perceived the worth of O'Neill's **Beyond the Horizon**. Here he is in that play

meringue." Opined the respected Clayton Hamilton, "This is the first tragedy that has been contributed to the drama of the world by an American playwright."

Switching to evening showings, the grim **Beyond the Horizon** proceeded to run for 111 performances. The only complaints about it involved length. According to one viewer, "An audience goes to the theatre to sit for an hour or so, not for a day. Mr. O'Neill seems to think that time is a negligible element in the development of his ideas." It was a sentiment that would be heard often throughout the decade.

Beyond the Horizon won O'Neill his first of four Pulitzer Prizes. **The Emperor Jones**, also presented at the Provincetown in 1920, proved too big for the Village and moved uptown. **Anna Christie**, offered on Broadway in 1921, earned O'Neill his second Pulitzer Prize.

Broadway had found its titan at the very beginning of the decade.

Roundup

As the best plays of the year, critic Burns Mantle of the **Daily News** chose **Beyond the Horizon**; **Deburau**, an adaptation of a Sacha Guitry play by Edward Sheldon, with Lionel Atwill; **Enter Madame**, by Gilda Veresi and Dolly Byrne; **The First Year**, a wholesome comedy by and with Frank Craven; **The Bad Man**, by Porter Emerson Brown, with the much admired Holbrook Blinn; **The Skin Game**, a war play by John Galsworthy; and **Mama's Affair**, a comedy about a hypochondriac by Rachel Burton Miller.

Holdover hits from 1919 were **Abraham Lincoln**, by England's John Drinkwater, with Frank McGlynn; **The Famous Mrs. Fair**, by James Forbes, with Blanche Bates, Henry Miller, and Margalo Gillmore; **Declassee**, by Zoë Akins, in which Ethel Barrymore gave a highly praised performance; **Jane Clegg**, by St. John Ervine, the first success of the new producing group known as the Theatre Guild; **The Jest**, by Sem Benelli, with John and Lionel Barrymore; **Adam and Eva**, by Guy Bolton and George Middleton; and **Clarence**, by Booth Tarkington, with Alfred Lunt, Helen Hayes, and Glenn Hunter.

Surrounding these plays were a host of others. John Drew was in **The Cat Bird**, Margaret Anglin in **The Woman of Bronze**, Florence Reed in **Three Live Ghosts**, Frances Starr in Edward Knoblock's **One**, Grace George in **The 'Ruined' Lady**, Eva Le Gallienne and Sidney Blackmer in **Not So Long Ago**, Maxine Elliott in **Trimmed in Scarlet**, and Ina Claire in **The Gold Diggers**, a title prophetic of the decade to come.

William Faversham starred in **The Prince and the Pauper**; a young English actor named Leslie Howard, who would become more famous as the decade progressed, made his American debut in **Just Suppose**, with Patricia Collinge and Geoffrey Kerr; Rod La Rocque, destined to be a top silent-film star, supported Alice Brady in **Anna Ascends**; William Powell, headed for fame in talkies, scored in **Spanish Love**; Edward Arnold appeared in **She Would and She Did**; Jeanne Eagels was in **The Wonderful Thing** and Charles Ruggles in **Ladies' Night**.

John Barrymore, having finished with **The Jest**, played his first Shakespearean role in **Richard III**; brother Lionel starred in Eugene Brieux' **Letter of the Law**; Laurette Taylor was visible in **One Night in Rome**, by husband J. Hartley Manners; David Belasco's sultry star Lenore Ulric dominated **The Son-Daughter**, about the mystic East; Pauline Lord and George Gaul were in **The Big Game**, about the Canadian wilderness; June Walker was in **My Lady Friends**; Walter Hampden played **George Washington**; lovely Doris Kenyon left films to appear in **The Girl in the Limousine**; veteran Otis Skinner starred in **Pietro**; Nita Naldi, late of girl shows, spoke ten lines in **The Bonehead** and got herself a larger part in **Opportunity**; Roland Young, Glenn Anders, and Elise Bartlett were in **Scrambled Eggs**; and Leo Carrillo was in **Lombardi, Ltd**.

The Famous Mrs. Fair, top hit as the decade dawned, boasted Henry Miller (standing), Margalo Gillmore, Blanche Bates, and Jack Devereaux.
Miss Gillmore became one of outstanding
young actresses of that era.

Scandal, with Francine Larrimore
and Charles Cherry, employed tense histrionics to expose secrets
of contemporary high life.

In the musical-comedy field, Marilyn Miller triumphed in her first big hit, **Sally**, with rubber-legged Leon Errol, music by Jerome Kern, book and lyrics by Guy Bolton and P. G. Wodehouse; blackface comic Frank Tinney went partially whiteface in **Tickle Me**; **The Night Boat** had Hal Skelly; **Honey Girl**, Lynne Overman; Nora Bayes was in **Her Family Tree**; Joe E. Brown and Frank Fay in **Jim Jam Jems**, with Ned Sparks and Harry Langdon deep in a large cast; Fred and Adele Astaire danced but did not sing or speak in Fritz Kreisler's **Apple Blossoms**; eccentric dancer Jack Donahue was a personal hit in **Angel Face**; and—note this!—**Poor Little Ritz Girl**, music and lyrics by Richard Rodgers and Lorenz Hart, with an assist from Sigmund Romberg, opened at the Central Theatre and ran for 119 performances.

In the dazzling world of revue, the **Ziegfeld Follies**, fourteenth edition of this sumptuous spectacle, offered the comedy of Fannie Brice, W. C. Fields, and the clever Van and Schenck. The first edition of **George White's Scandals**, a younger, breezier revue than the **Follies**, had been presented in 1919, starring the producer himself and Ann Pennington, "the girl with the dimpled knees." In addition to his **Scandals**, White's great contribution to the Twenties would be the dances Charleston and Black Bottom, both of which he claimed to originate.

Scandals of 1920 boasted Ann Pennington, La Sylphe, Lou Holtz, Lester Allen, tunes by young George Gershwin; Ed Wynn's **Carnival**, was by and with Ed Wynn himself; Eddie Cantor and Bert Williams, or vice versa, were to be seen in **Broadway Brevities**; the Shubert's annual **Passing Show**, never as tasteful or elegant as a **Follies**, provided Willie and Eugene Howard, Marie Dressler, and J. Harold Murray.

The figure in the spotlight was in blackface, with a wide rim of light greasepaint outlining his mouth. On his hands were the whitest of gloves. He was down on one knee, startling gloves outstretched to the audience, singing in an attention-commanding voice, "I'd walk a million miles for one of your smiles, My Mammmmmm-y."

Newest theatre in town was the Jolson, Shubert-built and owned, on Seventh Avenue between 58th and 59th Streets. Fittingly, its initial production was Al Jolson in **Bombo**, book and lyrics by Harold Attridge, music by Sigmund Romberg.

It may be hard to believe, but the plot of this musical comedy involved Christopher Columbus and his voyage of discovery. Bombo was a Negro deckhand aboard Columbus' ship; this was necessary because in those days Al Jolson made his stage appearances in blackface. In the show, Bombo's native wit and wisdom endeared him to Columbus, who allowed the blackface character to barter with the Indians. This provided many laughs. One of the biggest was "Give me Brooklyn, and I'll give you a pair of rusty scissors."

Altogether, the book of **Bombo** was such an inconsequential affair that some nights at 10:15 the magnetic star of the show stepped to the footlights. Pointing to the rest of the cast, he said, "These folks have been workin' hard tonight. Why don't we tell 'em to go home and just let Jolie sing?" The audience roared its approval; these were words they thirsted to hear. Al Jolson, a man truly exalted when alone on a stage, was likely to sing until one in the morning. There is no record that anyone ever walked out of a theatre when he did.

The Al Jolson of the Twenties was less an entertainer than a phenomenon. He was a small, solid man who looked bigger onstage, and his ability to electrify people with his voice was unsurpassed as he made top hits of such songs as "Mammy," "Avalon," "Swanee," "April Showers," "California, Here I Come," and a host of others. Though he did not have the exposure of movie stars like Charlie Chaplin and Douglas Fairbanks, his phonograph records sold in the millions and he was probably the best-known entertainer in the land. "He was the King—and the King could do no wrong," said Eddie Cantor. To comedian Lou Holtz "Jolson was the greatest." Newspapers unhesitatingly called him the world's greatest entertainer. Without qualification, his ego can also be called the most monumental ever known on Broadway.

Jolson may have reached his eminence because he gave everything he had to every song and to every audience. Published at the time of **Bombo** was **The Seven Lively Arts**, a book by Gilbert Seldes that informed the contemporary public that the show-business stars they took for granted were among the greatest in history. In it the author gave almost as much space to Jolson as to Charlie Chaplin, noting among much else the exaltation of his singing.

In **Bombo**, a star vehicle if ever one existed, Al Jolson flirted with
Vivienne Oakland.
The great Jolie still felt unaccountably
shy before audiences
and liked to appear in blackface until his epochal movie debut in 1927.

Offstage, Al Jolson
was a monomaniac, alternately affable and arrogant.
But, says Irving Caesar,
his gifts were so great that friends willingly overlooked
his personal faults.

Wrote Seldes, "In Jolson, there is one thing you can be sure of—that whatever he does, he does at the highest possible pressure . . . . On the great nights when everything is right, Jolson is driven by a power beyond himself. One sees that he knows what he is doing, but one also sees that he doesn't half realize the power and intensity with which he is doing it. In those moments I cannot help thinking of him as a genius."

Jolson kept the water running in the sink of his dressing room to drown out the applause won by others in a show; he wanted every bit of it himself. When singing onstage he seemed to soak up the approbation and approval of a crowd through the pores of his skin; when sick, his health was visibly improved by applause. Offstage he was tense and restless, always appearing to wish to be somewhere else. With a spotlight bathing him in its glow, he was supremely content—"the totality of one human being," Seldes says. "Keep it up, I love it!" Jolson shouted back at crowds applauding him.

At the Winter Garden, where he scored his first Broadway success, Jolson made the Shuberts tear out precious aisle seats and build a runway out into the auditorium. When showgirls paraded along it, this was called the Bridge of Thighs. Jolson used the runway to prance up and down, then sit on its edge and chat with the audience, for he was as glib with words as with songs and a master of the sly innuendo, the knowing wink, and the smart wisecrack. From time to time he went through the motions of exiting from the stage, evoking wild clapping to bring him back. Appearing again, he yelled the words most often associated with his name—"You ain't heard nothin' yet!" Or sometimes it was "You ain't **seen** nothin' yet!"

One of his associates said, "He would never save up anything for the next scene, the next act, or the next day. Even at rehearsal, he would never hold back, no matter how we pleaded with him. He seemed to have enough lung power for an army." Almost without effort, Jolson's strong, vibrant voice was able to fill a theatre; serious musicians compared his range and tone to a violin. In 1919 he impulsively rented the Boston Opera House for a concert backed by fifty long-hair musicians; the performance was a success, with two thousand people turned away.

Yet it is a mistake to think of Jolson only as a singer. In talking pictures, where he pioneered, his roles were serious, his acting wooden. On the musical-comedy stage, though, he was a sure-footed comedian with a honed sense of hokum who enjoyed the laughter of an audience as much as applause. In one show he played a gondolier in a sketch. "Do you know the ruins of Florence?" the straight man asked him. "Know 'em?" Jolson replied. "I ruined 'em." Said Jolie to an interviewer, "If I don't get a laugh at that line, I drop the oar on the guy's head and **make** 'em laugh."

Al Jolson (born Asa Yoelson) was brought to the United States from Russia at age eight, son of a stern rabbi father and understanding mother. The family settled in a poor section of Washington, D.C., and one afternoon Al returned from school to find his mother in her death throes. The shock may have contributed to the yawning insecurities that haunted his life and made him crave constant reassurance and public approbation.

He and his older brother Harry earned money by singing popular songs before the porches of Washington hotels, where the politicians in rocking chairs tossed pennies, nickels, and dimes. The two boys spent most of their loot on seats in the top galleries of vaudeville houses. When an angry father bore down on them, Harry ran away to Broadway and Al followed. He was eleven years old, a boy soprano who could also whistle melodiously. He returned ingloriously to Washington but soon took off again with Walter Main's Traveling Circus. From there he moved to burlesque as a boy singer. There were few jobs and between them he was broke and hungry, sleeping in hallways or on park benches.

When his voice changed he again returned home, but not for long. Appearing in cheap vaudeville, he whistled until his voice developed into a vibrant baritone. Told to take part in sketches, he delivered lines in stiff, self-conscious fashion. Another actor on the bill suggested he overcome nerves by appearing in blackface. It worked; uncertainties seemed to vanish. From then on he wore burnt-cork makeup and a black suit, creating the image of a black Sambo with a white rim around his lips and white gloves. This was the Al Jolson known to the early Twenties.

Young Al toured for years in small-time vaudeville, then polished his skills with the famed Lew Dockstader Minstrels, becoming more popular than Lew himself. A vital moment in his career came in 1909 when he was booked alone into Hammerstein's Victoria in New York. Hammerstein audiences, notoriously tough, specialized in shattering the morale of fresh acts. Usually this was done by noise. Jolson strutted out into bedlam, thought fast, put two fingers in his mouth, and emitted a piercing whistle. It brought silence, and he said, "I've rehearsed hard in order to please you, and you've paid money to see me. So let's get going!"

Two years later, at age twenty-four, he performed a similar feat in *La Belle Paree*, the Shubert extravaganza opening at the Winter Garden, then the most elaborate theatre the city had ever seen. Until he appeared onstage the revue was a bore. With him, it perked up and his Broadway career commenced. Under the Shubert banner he appeared in shows like *Vera Violetta*, *The Whirl of Society*, and *Dancing Around*, which ran two years. As a star, he played in *Honeymoon Express*, *Robinson Crusoe, Jr.* (he was Friday), and *Sinbad*, where he introduced "Swanee," "Rock a Bye Your Baby," and "Mammy." Jolson kept inserting new numbers into his shows, no matter how the programs read, and one way or another sang during *Bombo*'s Broadway run and nationwide tour "April Showers," "Yoo-Hoo," "Toot-Toot-

Tootsie," "Dirty Hands, Dirty Face," "I'm Goin' South," and "California, Here I Come." One Christmas he put an ad in *Variety* that read, "Everybody likes me! Those that don't are jealous! Anyway, here's wishing those that do and those that don't a Merry Christmas and a Happy New Year—AL JOLSON."

Sunday theatrical performances were against the law in New York City, but the crafty Shuberts got around this by giving special Sabbath shows at the Winter Garden and advertising them as concerts or recitals. Shubert stars were featured at these performances. Al Jolson was one, and sometimes he took over as a one-man show to make his famous Sunday nights at the Winter Garden. At them he sang twenty or thirty songs, yelled, "You ain't seen nothin' yet!" and did twenty or thirty more. "This is Jolie singing to ya," he bellowed at audiences, as if they didn't know.

One night, singing "You Made Me Love You," he felt a painful twinge in his leg. Sinking to one knee, he stretched out his white-gloved hands to the auditorium as if in supplication. The crowd loved it, and this pose became another of his trademarks.

Success that should have satisfied any man failed to assuage the rampant competitiveness of his nature. A king-size ego told him nobody must outdo Jolie. At rehearsals there were shouting scenes and temper tantrums if he did not get his own way. Yet at times competitiveness paid off. During a Liberty Loan benefit during World War I, he appeared after Enrico Caruso, who had dazzled the crowd by rendering "Keep the Home Fires Burning" and other war songs. It did not seem possible that anyone could top him. Yet Jolson leaped nimbly out and shouted, "You ain't heard nothin' yet!" Then he proceeded to make the audience forget Caruso.

At the time of *Bombo* Jolson was earning $2,000 a week, plus one-quarter of the weekly gross. There were seldom empty seats in a Jolson house, and the percentage brought his salary up to $5,000 a week. Add to this another $5,000 from the sale of his phonograph records; at one point his burlesque of opera's "Toreador Song" swept the nation. His shows usually ran one year in New York and another on the road, so he could be busy all the time. Occasionally he professed to be tired and took vacations, but soon was back center-stage again.

What was the great Jolson really like? Offstage he was brisk and aggressive, fast-talking, fast-thinking. Yet onstage or off he believed himself thoroughly relaxed. "You should take it easy, the way I do," he told people. He handled himself like a prize possession, smoking and drinking sparingly, never losing a night's sleep. He hated (or feared) being alone and traveled with an entourage. (Was he the first big-shot entertainer to do so?) There were pals, tipsters, and court jesters, yes-men. "If it was Monday and he said Wednesday, you had to agree with him," one said. He wanted the world to think of him as "Jolie," the name he coined for himself. But he did not like being called that to his face.

He was long on life's experiences, short on formal education, and his grammar left much to be desired; purposely or not, he never quit saying "ain't." Eddie Cantor and George Jessel were close to him, but he counted few other actors among his friends, since their egos might vie with his. He liked to dominate a group by his theatrical glamour, and his pals were sportsmen, gamblers, song pluggers, and sycophants. He was a hypochondriac who tirelessly gulped pills and nostrums while nursing imaginary diseases. His sense of humor was sharp; he told jokes well and appreciated those well told by others.

Like most top entertainers, he could be alternately arrogant and pleasant. Pearl Sieben, who wrote a book about him, sees a chameleon: "He was kind, sentimental, and charitable to a fault; he was arrogant and surly; he was a braggart; he was crude and untutored." Later, when his career crumbled, he was subject to fits of morose melancholia, but on Broadway ego rode high. Complimented on his ability to pick the right songs, he exploded, "A song don't have to have anythin'! It's all in the delivery. Why, I could pick up a telephone book and make the folks cry if I wanted to!"

He was not stingy with money, nor could you call him extravagant. "He was always very generous with his talent," says Irving Berlin. Most of his $10,000-a-week intake went to a business manager who wisely invested in buildings and real estate. When he made **The Jazz Singer**, the first movie in which an actor spoke, his pay was largely in Warner Brothers stock, which zoomed upward after the premiere. He lost $750,000 in the stock-market crash of 1929, but it hardly mattered. On his death he left $4,000,000 to charity but not a penny (or anything) to his longtime personal manager, accompanist, or chauffeur.

A man's man who relished the company of males, he loved to gamble, especially shoot craps, and seemed to win more often than lose. He was conspicuous at championship prize fights and horse races and one summer reputedly won $100,000 betting on the horses.

But he was a man's man who liked women. He married four times, and as a glittering stage luminary found countless willing sex-partners among the showgirls and chorines of Broadway. Yet he never begat a child, a fact that gnawed. In 1920 he married for the second time, taking as his bride a chorus girl in **George White's Scandals**. His first two wives (they preceded Ruby Keeler) were pretty girls who feared the pitfalls of marrying a peak performer with an overweening ego. Yet the more they resisted, the more ardent he became. Following the marriage, he turned neglectful, just as they knew he'd be. His real spouse was the spotlight, and no woman could ever take its place.

Between 1911 and 1926 Jolson had nine consecutive hit shows on Broadway. When **Bombo** closed to go on tour, Mayor Hylan of New York wired, "New York has been proud to have you as you have enhanced the Broadway scene." After the tour, **Bombo** returned to the Jolson Theatre and became a hit again.

In the actors' strike of 1919, the self-centered Jolson sided with George M. Cohan in opposing Equity. The profession never forgave Cohan but did not care about Jolson. With **Bombo**—and its successor, **Big Boy**—he succeeded in dethroning Cohan as Mr. Broadway, his brassy personality, magical voice, and supercharged delivery seeming to typify the advent of the Twenties, Prohibition, and the Jazz Age. He remained Mr. Broadway until 1926, when he went to Hollywood to make **The Jazz Singer**, the film that dealt a body blow to a legitimate theatre that had so well rewarded Al Jolson.

Hit songs from 1921 Broadway musicals—the kind remembered by old-timers and still occasionally heard:

"April Showers" (Silvers/De Sylva), from **Bombo**
"Everybody Step," "Say It with Music" (Berlin), from **Music Box Revue**
"I'm Just Wild about Harry" (Sissle/Blake), from **Shuffle Along**
"Ka-lu-a" (Kern/Caldwell), from **Good Morning, Dearie**
"My Man" (Willemetz/Charles/Pollock), from **Ziegfeld Follies**
"The Sheik of Araby" (Smith/Wheeler/Snyder), from **Make It Snappy**
"Song of Love" (Donnelly/Romberg/Schubert), from **Blossom Time**
"Three O'Clock in the Morning" (Robledo), from **Greenwich Village Follies**

TWO WEDDINGS

No plaque adorns the premises at 130 West 70th Street in Manhattan, in the early Twenties a theatrical boardinghouse run by Dr. Rounds, a female medico who favored play folk as paying guests.

Yet it was here that Lynn Fontanne and Alfred Lunt—she on the third floor, he in the basement front—lived at the time of their marriage. For a time their most frequent guest was a pale, intense, self-assured young man who had arrived the summer before from London with a bundle of playscripts and seventy-five dollars in his pocket. He was Noël Coward, and in Lynn's comfortable upstairs quarters the three endlessly discussed dreams for themselves and the theatre. It is interesting to note that individually and collectively these dreams came true.

At this point, Alfred and Lynn were not the glamorous creatures they later seemed as the Lunts. He was a young man described as shy, repressed, and neurotic. She was thin, angular, and pigeon-toed. Both were comedians in the theatre—friend Robert E. Sherwood went so far as to call them *eccentric* comedians—and physical beauty was not an important part of their skills. For the play **Clarence**, Alfred had adopted a funny, stomach-forward stance that most people thought his own. Gawky Lynn did not care how she looked onstage or off, provided she got laughs from an audience. Not until they began acting together as a team did the two work at being glamorous. Then their combined genius turned him into a handsome, polished man and her into a regal beauty.

Still, they were successful at the time of their marriage. Late in 1919 Alfred had opened in **Clarence**, a comedy written expressly for him by Booth Tarkington. The young actor had devised comedy techniques easier and more naturalistic than those in favor at the time, and he was so good in **Clarence** that the first-night audience chanted ''Lunt, Lunt, Lunt!'' after the fall of the curtain. Helen Hayes, his leading lady, has recalled, ''That opening night was as wildly exciting as Armistice Day.'' Critics rated **Clarence** the best light comedy yet written by an American.

Two years later—in August 1921—Lynn enjoyed a comparable triumph, appearing in the title role of **Dulcy**, a play by the new team of George S. Kaufman and Marc Connelly. Kaufman was a leg-man in the drama department of **The New York Times**, while Connelly performed the same function on the **Morning Telegraph**. Finding that they laughed at the same things, the pair set out to write a play together. Borrowing the character Dulcinea from the ''Conning Tower'' column conducted by Franklin P. Adams (F.P.A.), they wrote three acts about an adorable dumbbell who uttered bromides while all hell broke loose around her. ''Live and let live is my motto'' was one of her pet phrases. ''All's well that ends well, I like to say'' was another. **Dulcy**, too, was hailed as one of the best American comedies and Lynn's performance won raves.

Alfred Lunt
first scored on Broadway with a low-comedy performance
in Booth Tarkington's *Clarence*, a role tailored especially
for him. He and Lynn Fontanne were engaged to marry on his night of triumph.

Lovely Lynn Fontanne
had been brought to New York from London
by Laurette Taylor. At first she was an actress
whose comedy performances bordered on slapstick; however, she secretly aspired
to high comedy and drama. Her success in the Kaufman–Connelly *Dulcy* proved as great
as Alfred Lunt's in **Clarence**.

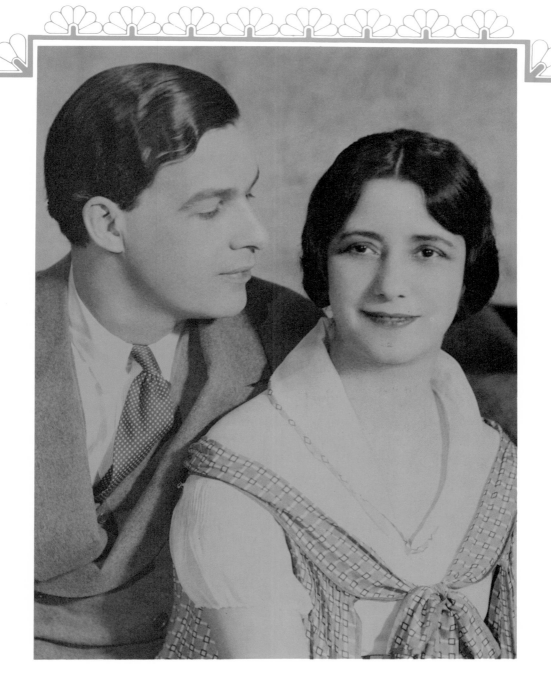

After *Clarence* and *Dulcy*,
Alfred and Lynn were prosperous enough to marry during a
lay-off week. In the minds of both lay hopes of acting together.

Noël Coward, at this point, had few funds; so far the Broadway theatre had not been hospitable to him. Living in Greenwich Village, he survived by rewriting his numerous play scripts into short stories and selling them to magazines like **Vanity Fair**. He had known Lynn in London, recalling her as "a scraggy, friendly girl with intelligent brown eyes and a raucous laugh."

When he arrived in New York, writes Coward, "Lynn and Alfred were, to put it mildly, 'courting.' " Nonetheless, the duo became a trio. Nightly over dill pickles and delicatessen potato salad they evoked a future divided into four parts: 1) Alfred and Lynn were to marry; 2) they would become popular enough to insist on acting together; 3) Noel would write plays and also act in them; 4) after all three had become sufficiently important—"poised serenely on that enviable plane of achievement" is the way Noël put it—they would perform triumphantly together in one of his plays. And that, of course, is what happened with **Design for Living** in 1933.

The theatre had been good to Alfred and Lynn—as it shortly would be to impecunious Noël. Lynn was born at a mysterious date in Essex, a few miles north of London. As a child she was encouraged to perform: "I was thought by my family to be a talented actress from the time I was born." Lynn's mother took the child to Ellen Terry, and this great actress agreed to accept her as a pupil-protegée. Among the words of wisdom offered by Miss Terry were, "Think of the meaning of the words you are speaking, and let the words pour out of your mouth."

Through Miss Terry teenage Lynn got professional jobs in pantomime, then bits in London plays. In one she did well enough to attract the attention of America's Laurette Taylor, currently the toast of London in **Peg o' My Heart**. When Miss Taylor returned to the United States, Lynn came along as part of her acting company. In her first New York role she scored a personal success. Wrote one audience member, "She riveted your attention from the moment of her first appearance. Somewhere in the middle of the second act she had an emotional scene and so true was she—so touching and so vivid—that her exit brought the house down."

Alfred Lunt, born in Milwaukee on August 9, 1892, was the son of a vigorous mother who took him to every entertainment she could find, be it Shakespeare or vaudeville. In no time he too was theatre-struck. After two years of college in Wisconsin he transferred to the Emerson School of Oratory in Boston. One afternoon he walked into the Castle Square Theatre, which housed one of the finest repertory companies in the country. "I want to go on the stage," he said in a small voice. "Can you start Tuesday?" came the unexpected reply.

In the Castle Square company Alfred specialized in playing old and middle-aged men. "He was obsessed by the theatre," writes Maurice Zolotow, biographer of the pair. It was noted that he not only studied his own techniques and those of other actors but audience reactions as well.

Breaking loose from Boston, Alfred toured with Margaret Anglin, Laura Hope Crews, and Lily Langtry, three actresses whose careers had seen better days. In 1917, at age twenty-five, he made his New York debut in something called **Romance and Arabella**. Next he appeared in Booth Tarkington's **Country Cousin**. The author was so impressed by him that he said, "Alfred, I'm going to write a play for you." With this, George C. Tyler (who would produce) signed the actor to a two-year contract and sent him to Washington to do repertory. Already in the Washington company was Lynn Fontanne. From the first the two enjoyed acting together, rehearsing together, and **being** together; they were falling in love.

Love really bourgeoned while Alfred appeared in **Clarence**. Helen Hayes was bitterly jealous as each night after the final curtain Lynn arrived to claim her man. Later, while Lynn played **Dulcy**, Alfred was to be seen opposite Billie Burke in **Intimate Strangers**, another play by Booth Tarkington. **Intimate Strangers** was playing Atlantic City, and when it closed for a week's vacation Alfred rushed back to New York. One morning he and Lynn were sitting on a bench in Central Park when suddenly Alfred said, "Let's get married. Now! Immediately!" Without stopping to tell anyone, they tore downtown to the Municipal Building. Both were (then and always) absent-minded, and Alfred found he did not have enough money to pay for the license. Lynn, naturally, had forgotten her purse. Alfred borrowed two dollars from a witness, and the knot was tied.

The two honeymooned in Atlantic City, where Alfred resumed his role. Billie Burke seemed so upset by the barrenness of their New York ceremony that the two decided to marry again in a more elaborate religious ceremony. Afterward, Miss Burke threw a lavish reception.

Now they were important enough to be interviewed together, and a scribe from **Theatre Magazine** found them happily interrupting each other over afternoon tea. They tenderly called each other "Betsy" and "Bill," and Alfred revealed that his real name was Ecklunt.

Next, the pair began to badger George C. Tyler about acting together, but the crusty producer vetoed the idea as self-indulgent. So the second rung of their private ladder of success would have to wait. As for Noël Coward, he had returned to London and from there was taking new steps to conquer Broadway.

The marriage of Katharine Cornell and Guthrie McClintic was a somewhat more conventional affair. At least, it took place at the home of the bride's aunt, but it was no less a theatre event for that.

Katharine Cornell was a daughter of a stage-struck Buffalo physician. She came east to attend Miss Merritt's Finishing School of Girls at Mamaroneck, New York, where theatrics were taught by a young woman named Theresa Helburn. In other moments Miss Helburn was active in a New York theatre group known as the Washington Square Players, which aspired to present better plays on Broadway than the

Katharine Cornell married Guthrie McClintic just before starting rehearsals of ***A Bill of Divorcement***. For a time she stood out as the celebrity of the family; however, McClintic soon achieved recognition as a stimulating new producer-director.

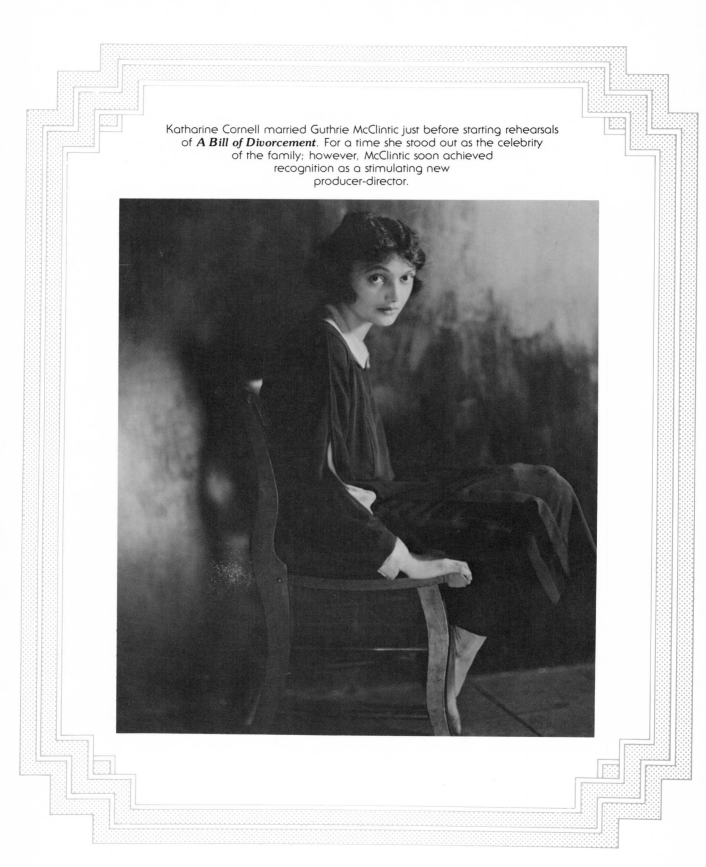

42

Few men
in all history have been
as powerful as the Broadway producers of the Twenties.
Though bested in the Actors' Equity strike of 1919,
they still retained iron control over plays and casts, able to
hire and fire at will. Most picturesque of the group was David Belasco (*left*).
Indoors he labored amidst a colorful clutter; outdoors he reversed his collar in
clerical fashion, earning the respectful title "Bishop of
Broadway." By far the most powerful producers
were the brothers Shubert—the awesome
"Mr. Lee" and "Mr. J. J."
Few ever saw Mr. Lee laughing as he is
here (*above left*), for he was a sinister Gray Eminence
(if Belasco rated "Bishop") who produced more plays annually
than any rival. Boorish and belligerent, brother J. J. took care of
the musical aspects of the Shubert empire, which featured revues like **Passing Shows**
and **Artists and Models**, along with such operettas as **Blossom Time** and
The Student Prince. Typical of a newer breed of producer
was Brock Pemberton (*above right*), formerly of the drama department
of **The New York Times**. Witty and human,
Pemberton was one of those who gave
producers a good name.

Rialto had ever seen. Because of Theresa Helburn, Katharine Cornell made her stage debut in tiny parts with the Washington Square Players.

If the theatre was kind to the Lunts—and to Katharine Cornell—it had been a place of trial and tribulation for Guthrie McClintic. Sensitive son of average parents, he grew up in Seattle. There the local stock company was run by Laurette Taylor's husband, who featured his wife in diverse roles. (After he deserted her Laurette propelled herself to New York.) On viewing his first stage performance, young Guthrie decided that he too must act. An unsympathetic family scraped up the money to send him to New York to study at the American Academy of Dramatic Art. Two years later he graduated and, almost penniless, began the rounds of producing offices and agents.

McClintic was not impressive-looking, and few parts came his way. He went out on road tours, only to be stranded in faraway places. Returning to New York, he resumed the dismal rounds. One desperate day he wrote an impassioned letter to Winthrop Ames, whose sanctum he had been unable to penetrate. To his amazement Ames replied, offering him the post of stage manager on a new play.

It wasn't acting, but it meant eating. McClintic accepted and gradually became one of the top stage managers on Broadway, working for Ames and William A. Brady. But he still wanted to act and one night investigated the struggling Washington Square Players. There, for the first time, he glimpsed the dark, glowing, swanlike beauty of Katharine Cornell.

A firm believer in the supernatural, McClintic claimed that several times his life had been affected by signs from above. Looking at Katharine, he heard a still, small voice say, ''Some day you'll marry that girl.'' But McClintic was already married, and the possibility of a second romance seemed remote.

Still determined to act, he spent a summer with the Jessie Bonstelle Stock Company in Detroit. Katharine Cornell—or Kit, as he began calling her—was also in the company. This time the two fell in love. As a result, Guthrie began steps toward a divorce. Weary of stage managing, he also decided to produce and direct his own plays. All he needed was the right one, and it came his way in A. A. Milne's **The Dover Road**.

Meantime, Kit had been selected to play the girl in **A Bill of Divorcement**, by Clemence Dane. Guthrie got his divorce, and the two were married just before Kit reported at rehearsals. She and the play succeeded, and for a few months Guthrie lived in her shadow. Then **The Dover Road** opened to excellent reviews, making him important, too.

So began two marriages that lasted through decades and did much to enrich the American drama.

Drama critics
were "personalities" in the Twenties.
Most envied was George Jean Nathan (*above left*),
here caricatured by John Held, Jr. Perennially youthful,
he was a man about town, wit, ladies' man, prose stylist, and dandy
who could easily be called Broadway's boulevardier. Nathan's
mind was a theatrical encyclopedia, and his criticism in
The American Mercury had almost as much
effect on the young
as the pronouncements of his sidekick, H. L. Mencken.
Alexander Woollcott (*above right*), aisle sitter for **The Times**, **Herald**, **Sun**,
and **World**,
carried drama criticism
to the masses, his wild enthusiasms
making theatre as exciting as baseball. Rating emotion over
balanced judgment, he figuratively tossed hat in air over favored plays and
performers. Admirers at the Algonquin Round Table dubbed him
"the smartest of Alecs."

Dream cast
of **Lilies of the Field**, a play about kept women, included Alison Skipworth, Pauline Garon,
Marie Doro, Evelyn Duncan, Josephine Drake, and Cora Witherspoon.
The locale was Maisie's boudoir.

Grace George, the dainty but strong-willed mate of producer William A. Brady, was a busy star. One triumph was in St. John Ervine's *The First Mrs. Fraser*.

In the Golden Age
of Comedy, onetime juggler W. C. Fields
fought his way to the top rank in the *Ziegfeld Follies*.
It may be hard to believe, but offstage Bill Fields was a fine-looking man.

ROUNDUP

As the best plays of the year critic Burns Mantle picked Eugene O'Neill's **Anna Christie**, rewritten with emphasis on an Anna notably played by Pauline Lord rather than on father Chris Christopherson, portrayed by George Marion; **The Green Goddess**, with the inscrutable English star George Arliss; **Liliom**, by Ferenc Molnar, with Joseph Schildkraut and Eva Le Gallienne; **Mary Rose**, a psychic drama by J. M. Barrie, with Ruth Chatterton; **Nice People**, by Rachel Crothers, with Francine Larrimore, Tallulah Bankhead, and Katharine Cornell, **The Emperor Jones**, by Eugene O'Neill, with Charles Gilpin in the title role (Paul Robeson played it in a later revival); **A Bill of Divorcement**, by Clemence Dane; **Dulcy**, by George S. Kaufman and Marc Connelly; **Six-Cylinder Love**, by William Anthony McGuire, with Ernest Truex, June Walker, and Hedda Hopper; **The Dover Road**, by A. A. Milne, with Charles Cherry and Winifred Lenihan; and **The Circle**, by Somerset Maugham, with John Drew and Mrs. Leslie Carter.

This was a remarkable year for revivals, with stars of prewar years striving valiantly to shine again in plays that had made them famous. Among them were Laurette Taylor in **Peg o' My Heart**, Doris Keane in **Romance**, David Warfield in **The Return of Peter Grimm**, Frances Starr in **The Easiest Way**, William Faversham in **The Squaw Man**, and Wilton Lackaye in **Trilby**. John Drew and Mrs. Leslie Carter, two titans of the past, were appearing in an up-to-date play by Somerset Maugham. E. H. Sothern and Julia Marlowe, also titans, offered Shakespearean repertory.

Plays that found high favor with the public were the long-running mystery **The Bat**, by Mary Roberts Rinehart and Avery Hopwood; **The Charm School**, by Alice Duer Miller and Robert Milton; **Miss Lulu Bett**, by Zona Gale, with Carroll McComas as Lulu; **Daddy Long Legs**, by Zoë Akins, with Marjorie Rambeau; Otis Skinner with daughter Cornelia in **Blood and Sand; Rollo's Wild Oat**, by Clare Kummer, with Roland Young; and **Bluebeard's Eighth Wife**, with Ina Claire; in **The Nightcap** a butler named Charles was played by Ronald Colman.

Also Lina Abarbanell and Lionel Atwill in **The Grand Duke**; Margaret Anglin in **The Trial of Joan of Arc**; Lou Tellegan in **Don Juan**; Helen Hayes in **Golden Days**; Elsie Ferguson in **The Varying Shore; Mr. Pim Passes By**, by A. A. Milne, with Dudley Digges, Helen Westley, and Laura Hope Crews; George M. Cohan in the mystifying **The Tavern**; Billie Burke and Alfred Lunt in **The Intimate Strangers**, by Booth Tarkington; Wallace Eddinger in **Captain Applejack**; Mr. and Mrs. Charles Coburn in **French Leave; Follies** graduate Lilyan Tashman in **A Bachelor's Night**; and Glenn Anders and Hazel Dawn in **The Demi-Virgin**, an Al Woods production that got in trouble with the police because of its title.

Lionel Barrymore's **Macbeth** was poorly received (John's **Richard III** was a sensation) and Eugene O'Neill's **Diff'rent** garnered little praise. **Tarzan of the Apes**, with Ronald Adair, laid an egg.

In the blithe fields of musical comedy and revue the Shubert's **Blossom Time** began its exceptional career as a favorite with the operetta-conscious; Ed Wynn hit the heights in **The Perfect Fool**; the brightly titled **Good Morning, Dearie**, music by Jerome Kern, starred Louise Groody and Oscar Shaw; De Wolf Hopper, Nora Bayes, and Lew Fields embellished the oddly titled **Selwyn's Snapshots of 1921**; the Fairbanks Twins were **Two Little Girls in Blue**; the clever Duncan Sisters in **Tip-Top**; Mae West, former vaudeville headliner, in **The Mimic World**; Grace Moore, destined for operatic fame, was barely visible in Ned Wayburn's **Town Gossip** (the season before she had a smaller part in **Hitchy-Koo**, with Irene Bordoni); Sam Bernard, Joseph Santley, and Ivy Sawyer were in Irving Berlin's **Music Box Revue**; Frank Crumit and Julia Sanderson in **Tangerine; The Love Letter** had Fred and Adele Astaire; **George White's Scandals** boasted Ann Pennington, Charles King, Lester Allen, and Aunt Jemima; in the **Ziegfeld Follies** were W. C. Fields, Fannie Brice, Raymond Hitchcock, Ray Dooley, and gorgeous Mary Eaton.

HAMLET OF THE CENTURY

The actor who emerged from the stage door of the Sam H. Harris Theatre was a bit over medium height, with exceedingly broad shoulders. His suit was rumpled and messy, yet he managed to wear it with an air of rakish elegance. His hat, tilted jauntily over one eye, might have been expensive once, but it looked like the veteran of a thousand gutters. Yet this, too, was worn with sublime assurance.

On the sidewalk a cluster of newspaper photographers waited. Recognizing one as an old friend and boozing companion, the actor gave a snort of approval and said, "Ah, you sweet-scented bastard." However, the atmosphere chilled as another shouted, "Look this way, Jack." The actor swung his broad-shouldered body to bestow a withering glance. Sensitive nostrils flaring, he snapped in syllables etched in venom, "Why be so formal? Just call me *kid*."

Such was John Barrymore, youngest member of the Royal Family of the Theatre, at the peak of his career—during those 101 incomparable days when he played Hamlet on Broadway and was saluted by critics as the Hamlet of the Century. Nothing has happened since 1922 to alter this verdict. These were indeed Barrymore's finest hours and just possibly Broadway's.

John Barrymore! Women who saw him onstage thought he was the handsomest male they had ever seen, and men were forced to agree. His outstanding attribute was a sharp, flawless profile of which Heywood Broun had written, "It slides into a scene like an exquisite paper knife." Until he appeared in *Peter Ibbetson* in 1917 Barrymore had worn a mustache. He shaved it off for this production, and at his first appearance onstage a collective gasp swept the women in the audience.

Yet the actor seemed perversely ashamed of his good looks and sought to downgrade them whenever possible. Offstage he liked to walk around in old clothes with a stubble of beard on his face. He bathed as seldom as possible and usually was shrouded in the fumes of body odor. But always his mind was mordant and rapier-like, his sense of humor diabolical.

John Barrymore was forty years old at the time of his *Hamlet*, the son of actor Maurice Barrymore and his actress wife Georgie Drew Barrymore. He was a nephew of John Drew, courtliest of theatrical stars, and brother of Ethel, called the First Lady of the Theatre, and Lionel, hailed as the finest character actor on Broadway. Taken together, the Barrymores were certainly the Royal Family of the Theatre.

As a young man John had dreamed of being a newspaper cartoonist, sketch artist, or caricaturist. He had even worked as an artist on Manhattan newspapers. But his family name and striking good looks made it easier for him to earn a living as an actor. His first success came in 1909

In his glorious prime,
John Barrymore was probably America's
finest actor. Having risen from light comedian to matinee
idol to tragedian, he capped his New York career with **Hamlet**. Artists
clamored to sketch this handsomest of males, and one who
succeeded during the run of **Hamlet** was
John Singer Sargent.

with the comedy *The Fortune Hunter*, and after it he mused, "In all the other arts, poor bastards starve, freeze, and strip their souls year after year. In this stage paradox, success comes overnight."

Over the next ten years Barrymore acquired an enviable reputation as a light comedian. While working at night, he made early silent pictures during the day. Usually these were farcical comedies, and in the hinterlands Barrymore rated second only to Charlie Chaplin as a funnyman.

But even then the actor was surrounded by people who believed he could become something more than a *farceur*. Among them were his sister Ethel; playwright Edward Sheldon, author of *Salvation Nell* and *Romance*; and Alexander Woollcott, who spoke for all when he expressed the belief, "This apparently raffish clown has genius." Barrymore's well-wishers thought he should be playing Shakespeare, for the actor was fond of quoting what he called the Bard's iambic perfections. In addition, his own robust, picturesque vocabulary had a distinct Shakespearean flavor.

However, Barrymore had other interests. He had begun to drink (in emulation of his father) at age fourteen and had kept it up relentlessly since, despite excruciating hangovers and unpardonable social lapses. At his drinking best, he was suave and debonair. But whatever his condition, he was happiest when drinking.

He had been introduced to sex at an equally early age, when a girl friend of his father's beckoned the attractive youth into a bed just vacated by his parent. As an actor, females sent Barrymore mash notes, flowers, and exposed themselves invitingly in his path. Barrymore would rather drink than make love but liked to finish off a night of revelry in a warm bed beside a warmer body. "Girls are just girls to him," said his friend Ashton Stevens, "and the plural suited better than the singular."

Despite this, Barrymore was an incurable romantic who fell in love every seven years and, when he did, behaved like a smitten adolescent. In 1917 he met and married his second wife, poetess Michael Strange, and at the time of *Hamlet* this union was turbulently breaking up. Yet it was during this marriage that Barrymore began to agree with his friends about undertaking more serious roles. After *Peter Ibbetson* (in which Lionel played the villainous Colonel Ibbetson), he played in Galsworthy's *Escape*, *Redemption*, and *The Jest*, also with Lionel. Finally, in 1920, he starred in a successful *Richard III*.

Strangely enough, Barrymore's voice had been his weak point. His vocal cords tired easily, and the tones emerging from his larynx were furry and undistinguished compared to his smashing appearance. Barrymore had not contemplated doing Shakespeare until good fortune led him to Margaret Carrington, a voice teacher and sister of actor Walter Huston. Mrs. Carrington believed that in an actor's voice "thought and soul must find their way into vibrations of depth and beauty—it is beyond soul, it is a communication of spirit."

Barrymore's stormy marriage to poet-playwright Michael Strange headed for the
rocks before **Hamlet**, and many thought marital furies added
to the glowing fire of his performances. Here the
couple try to look compatible.

Barrymore's *Hamlet*
proved he had delved deeply into the writings
of a newly popular Sigmund Freud. His was a cerebral performance
with overtones of neurosis. With him is Blanche Yurka as his mother, the Queen.

Barrymore worked tirelessly with Mrs. Carrington before **Richard III**. The result was a voice of which he was complete master, able to shape every syllable, sending chills up the spines of an audience, or making them rock with laughter at a swift nuance. At last he was at peak power. "His wine is from his own vine," commented producer Arthur Hopkins.

When preparing **Hamlet** he also studied with Mrs. Carrington. The pair threw out notes and guidelines laid down by others and worked on it like a newly written script. Their interpretation was intellectual rather than active—"more brains than blood," a critic would say. In those days Freudian psychoanalysis was making its first impression on the mind of the world, and the alert Barrymore perceived an Oedipus relationship between Prince Hamlet and his mother. Blanche Yurka, who played the Queen, was actually younger in years than Barrymore. Though made up to look older, she had a young air, allowing for certain implications of incest. "To my Mother, from her wildly incestuous son," read Barrymore's Christmas card to her that year.

Broadway knew of the preparations for **Hamlet** and expected it to be the highlight of the 1922-23 season. Rehearsals began, with Blanche Yurka as the Queen and Tyrone Power, Sr., as Claudius. Sensitive Arthur Hopkins was producer and the sets were by Robert Edmond Jones, most admired scenic designer of the time. Jones built a vast stairway with three platforms and a great arch forming a soaring background. Said one expert, "The fluidic lighting of this set complied with and accentuated the stark aspects of the tragic action."

Barrymore did not let the public down. A few of those who sat in the audience on opening night may have disapproved of the amount of cutting he and Mrs. Carrington had done; others may have objected to the Oedipus aspect of the mother-son relationship. But the majority of first-nighters believed Barrymore's Hamlet the finest they had ever seen.

Looking back on it, Blanche Yurka saw "a passionate, bitterly humorous reading of the part." Critics of the day were not so analytical. "The Hamlet of the Century," one wrote and the rest agreed. Percy Hammond saluted "so beautiful a picture, so clear an analysis, so untheatrical an impersonation, and so musical a rendering of Shakespearean song." Wrote another: "There has never been such a great actor at any time; there never has been such shattering beauty in art." In the **Nation**, Ludwig Lewisohn wrote, "Other actors can act Hamlet, but John Barrymore **is** Hamlet." Brother Lionel took it in stride, saying, "You must take into account that when the Bard wrote **Hamlet**, he had Jack in mind."

Barrymore himself reacted with typical perversity, telling an interviewer that Hamlet was the easiest role he ever played. "You can play it standing, sitting, lying down or, if you insist, kneeling," he explained.

"You can have a hangover. You can be cold sober. You can be hungry, overfed, or just have fought with your wife. It makes no difference as regards your stance or your mood. There are, within the precincts of this great role, a thousand Hamlets, any one of which will keep in step with your whim of the evening."

Yet the success of *Hamlet* brought another problem. Over the years it had been noted that Barrymore was an actor who did not really enjoy acting. He liked the preparation and rehearsal of a role but after opening night quickly grew bored. Said producer Hopkins, "Once the excitement has passed, the part interests him no more."

This was true with *Hamlet*—though his admirers hoped it wouldn't be. Barrymore's best interpretations probably came at dress rehearsals and opening night. After that he grew erratic. Sometimes his words snapped and crackled electrically, but just as often the lines were slurred, more from indifference than drink. Recalls Blanche Yurka, "Each night some scenes would be superbly played, while others were perfunctory, and they were never the same scenes twice." He also displayed attacks of nerves surprising in so experienced an actor. The Moscow Art Theatre, led by the great Constantin Stanislavsky, visited New York and the Russians attended a performance of *Hamlet*. Their presence rendered Barrymore so jittery that he gave a ragged performance and sent the Russians away disappointed.

Broadway buzzed with speculation over how long this *Hamlet* would continue. One evening playwright Marc Connelly encountered the actor and asked him. "Everybody wants to know that," Barrymore replied. "What do they think this is—a tugboat race?"

The question was settled when a delegation of distinguished older actors and authors entered Barrymore's dressing room. They were men who had seen and admired Edwin Booth's *Hamlet*. Booth had set a record by giving 100 consecutive performances on Broadway, and the gentlemen asked Barrymore to terminate his production at ninety-nine, thus allowing the Booth record to stand. The actor was annoyed and snapped, "I'll play mine one hundred and one times." And he did.

Still, he was not through with *Hamlet*. He was determined to play the role in London, though English producers and public did not seem interested. Finally, Barrymore all but produced it himself. His *Hamlet* was praised in London, and he performed for twelve weeks. But the star's growing boredom was apparent as he took one curtain call with a pet monkey on his shoulder and another clutching a saxophone.

Returning to the United States, he started to tour in *Hamlet*, then abruptly closed in Cleveland. The Warner Brothers of Hollywood had offered him a contract at $75,000 a film, plus overtime and approval of casts and sets. To sweeten this further, the studio promised to pay his rent and living expenses. By now Barrymore had made some forty movies and knew that in them he could create his characters, then forget them after one appearance before the camera; in Hollywood, there would be no more playing the same roles night after night. "On the stage, I have to work hard for a fairly small salary," he told an interviewer. "In Hollywood, I can loaf and earn ten times more."

He traveled to Hollywood in 1925 to become one of the film immortals. Not until 1940 did he reappear on Broadway and then as a wreck from drink who clowned through a play also featuring his nineteen-year-old bride.

Did he think back on 1922 and *Hamlet*? He must have. Broadway had known him in his finest hour. "The Hamlet of the Century," he had been called, and the tribute still held valid. John Gielgud, Leslie Howard, Maurice Evans, Richard Burton—none of the others who played the role since have come anywhere near matching his fire. It is not likely anyone ever will.

SHORT TAKE

Probably no actor in history was as temperamental onstage as John Barrymore. He expected audiences to maintain total silence while he emoted. When they failed, he reacted.

Coughing in an audience especially annoyed him. One of his favorite responses was to cough along with the cougher until the latter was shamed into stopping. Once, when a man's hacking cough kept interrupting his lines, he strode to the front of the stage and intoned, "Will somebody please throw a fish to that seal!"

In *Peter Ibbetson*, a piece of business had him picking up a bouquet dropped by the Duchess of Towers, pressing the flowers to his lips, and tenderly murmuring "*l'amour.*" It was a scene that kept audiences transfixed, but one night a girl in the balcony gave a nervous giggle. Barrymore leaped out of his role to shout, "Damn it! If you think you can play this part better than I can, come down here and do it." With that, he hurled the bouquet into the audience. It struck a woman in the face, injuring her eye.

Not only audiences bugged him. During one major scene a stage electrician focused his light on Barrymore's feet rather than face. In a fury Barrymore stormed into the wings, felled the electrician with an uppercut, and returned to his acting onstage.

Barrymore did not always come out ahead. One night he strode to the footlights and fixed a cougher with a baleful, unblinking stare. The offender stirred, laboriously got up from his seat, adjusted a pair of crutches, and struggled up the aisle. Acutely embarrassed, Barrymore for a time left audiences alone.

SEVENTH HEAVEN

Austin Strong's **Seventh Heaven**, with Helen Menken, Frank Morgan, and George Gaul, was a hit when produced in October 1922 and a greater success when made into an early talkie with Janet Gaynor and Charles Farrell. Assisting the movie was the haunting theme song "Diane."

The lurid plot of **Seventh Heaven** is one the world should not be allowed to forget. It tells of two sisters, Nina and Diane, adrift in Paris just before World War I. In their slum quarters, Nina has turned brutal and bestial from absinthe and with a black-snake whip drives her sweet sister into thievery and occasional prostitution.

One day Chico, a debonair sewer worker, rises from a manhole to find Nina in the act of whipping Diane. He rescues the young girl and takes her to his room on the rooftops of Paris. War has just broken out and in three days he will be called to the colors to fight for **la belle France**. In that time he falls in love with Diane and the two marry by pledge just before he leaves.

Over four years Diane waits patiently and honestly for his return. At one point she even grabs the whip from her fiendish sister and lashes her back. Then, on Armistice Day, she hears that Chico has been killed. Cursing **le bon Dieu** for this bitter tragedy, she accepts the caresses of a lover. As she does, Chico steps in the door. But he is blind and does not realize that Diane is in another man's arms. Diane chases the interloper, and she and Chico are ecstatically reunited.

Curtain . . .

Bad sister (Marion Kerby) whips good sister (Helen Menken)
in the lurid *Seventh Heaven*, produced by John Golden

Both the Provincetown Players and the Washington Square Players were born in Greenwich Village. Indeed, for a time in pre-World War I days the two comprised a single amorphous group, consisting of theatre-conscious young idealists who had flocked to Manhattan's Bohemia. Then the group split, with the Provincetown spin-off becoming known for the discovery of Eugene O'Neill. The Washington Square Players went on to achieve greater distinction, for they became the Theatre Guild.

The reason for the split between these two groups was simple to comprehend. Those on the Provincetown side believed in encouraging native-born playwrights, then presenting them in off-Broadway surroundings. The Washington Square Players marched to a different drummer. They were determined to invade Broadway and put the contemporary theatre to shame.

As seen by Lawrence Langner, a practicing patent attorney and playwright who was an ever-vital figure of the Guild, "The Provincetown was always a more personal expression of the authors behind it than was our group, with the result that it tended its authors more than its audiences . . . It was frankly experimental as to plays, while the Washington Square Players were attempting to present productions which would be in healthy competition with the plays on Broadway."

However, there was more. The Washington Square group steadfastly believed that at first they should present only the plays of European authors in order to establish higher standards for American playwrights. Once American writers had developed enough, they too would be produced. The Players were also violently opposed to any star system in the theatre. Never, its members vowed, would the name of an actor appear above the title of a play in one of their productions.

True to this, the Washington Square Players gave their first productions at the uptown Bandbox Theatre. Between 1915-17 they offered three long plays and sixty-one short ones, including one by Eugene O'Neill and another by Theodore Dreiser. But as often as possible foreigners like Shaw, Maeterlinck, Chekhov, and Leonid Andreyev were the authors.

Came World War I and the group disintegrated, some members joining the Army to fight and others performing various war jobs. After the armistice the spirit still flared, and it was decided to proceed even more ambitiously as the Theatre Guild. Further, it was determined to present only full-length plays—"a professional theatre, to present plays of artistic merit not ordinarily produced by the commercial managers."

One especially important part of the credo was to raise money by selling seats on a subscription basis—that is, subscribers would pay in advance for a season of five or six plays. Ideally, this would eliminate the headaches involved in finding financial backing for each production.

There was something splendid about the spirit of these eager amateurs! For proof, take the fact that they softened the callous heart of Lee Shubert, who before the war gave them easy terms on the Comedy Theatre. Afterward, financier-philanthropist Otto Kahn let them use the Garrick Theatre on West 35th Street on a pay-rent-when-you-can basis.

The first Theatre Guild production at the Garrick—on April 19, 1919—was a Spanish **commedia dell' arte** costume play by the Nobel Prize winner Jacinto Benavente. A member of its large cast was Edna St. Vincent Millay. On opening night 150 pioneer Guild subscribers sat expectantly before the curtain, and their applause at the end was clamorous.

However, the critics did not agree, and the run was short. A month later the Guild was down to its last dollar as the curtain rose on a second play, St. John Ervine's **John Ferguson**, with Dudley Digges, Augustin Duncan, and Helen Westley. This turned out to be a happy hit that ran through the summer of 1919. During the Actors' Equity strike it was the only play open, for the Guild had signed with Equity before the walkout began.

The next two plays were failures, but once more the day was saved by St. John Ervine and **Jane Clegg**, with Margaret Wycherly. Then came Shaw's **Heartbreak House**, and with this the Guild became Shaw's official American producer. "Shaw was the backbone of the Guild in the early days," writes Langner. "We used to say, 'When in doubt play Shaw.'"

By now the Guild had shaken down to a working organization. Theresa Helburn, executive director, was also a member of the six-person board that picked the plays to be produced and the casts to appear in them. Other members were patent attorney Lawrence Langner, play director Philip Moeller, moneyman Maurice Wertheim, actress Helen Westley, and scenic artist Lee Simonson. "Each member was talented in a particular manner," says Langner, "and our results were the sum of these talents."

Philip Moeller, who directed most of the important Guild plays, was a firm believer in natural, character-motivated acting, and the example of the Guild did much to establish a more relaxed style of acting in the American theatre. Moeller, incidentally, was the first director ever to tell an actor to use pear-shaped tones. The actor was Ireland's J. M. Kerrigan, and he coolly inquired, "Which end of the pear would you like first?"

The six Guild board members were known to argue fiercely among themselves as they selected productions. Yet from the midst of turmoil emerged, between 1920-25, such noteworthy plays as **Mr. Pim Passes By**, by A. A. Milne; **Liliom** and **The Guardsman**, by Ferenc

The importance of the Theatre Guild in drama of the Twenties cannot be overestimated.
This ardent group of amateurs-into-pros first scored with St. John
Ervine's **John Ferguson**. But it was George Bernard Shaw
who brought immortality by assigning to the Guild rights
to his plays. **St. Joan**, with Winifred Lenihan,
rocked the theatre universe.

After establishing European drama on Broadway, the Theatre Guild turned to native playwrights. One daring production was the impressionistic *Processional*, by John Howard Lawson. Seen here are June Walker and George Abbott, who went on to an impressive career as collaborator, director, producer, and nearly everything else.

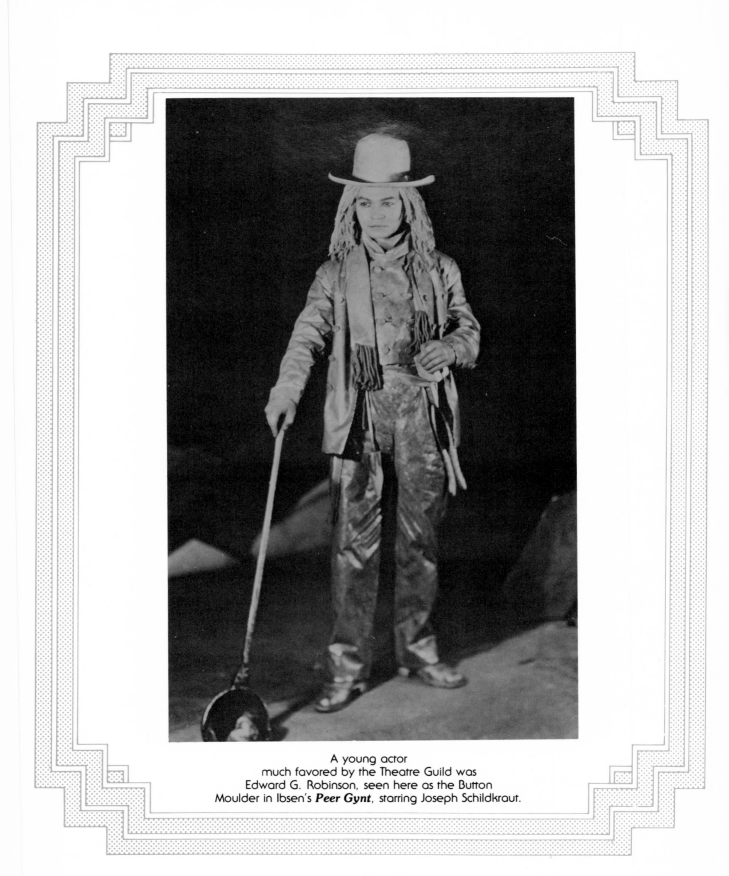

A young actor
much favored by the Theatre Guild was
Edward G. Robinson, seen here as the Button
Moulder in Ibsen's **Peer Gynt**, starring Joseph Schildkraut.

Molnar; *He Who Gets Slapped*, by Leonid Andreyev; *Peer Gynt*, by Henrik Ibsen; *R.U.R.* by Karl Capek; *Fata Morgana*, by Ernest Vajda; and *Heartbreak House*, *Back to Methuselah*, *The Devil's Disciple*, *Arms and the Man*, *St. Joan*, and *Caesar and Cleopatra*, by George Bernard Shaw.

Even so, the Guild had ups and downs, for its policy was to sink the profits of successful productions into others that might not do as well. No money was earned, and little praise gained, from the likes of Galsworthy's *Windows*, Lenormand's *The Failures*, or Verhaeren's *The Cloister*. In order to keep the Garrick stage clear for its six productions a year, the Guild moved its hit plays into other theatres. Thus, *Liliom* was transferred to the Fulton Theatre, where it ran 311 performances, and *Mr. Pim Passes By* went to the Henry Miller, where it played 232.

The Guild tried to get top actors for its efforts, and among them were Richard Bennett and Margalo Gillmore (*He Who Gets Slapped*), Joseph Schildkraut and Eva Le Gallienne (*Liliom*), Lionel Atwill and Helen Hayes (*Caesar and Cleopatra*), Winifred Lenihan (*St. Joan*), Dennis King (*Back to Methuselah*), and Basil Sydney (*The Devil's Disciple*). Playing a small part in *Peer Gynt*, in which Schildkraut had the title role, was Edward G. Robinson.

In its first season the Guild had 500 subscribers; in the second, 1,300; and by 1923, 6,000. By then the organization had begun presenting the works of American playwrights, among them Elmer Rice's *The Adding Machine*, Sidney Howard's *They Knew What They Wanted*, and John Howard Lawson's *Processional*. Fed up with the dilapidated Garrick, the Guild began raising $600,000 by the sale of bonds to build its own theatre. A site on West 52nd Street was picked and two years allowed for construction.

Broadway's feelings about the Theatre Guild were mixed. Rival producers still considered it upstart, arty, and amateur; they could never understand how the Guild shoved aside successful plays to concentrate on new ones.

"The play's the thing" was ever the Guild motto, and the salaries paid to actors, even to stars, were the barest minimum. In 1924, when the Lunts came to the Guild for *The Guardsman*, they were paid $250 a week together, *not singly*. Why did the Lunts do it? In part because they liked the play, but mainly because of an aching desire to play opposite each other.

Still opposed to the star system, the Guild did not compensate for its low wages by putting an actor's name in lights. "We are an art theatre, we do not make money," Theresa Helburn told any stars who demanded this. "Think instead of the prestige of acting for us." Guild roles were usually fine roles, and most actors succumbed to her blandishments. However, the acting profession believed the Guild was indifferent to salaries because its board members had extra-theatre means. Langner, for instance, had his thriving patent business, Moeller had a wealthy father and Miss Helburn a rich husband.

But the Guild continued to flourish and by mid-decade was speeding along like an idea whose time had come. In April 1925 the Guild Theatre opened with Shaw's **Caesar and Cleopatra**, and by then the subscribers list ($15 a season) was swollen by those who considered Theatre Guild membership a mark of cultural status.

And while still at the Garrick, the Guild put on a show that showed its rare flexibility. This was **The Garrick Gaieties**, music by Richard Rodgers, lyrics by Lorenz Hart. This refreshing revue was performed by younger actors—Sterling Holloway, Romney Brent, Philip Loeb, Libby Holman—who worked for the Guild and rehearsed in off hours. Soon the whole town was humming "Manhattan" and "Sentimental Me" from the arty Theatre Guild's musical comedy.

LONG TAKE—ROSIE MURPHEYSKI

The comedy titled **Abie's Irish Rose** opened on the night of March 23, 1922. Destined to be one of the theatre miracles of all time, it ran on Broadway for 2,327 performances, or five years and five months. In this time, it served as the butt of a million jokes, in revues, vaudeville, burlesque, and elsewhere.

Abie's Irish Rose was no overnight hit but took about a month to tap its rich vein of lowbrow audience. During that period author Anne Nichols, a devout believer in her brainchild, frantically borrowed money to keep her play running. One of her biggest loans reputedly came from Arnold Rothstein, the shadowy big-time gambler.

Anne Nichols' unpretentious hit dealt with young Abraham Levy, who at the end of World War I brought home as his bride Rosemary Murphy, a girl he met in France as she entertained the doughboys. Knowing his family, Abie introduced the blushing beauty as the onetime Rosie Murpheyski. Soon the Murphy clan came to visit, and you can take it from there. Miss Nichols, already a playwright, had heard of a similar situation in life and immediately went to work on her typewriter.

Amazingly enough, Alexander Woollcott gave **Abie's Irish Rose** a good notice, but other first-night critics were not so charitable. One called it "cheap claptrap," while others employed words like "ridiculous," "idiotic," and "stupid." The New York **World** deemed it beneath mention.

Placed in the worst spot was Robert Benchley, then the play reviewer of the humor magazine **Life**. Benchley gave the alleged comedy a scathing review, evoking the image of a latter-day Paul Revere galloping up and down Broadway to proclaim, "**The Rotters** is no longer the worst play in town—**Abie's Irish Rose** has arrived!"

Phenomenal was—and is—the word for **Abie's Irish Rose**, which ran more
than five years on Broadway. In all, playwright Anne Nichols
made over $6,000,000 from her mixed-marriage brainchild.
Marian Shockley played the Irish Rose, Richard Bond Abie, Al White Abie's father.

Each week *Life* provided capsule comments about plays on the Rialto, and throughout *Abie's* seemingly endless run Benchley thought up new cracks at seven-day intervals. One was: "People laugh at this every night, which explains why democracy can never be a success." Another: "Where do the people come from who keep this one going? You don't see them on the streets in the daytime." After *Abie* had run a year he wrote, "We give up!" In 1924 he said, "In another two or three years we'll have this play driven out of town." In 1926 it was "Closing soon (only fooling)."

Despite the scorn it aroused among the intelligentsia, *Abie's Irish Rose* appealed mightily to average members of the general public. At one time six road companies of *Abie* crisscrossed the country, with others touring England and Australia. There would have been more touring if the author had not called a halt because of taxes. *Abie's Irish Rose* became such a big business that at one time *Variety*, the show-business bible, devoted an entire issue to it.

Abie's Irish Rose finally closed in October 1927.

Hit songs from Broadway shows, 1922:
"Carolina in the Morning" (Kahn/Donaldson), from *The Passing Show*
"Crinoline Days," "Lady of the Evening" (Berlin), from *Music Box Revue*
"Stairway to Paradise" (Gershwin/De Sylva), from *George White's Scandals*
"A Kiss in the Dark" (Herbert/De Sylva), from *Orange Blossoms*
"Way Down Yonder in New Orleans" (Creamer/Layton), from *Spice of 1922*
"Toot, Toot, Tootsie" (Kahn/Erdman/FioRito/King), from *Bombo*

ROUNDUP

As the best plays of 1922 Burns Mantle selected **Rain**, adapted from Somerset Maugham's short story by John Colton and Miss Clemence Randolph; **He Who Gets Slapped**, by Leonid Andreyev with Richard Bennett and Margalo Gillmore; **Loyalties**, by John Galsworthy; **Why Not?** a comedy by Jesse Lynch Williams; **The Fool**, by Channing Pollock; **Merton of the Movies**, adapted from Harry Leon Wilson's novel by George S. Kaufman and Marc Connelly, with Glenn Hunter and Mary Nash; **The Old Soak**, by Don Marquis, based on a character invented by the author for his "Sun Dial" column in the New York **Sun**; and **R.U.R.**, by Karel Capek, which introduced the word **robot** to the language. And who played two of the robots? None other than Spencer Tracy and Pat O'Brien, young actors who had yet to speak a word on the stage.

Because John Barrymore's **Hamlet** was an old play, it could not be listed as a "best," even though many considered it the most worthwhile production of the year. This was also the year of the first American production of Luigi Pirandello's **Six Characters in Search of an Author**.

Plays that delighted theatregoers were **Seventh Heaven**; **The Torchbearers**, by George Kelly, with Alison Skipworth and Mary Boland; **The Awful Truth**, with Ina Claire; **To the Ladies**, by Kaufman and Connelly, with Helen Hayes and Otto Kruger; **Lawful Larceny**, with suave Lowell Sherman; **The Cat and the Canary**, another Mary Roberts Rinehart chiller, with Henry Hull and Florence Eldridge.

Also **Shore Leave**, with Frances Starr; Grace George in **Marie Antoinette**, with Pedro de Cordoba; Doris Keane in **The Czarina**, supported by Basil Rathbone; **The Rubicon**, with Edna May Oliver; **The Truth about Blayds**, by A. A. Milne, with Leslie Howard and Frieda Inescourt; **Dreams for Sale**, with Helen Gahagan; **Lonely Heart**, second Broadway appearance of Ann Harding, who was complimented by a critic for her "astonishing wealth of golden hair"; Laurette Taylor in **The National Anthem**; Henry Miller and Ruth Chatterton in **La Tendresse**, Billie Burke in **Rose Briar**; Alice Brady in **Drifting**; Jane Cowl in **Malvaloc**; and **Kempy**, by and with folksy J. C. Nugent and son Elliott.

A major disappointment was David Warfield in **The Merchant of Venice**, presented with much fanfare by David Belasco. Star and producer had planned this project for years, but it turned out listless.

The musical sensation of the year came from Russia! It was the intimate revue **Chauve-Souris**, which arrived on Broadway by way of London and Paris—a delightful, sophisticated Muscovite vaudeville, with its master of ceremonies an ingratiating, moon-faced Nikita Balieff. This revue had originated as a diversion for players of the Moscow Art Theatre and afterward expanded into a lively divertissement for the public, featuring Russian folk songs, dances, and burlesque dramatic

Melodrama
was a staple of the stage in the hallowed Twenties. Ann Mason,
Charles Trowbridge, William Courtleigh, Clarence Derwent, and
Ben Lackland register varying degrees of alarm
in *Last Warning.*

Irving Berlin's **Music Box Revues** turned out to be the super-successes
everyone anticipated. In them, Grace Moore warbled
Berlin melodies like "What'll I Do?"
and lovely Miriam Hopkins
(center) was one of the Seven Little Musical Notes. But the tasteful shows
proved too expensive and were dropped after 1924.
The Music Box Theatre still stands.

sketches. Its most popular act was "Parade of the Wooden Soldiers," with its catchy music. Balieff remained in this country and offered several other editions of his **Chauve-Souris**, but none met with the high approval of the first.

Other shows with music were **The Lady in Ermine**, with Wilda Bennett; **The Gingham Girl**, with Helen Ford and Eddie Buzzell; **Sally, Irene and Mary**, with Eddie Dowling; Joseph Cawthorn and Robert Woolsey in **The Blue Kitten**; Peggy Wood in **The Clinging Vine**; Charles King in **Little Nelly Kelly**; Eddie Cantor in **Make It Snappy**; Clark and McCullogh, Charlotte Greenwood, and John Steel in Irving Berlin's **Music Box Revue**; and Hal Skelly and Queenie Smith in **Orange Blossom**.

Fred and Adele Astaire appeared in **For Goodness Sake**, a musical tailored to their talents. This year W. C. Fields was to be found in **George White's Scandals**, along with Paul Whiteman's Orchestra. **The Passing Show of 1922** starred the comics Willie and Eugene Howard; also in it was a young monologist named Fred Allen, making his debut.

GREAT GLORIFIER

The best people in town turned out for premieres of a *Ziegfeld Follies*
As the stock market hit new heights, paper-profit millionaires prolifer-
ated and, along with men of entrenched wealth, fought to pay $22 at
the box office (or as high as $100 at ticket speculators) for tickets to
Follies openings at the New Amsterdam on West 42nd Street, which
was Florenz Ziegfeld's favorite theatre until he opened his own uptown. On the arms of escorts, women who attended tried vainly to
look as beautiful as the girls onstage were certain to be.

Next morning's papers treated the premiere as a social occasion, reporting (as one did) the presence of Mr. and Mrs. Vincent Astor, Mr.
and Mrs. Donald Wagstaff, Ambassador to Germany James W. Gerard
and Mrs. Gerard, Mr. and Mrs. William Randolph Hearst, Mr. and Mrs.
Herbert Bayard Swope, Mr. and Mrs. Julius Fleischmann, and Mr. and
Mrs. John Ringling.

The *Ziegfeld Follies of 1923* was not one of your great editions. It was,
for instance, far from the editions of 1917 and 1918, which between
them offered Will Rogers, Eddie Cantor, W. C. Fields, Ed Wynn, Fannie
Brice, Marilyn Miller, and Leon Errol. Today the eyes of nostalgia
hounds grow misty at the thought of such productions, and they wonder
what it would be like to sit through a *Follies* and watch these greats in
their hilarious heyday.

The greatest novelty adhering to the *Follies of 1923* was that it opened
in October, when the superstitious Ziegfeld preferred openings in the
summer. But the *Follies* of the previous year, regarded indifferently by
the critics, had turned out to possess a magic allowing it to run through
one year and far into the next. Will Rogers had starred in that edition,
along with Gilda Gray, famed for her ability to do the quiver-dance
Shimmy. But the probable reason for the extraordinary run of this *Follies* was the presence of Gallagher and Shean, vaudeville veterans
who in this show introduced a nonsense song that swept the country.
Titled "Mr. Gallagher and Mr. Shean," its numerous verses ended "Ab-
solutely, Mr. Gallagher?" "*Positively*, Mr. Shean."

The *Follies of 1923* boasted the comic talents of Fannie Brice and
Eddie Cantor. Strange to say, however, the proud producer of the
Follies, along with a considerable portion of his audience, was less
interested in the funny folk of a Ziegfeld show than in the girls, the sets,
the costumes, and possibly the music. For the name Florenz Ziegfeld—
feld, never *field*—represented the absolute ultimate in sumptuous
good taste. Ziegfeld's ability to pick beautiful girls and garb—or
ungarb—them in spectacular and revealing fashion was unsurpassed.
Instinctively this man understood the delicate line between taste and
vulgarity and trod it like a tight-rope artist.

Far from a frantic Times Square,
Billie Burke, most charming of actresses, was
Mrs. Florenz Ziegfeld in private life. Here she posed at country estate
with husband, daughter Patricia, and
sundry canines. Ziegfeld loved his Billie but shamelessly
shopped around among **Follies** beauties.

Flo Ziegfeld himself was a man loved or liked by few but admired and envied by many. Lean and hawk-faced, with a nasal singsong voice, he posed before the world as imperturbable and ever-charming. Actually he was vain, insecure, and a cruel taskmaster over those wooed into his employ. In theatre and private life extravagance was Ziegfeld's trademark, his bit, his thing. Adorning his desk were three solid gold telephones; a fleet of limousines drove him and friends around town, and private Pullmans and yachts carried him afar. He once gave Eddie Cantor a Rolls-Royce merely because the comedian said he had always wanted one.

When a designer of a Ziegfeld show asked the producer to choose between a fabric that cost $5 a yard and another at $30, Ziegfeld unhesitatingly picked the latter. At other times he ordered costumes sewed with gold and silver thread. In relaxed moments during rehearsals he pitched $20 gold pieces with showgirls and made sure they won. On opening nights every *Follies* girl got an expensive bouquet from Mr. Ziegfeld, and during the run of the show he rewarded (or propositioned) his favorites with diamonds.

The sums Ziegfeld spent on his shows may not seem large today, but in the Twenties they were astronomical. The *Follies of 1907* cost $19,000; by 1920 the sum was $100,000. By the end of the decade a *Follies* cost $300,000 so that, with operating costs and other running expenses, it was impossible to make a profit or even a return of the initial investment. At one point in the Twenties Ziegfeld had an enviable clutch of hits in a *Follies*, *Kid Boots*, *Show Boat*, *The Three Musketeers*, and *Rio Rita*. According to Broadway rumor all lost money because of the producer's lavishness.

Yet Ziegfeld never changed his prodigal ways; there were always plenty of millionaires flattered to invest in his shows. Only the stock-market crash of 1929 stopped him, and even then he put on a *Follies of 1931*, two years after the world as he knew it fell apart.

Every advertisement for a *Follies* carried the line "Glorifying the American Girl." There were about 100 glorified girls in a *Follies* and fifty more in the *Ziegfeld Midnight Frolic*, a supper show presented upstairs on the New Amsterdam Roof. To get his girls, Ziegfeld interviewed some 15,000 eager females annually. Those chosen for the *Follies* were immediately placed under the tutelage of stage director Ned Wayburn in a backstage finishing school and taught how to dress, walk, and talk like exquisite ladies. Ziegfeld never let his beauties appear in public unless dressed to glossy perfection.

Ziegfeld was as mystified as anyone by his ability to pick rare beauties. Asked his secret, he could only say, "They must attract men, you cannot define the quality." Of course, Irving Berlin said it best in his song for the 1919 *Follies* — "A pretty girl is like a melody/That haunts you night and day."

Sometimes you had trouble
seeing the girls for the costumes in the **Ziegfeld Follies**. Here Vivian Vernon is
a super-lavish butterfly.

Ziegfeld paid his gorgeous girls $75 a week when the Broadway going rate for showgirls was $30. Each girl had at least one precious individual moment in a **Follies**, usually when she swayed center stage to pause for a moment, the focus of all eyes. Her attire might be a diaphanous, ermine-trimmed costume that left her shapely legs free and opened elsewhere to reveal strands of pearls wrapped around a naked body. Usually the girls wore beautiful but incredible head-dresses. Some Ziegfeld showgirls were so surpassingly lovely that males came night after night just to watch them strut around. Two such were Justine Johnstone and a girl who called herself Dolores.

Follies girls had to change costumes between numbers, and it was also necessary to shift spectacular scenery. Ziegfeld would have been happy to put a tenor before the curtain at these moments, letting him warble a song the girls could pose to in the next number. But the producer was surrounded by henchmen who persuaded him the **Follies** needed laughs.

So Ziegfeld gave in and began hiring comedians like W. C. Fields, Ed Wynn, and Eddie Cantor from vaudeville. They did their acts and took part in sketches during costume and scenery changes. Ziegfeld heard the laughter these immortals evoked but was glum about it. He didn't even appreciate Fannie Brice, whom he hired as a singer, then grudg-ingly allowed to burlesque songs and play in sketches.

The Great Glorifier lived surrounded by girls, girls, girls. He married twice. His first wife was the chanteuse Anna Held ("I Just Can't Make My Eyes Behave"), who gave him the idea for the **Follies** and whose Gallic know-how helped him perfect a formula patterned after the **Folies-Bergère**. His second wife was effervescent Billie Burke, whom he presented in a number of nonmusical plays.

Both wives loved Ziggy deeply, and each had to grow accustomed to the fact that he dallied with girls he glorified. When Billie Burke accused him of spending a night with luscious Olive Thomas, the imperturbable gent sighed and said, "The trouble with you, Billie, is that you always pick the wrong girl!"

As Miss Burke teetered on the verge of leaving her spouse, she rationalized by saying, "He adores those girls, but he **loves** me." This fine distinction allowed her to remain at his side until he died.

THE GLORIFIED

The number of Ziegfeld beauties who advanced to theatrical or cinema fame is amazing. Among them were Ina Claire, Mae Murray, Billie Dove, Peggy Hopkins Joyce, Marion Davies, Nita Naldi, Dorothy Mackaill, Jacqueline Logan, Lilyan Tashman, and Paulette Goddard.

Helen Morgan danced in the back row of a musical comedy produced by Ziegfeld, then went on to be a nightclub singer, after which Ziggy hired her for his immortal **Show Boat**. Ruby Keeler danced and sang the leading role of **Show Girl**. Ziegfeld glimpsed Irene Dunne in an elevator of the New Amsterdam building; finding she was a singer, he cast her as Magnolia in the Chicago company of **Show Boat**.

Just to be in a **Follies** was the most exciting career for any beautiful girl of the Twenties. Glamour had not yet reached Hollywood, and there was no higher pinnacle for an aspiring—or pleasure-loving—beauty than to be glorified by Flo Ziegfeld.

One song extolling **Follies** girls called them "Adeles and Mollies/ Lucilles and Pollys." In short, all types, all kinds. Some had hidden husbands; others supported ailing mothers or put brothers through college. Kay Laurel, the first **Follies** girl to bare bosoms in a **Follies tableau vivant**, did so solely because it brought extra money. This **Follies** girl was shrewd, ambitious, and self-centered, saving herself and her pennies for a dramatic acting career that never quite eventuated.

Many **Follies** girls came from small towns and drab backgrounds— one actually grew up in McKees Rocks, Pennsylvania—and let the bright lights of Broadway go to their delectable heads. With the coming of the Jazz Age and Prohibition gin, revelry for these pampered darlings stepped up a thousandfold.

Ziegfeld Follies girls were widely supposed to be dumb, and a multitude of jokes called them muscle-bound between the ears. One went, "I met a **Follies** girl who's so dumb she thinks Einstein is a glass of beer." Yet some were smart and quick-witted. "How do **Follies** girls get minks?" one was asked. "The same way minks do," she answered. Much married Peggy Hopkins Joyce met a society dowager who wanted to know why she wed so often. "I owe it to my pubic," Peggy replied.

Some of the eye-filling showgirls put on airs. Kay Laurel, the girl who aspired to act, became so refined she said "Detroit" with the French pronunciation "Detrois." In her frivolous moments Kay had Reginald Vanderbilt and Clarence Darrow as swains. Lillian Lorraine, whose life became a compulsive quest for thrills, was probably the first **Follies** girl to demand that a man give her a present before taking her out. She appears on the record as saying, "I won't accept any gifts in only the low hundreds from my gentleman friends." After Lillian, any high-

In the days before Hollywood glamour,
Ziegfeld Follies Girls were the reigning beauties of the land. Typical
of envied ones were Lena Thomas and Jean Ackerman.

flying *Follies* girl expected an expensive bauble or a $100 bill (or maybe $1,000) just for stepping out with a guy.

Marion Davies, a *Follies* girl at fifteen, became a movie star and lifetime consort of publisher William Randolph Hearst, able to lend him a million dollars when his journalistic empire grew shaky. Another *Follies* girl married Tommy Manville and got his first million-dollar divorce settlement. One-name Dolores wed a man of great wealth and spent the rest of her life elegantly in the south of France.

Not all *Follies* girls did well; many were ill-starred. After playing opposite John Barrymore in *Dr. Jekyll and Mr. Hyde*, Martha Mansfield burned to death when her costume caught fire on a Hollywood set. Olive Thomas took an overdose of sleeping pills on her second Paris honeymoon with Jack Pickford, irresponsible brother of Mary.

Other *Follies* beauties, among them Hilda Ferguson and Marion 'Kiki'' Roberts, displayed a deplorable weakness for the tough gangsters then infesting Broadway. Naturally, the New York tabloids—*News*, *Mirror*, *Graphic*—vied with each other for scandal about *Follies* girls. Top space winner here was Imogene ''Bubbles'' Wilson, called by Ziegfeld the most beautiful blonde ever to adorn his shows. Her lengthy love affair with the middle-aged comedian Frank Tinney featured publicized sex, sadism, and suicide attempts.

The career of Justine Johnstone, considered an all-time beauty in Ziegfeld shows, proves *Follies* girls were not always self-centered pleasure cravers. For a time Justine dreamed (like Kay Laurel) of being a dramatic star and was encouraged by new husband Walter Wanger, who worked for the Theatre Guild and in time became a top Hollywood producer. After Justine made a few appearances in stock companies, the young couple went to London, where she enjoyed moderate success on the boards.

When the Wangers returned to the United States, Justine found her interest in the theatre gone. As Justine Wanger, she applied for a job as laboratory assistant at the New York College of Physicians and Surgeons. Her work was brilliant, and over the years she became associated with several important medical discoveries. Justine divorced Wanger in 1938 and quickly went back to her medical research.

SUNSHINE GIRL

Oddly enough, the girl most often associated with Ziegfeld was not primarily of the **Follies**. She was Marilyn Miller, never a showgirl but a topflight dancing star beloved by the audiences of every show she graced. Ziegfeld put her in the **Follies** of 1918 and 1919 as a featured dancer and through the Twenties offered her twinkling toes in a series of lavish musical comedies tailored to her talents. Incidentally, she claimed to be inventor of the name Marilyn by combining her own name, Mary, with that of her mother, Lyn.

Onstage Marilyn Miller was a ray of sunshine. One critic wrote of her adorable style and happy dancing. Guy Bolton and P. G. Wodehouse were authors of **Sally**, her first big hit, in which she sang Jerome Kern's "Look for the Silver Lining." Bolton cites her "wistful charm that went right to the heart." Wodehouse recalls her as projecting "a curious enchantment."

Marilyn Miller acquired her skills the hard way, for she began dancing at age four as part of a family vaudeville act. Even as a child she shone with bright good humor and audiences loved her. Yet this divine child, with backstage her schoolyard, knew four-letter words and longer ones as well; when necessary, she employed them with rare distinction.

After several tours in Europe with her family, Marilyn got featured billing in a Shubert **Passing Show**. Ziegfeld, who seldom discovered his own talent, saw her and won her away from the Shuberts by proving her under age at the time of contract-signing. He put her in the **Follies**, where her star-crossed skills caused a sensation. Then she went into **Sally**, which he co-produced with Charles Dillingham, and later into **Sunny**, pluperfect name for a Marilyn Miller show.

Tragedy lurked in the life of the Sunshine Girl. Her first husband died in an automobile accident three months after their marriage; Marilyn was in **Sally** then. With this she became a Jazz Age party-lover as wild as any **Follies** beauty. Next she married playboy Jack Pickford. It took five years, most of them apart, before this union dissolved. Ziegfeld had early pressed his amorous attentions on Marilyn and Broadway believed them intermittent lovers, even though Marilyn was known to prefer chorus boys. Still, she never removed a diamond bracelet he gave her.

Ziegfeld's affection for Marilyn could be measured in dollars and cents. He gave her a percentage of each show she starred in—something done for no other star. Marilyn did a toe-dance specialty in her shows, and each night Ziegfeld provided a brand-new costume for this number. The costumes cost $175 apiece.

Supernal Marilyn Miller,
the most popular musical-comedy star of the day,
projected angelic innocence to an ever-adoring public.
But in the bright slang of the Twenties, this girl knew her onions.

SHORT TAKE
REGRET

Your eyes were brown as autumn leaves.
Your ears like shells from tropic seas.
Your hair was black as Arctic eves.
BUT YOUR HEART HELD NO MORE LOVE THAN MINE.

Your brow was white, like driven snow.
Your cheeks were soft, quite soft (I know!).
Your lips as red as fires aglow.
BUT YOUR HEART HELD NO MORE LOVE THAN MINE.

O arms so molded for embrace!
O wealth of beauty, charm and grace.
You've gone! We both have lost the race.
FOR YOUR HEART HELD NO MORE LOVE THAN MINE.

—Earl Carroll, producer of
the *Vanities*

LAUGHS FROM THE REVUES

Will Rogers in a *Ziegfeld Follies*, on the paradox of Prohibition:

> If you think our country ain't Dry, just watch 'em vote.
> If you think our country ain't Wet, just watch 'em drink.

Willie and Eugene Howard, in a *Passing Show*:

> Eugene: Who's that lady I saw you with in the street?
> Willie: That was no street; that was an alley

> Willie: I had a dream about you last night. If it comes true you'll never have to work again.
> Eugene: What did you dream?
> Willie: I dreamed you were dead.

> Willie: Stop that awful singing.
> Eugene: I can't; the tune haunts me.
> Willie: No wonder it haunts you; you're continually murdering it.

> Willie: My father is a Southern planter.
> Eugene: He is?
> Willie: Yes, he's an undertaker in New Orleans.

Clark and McCullough, in a *Music Box Revue*:

> McCullough: Is that the Senator from Rhode Island?
> Clark: Yes—he was elected by an act of Providence.

> McCullough: What's dumber than one dumb Irishman?
> Clark: Two smart Swedes.

> Clark: That Senator over there was a dollar-a-year man during the war. The government is still suing him for ninety cents.

Moran and Mack (using the slowest of blackface drawls), in a *Greenwich Village Follies*:

> Moran: What's an alibi?
> Mack: An alibi is proving that you was where you was when you wasn't, so you wasn't where you was when you was.

> Moran: I hear you folks are gettin' rid of all your horses.
> Mack: Only white horses; they eats too much.
> Moran: You mean to say that white horses eats more than the others?
> Mack: Yes, the white horses eats twice as much as the black horses.
> Moran: How do you explain that?
> Mack: There's twice as many of 'em. We have four white horses and two black horses. So we're gettin' rid of the white horses and we're gonna get black ones.

Gallagher and Shean, in a *Ziegfeld Follies* (singing):

Oh! Mr. Gallagher—Oh! Mr. Gallagher,
What's the name of the game they play on the links?
With a stick they knock the ball,
Where you can't find it at all,
Then the caddie walks around and thinks and thinks.

Oh! Mr. Shean—Oh! Mr. Shean,
You don't even know a hazard from a green.
It's become a popular game
And you don't even know its name.

Sure, it's croquet, Mr. Gallagher!
No, lawn tennis, Mr. Shean!

Joe Cook, in an *Earl Carroll Vanities* (explaining why he won't imitate four Hawaiians):

I'm a poet. If I were to tell you who I really am, you certainly would be surprised. Many, many years ago I was tossing off so much poetry that, believe it or not, as you like, I found myself running out of ideas. Imagine the fix I was in! The crowds clamoring at my gates for more poetry, women and children being jostled in the mob. I said to myself, "Homer" (I was going under the name of Homer at that time), "you must give the world its poetry." And I just took myself in hand and dashed off a basket of poems. These my lackeys took out and threw to the crowds. Well, sir, the ungrateful knaves began publishing my work under their own names and—laugh and scoff though you may—they made fortunes and got to be famous. They even started a school of New Poetry, modeled after my masterpiece, my Song to a Cloud, which goes—

From a far-off conspicuous, unseen star,
In the spaces of dormant wealth,
Milady betokes the wondrous ode,
While glancing to tales of stealth.
In her gaze I ponder the wrath of it all,
Sublime though it might would be,
And methinks of the woodlands uncitied in fall,
But these thoughts gave great courage to me.
So my steed as he rose and the sparks from his heels
On the silence of midsummer's dream,
Would by morning be known to the ears of the world,
Nay, that and forever 'twould seem.
But they lacked of the fibre, and passed by unsung
Though the trees and the springs were abloom,
Yet in Black Bridle Bay
Yes, oft till this day
Would that thought of a deep dark maroon.

So you see the position I'm in. If the public will prefer such fellows as John Masefield, why should I, a man of my wealth, position, and influence, go out of my way to imitate the four Hawaiians?

FUNNY ONES—I

The 1920's stand as the Golden Age of Comedy, and it's ironic that the *Follies* produced by humorless Flo Ziegfeld proved the best contemporary showcase for top comic talent. Largely this was because of the high competence of Gene Buck, Ziegfeld's first assistant and a songwriter and all-around theatre hand on his own. Today, books have been written about these master comedians of the Twenties, their skills analyzed by such sober authors as Gilbert Seldes, Brooks Atkinson, and Max Eastman. In 1923 the titans stood firmly on their various pinnacles, while a generation of younger, aspiring comedians swarmed below. Here they are in the order of appearances in the *Follies*:

Fannie Brice was born Fanny Borach in a New York ghetto. A gawky girl with rubbery features and a good singing voice, she was a dynamo of youthful ambition, avid for attention and applause, who made her debut at Bowery amateur nights. She was one of the few stars spotted by Ziegfeld himself. He found the nineteen-year-old singing Irving Berlin's "Sadie Salome" with what has been called "hoydenish hilarity." Signed by Ziggy as a comedy singer, she convulsed everyone at rehearsals and was allowed to do comedy and take part in sketches. Indeed, she was so funny that the 1910 edition was called *Fannie's Follies*. Depending heavily on racial humor, she later sang songs like "Oy, I'm an Indian" and tossed away lines like "the gentile waters of the canal." Fannie immortalized the song "My Man" (lyrics by Channing Pollock), which reflected her own inability to choose the right men in private life. She also popularized "Rose of Washington Square," "Secondhand Rose," and novelty numbers like "Becky Is Back at the Ballet." Spelling her name both Fanny and Fannie, she finally opted for the latter. Offstage she was warmhearted and multitalented.

Ed Wynn came of a well-to-do Philadelphia family. Born Edwin Leopold (Ed Wynn—get it?), he spent ten years in vaudeville, joined the 1914 and 1915 *Follies*, in the latter battling with W. C. Fields over laughs. Ed Wynn then struck off on his own, with several "firsts" accruing. He was the first of this batch of comics to appear in his own shows, *Carnival* and *The Perfect Fool*, writing, directing, and producing them as well. So he became the first millionaire comedian. Ed Wynn was a clown given to lisps, chuckles, and nervous giggles, as well as tiny hats, insane costumes, and outsize shoes. Large horn-rim glasses brought him a look of perpetual puzzlement. He made friends with his audiences. Wandering around the stage holding a piece of rope, he wondered if he had found the rope or lost a horse. Again he confided, "I take a swallow of salad dressing every night so as to get up oily in the morning." Other laugh-getters were his silly inventions, among them corn on the cob on a typewriter carriage, and a coffee cup with a hole in the bottom to save pouring in the saucer. An emotional man with the right instincts, he can be called the conscience of the profession

Fannie Brice
ranked as the funniest woman on the boards
until Beatrice Lillie came along. After that, audiences divided.
Fannie began in early **Follies**, then starred in musicals. Her fine voice
established the song "My Man"; she could also move
audiences with serious emoting. But then
she'd turn ape.

Treasured
by young and old were Ed Wynn's
silly inventions. Here the giggly fellow demonstrates
how to eat a grapefruit without being squirted in the eye.

during the Actors' Equity strike of 1919. Asked the difference between a comic and a comedian, he replied, "A comic says funny things; a comedian says things funny."

W. C. Fields, also born in Philadelphia, left home as a boy because of parental cruelty. Determined to excel at something, he chose juggling and laboriously made himself the world's greatest, with worldwide vaudeville as his stage. Billed as the International Eccentric Tramp Juggler, he employed sight gags that evoked laughter as well as amazement at his skill. Fields relied more on humor after joining the *Follies* of 1915—such things as a trick billiard table or a piece of paper sticking to his foot at the beginning of a golf swing. Never by word, gesture, or glance did he admit the existence of an audience. In the *Follies* he wore a fake mustache clipped to his nose and became known for the catch phrase "Not a word to the folks." Fields' sonorous voice made all the difference. In pantomime, with the mustache, he looked and moved somewhat like Charlie Chaplin, but the pretentious tones of his raffish voice created his own hilarious self. He appeared in the *Follies* of 1915–18, 1920, 1921, and 1925 but never had top billing; Fannie Brice or Will Rogers were always ahead of him. For this and other reasons he was hostile to Flo Ziegfeld. In 1923 his nose was just growing red and globular. "I bruised it with a cocktail glass in my extreme youth," he explained.

Will Rogers came from Oklahoma, with Indian blood as well as the feel of show business in his veins. As Bill Fields became the world's greatest juggler, so Will set out to be the rope-twirler supreme. He succeeded. His offstage humor was so wry and observant that friends urged him to add patter to his act. One day he commented, "Yep, swingin' a rope's all right, provided your neck ain't in it." The roar of laughter turned him into a rope-twirling monologist. Top comics had trademarks—Fannie Brice the rubbery face, Wynn the lisp and giggles, Fields the phony elegance. Rogers had three—a wad of gum, Oklahoma drawl, and twirling rope. His humor was topical. "All I know is what I read in the papers," he'd begin and launch into pungent comments on the headlines. Flo Ziegfeld thought him unsophisticated for the *Follies* and put him in the *Midnight Frolics* on the New Amsterdam Roof; when his *Follies* chance came Rogers was a hit and appeared in the editions of 1917, 1918, 1922, 1924, and 1925. After that he became a number-one funnyman in movies. He liked to say, "I never met a man I didn't like" or "I never hated anybody or anything." Yet today a Broadway survivor says, "He was not liked in the profession. He was a money grabber, not as nice as he could have been."

Eddie Cantor, a fellow with a tireless sense of fun, was born in the ghetto. After starting at amateur nights, he was hired by Gus Edwards for his Kid Kabaret, along with George Jessel, Lila Lee, and Walter Winchell. Full of frenetic energy, he worked in blackface as a developing comic, his trademark being big eyes, round as banjos. Ziegfeld first

Eddie Cantor,
youngest comedy titan, was
probably the most popular funnyman of the theatrical
Twenties. Somehow his high-pressure antics fit the hysterical
times. Like Al Jolson, Cantor liked to appear in blackface, but not always.

Leon Errol, rubber-legged dancer, excelled in portraying stage drunks.
Yet he was also a deft comedian who brightened many *Follies*,
Marilyn Miller musicals, and other shows during
the magical decade. Caricature by Irving Hoffman.

saw him in the Earl Carroll musical **Canary Cottage** and signed him for the **Follies** of 1916–18, in which he appeared with Fields and Rogers. Angered by Eddie's activities in the Equity strike, Ziegfeld let him go to the Shuberts but lured him back for the two long-running musicals **Kid Boots** and **Whoopee**. Highbrows never thought much of Cantor, calling his jittery humor adolescent. But audiences loved him, perhaps because he seemed so eager to please as he pranced, danced, rolled his eyes, and rendered songs like "If You Knew Susie," a number given him by Al Jolson in a weak moment. Cantor wrote his own material and also did sketches for other shows.

Leon Errol appeared in more **Follies** than any other comedian but never quite became a master of comedy. Yet he was a very funny fellow indeed. Possessed of rubbery legs, he was both comedian and eccentric dancer. In one famed **Follies** number he played a souse who wandered into a ballet class, only to be mistaken by the girls for the ballet master. As he wove around the stage, the class dutifully followed his every movement. Like some comedians, the Australian-born Errol was conventional and humorless offstage and annoyed Ziegfeld by giving newspaper interviews deploring the morals and empty minds of **Follies** girls.

Such were the **Follies** funnymen, but there were others:

Willie and Eugene Howard never appeared in a **Follies** but did yeoman service in **Passing Shows** (from 1912) and **George White's Scandals**. Their act seldom varied from its origins in vaudeville, where they had done "The Hebrew Messenger Boy and the Thespian." A comic (Willie) and a straightman (Eugene) exchanged rapid-fire jokes, but material and delivery were so fresh that the public never got enough. Eugene Howard, a good-looking man with a sweet singing voice, seemed content to subordinate his talents to those of his scrawny, funny brother.

Clark and McCullough—Bobby and Paul—began in a circus and developed into a team where (like the Howards) McCullough was secondary to the funnier Bobby Clark. In time, McCullough killed himself, perhaps for this reason. Clark was a demon clown who scampered around the stage in a half crouch, leering, wearing painted-on goggles, and tapping the ashes from a cigar. "The king of the running fools," Brooks Atkinson called him. As Bobby ran, Paul McCullough, usually attired in straw hat and raccoon coat, watched with wide-eyed wonder. Clark and McCullough were the comics in the prestigious **Music Box Revues** and in one sang "Yes, We Have No Bananas" as part of an operatic quartet with Grace Moore. Later in the decade they went into **The Ramblers**.

There were more, so many more:

Charles Winninger, a dignified-looking funnyman who would score his biggest success as Cap'n Andy in **Show Boat** . . . Lou Holtz, who hit Broadway with Elsie Janis and Her Gang and stayed to tell his unsurpassed dialect jokes in the **Scandals** and other revues . . . Frank Fay, suavest of masters of ceremonies . . . Joe E. Brown, in show business from age nine, with the widest mouth ever . . . Phil Baker, a handsome fellow who played the accordion and worked with a stooge, or "annoyer," in a stage box . . . Moran and Mack, the Two Black Crows, with their drawling dialogues . . . Jack Pearl of the heavy German accent whose 1925 character was Herman Pffeifer . . . Shaw and Lee, two guys who worked without a change of expression . . . Joe Cook, with his wild inventions, wilder chatter, and inimitable introductions of himself as "Not the old Joe Cook, but the **old** Joe Cook."

SHORT TAKE

In September 1923 W. C. Fields opened in the musical comedy **Poppy**, with Madge Kennedy and Luella Gear. This was a new departure—a step upward, you might say—for the man who had first appeared as a juggler in vaudeville, then as a comedian in top revues.

By appearing in a book musical, Fields was pointing himself toward the phase of his career that brought lasting fame. At rehearsals for **Poppy**, Fields (as Professor Eustace McGargle) behaved as he would on future film sets. He took over the show, inserting his old comedy scenes into the action and generally dominated proceedings. Still, some vestiges of **Poppy's** plot remained. Wrote critic Heywood Broun, "Fields is so good a juggler that recognition of his ability as an actor was delayed until last night. . . . He creates an authentic and appealing character."

Not all the reviews were as favorable. Some critics faulted the simple-minded plot and others found (incredibly!) too much Fields.

Pondering the diverse notices, Fields uttered a line not supposed to be funny: "Why the hell should these guys be telling the public what to think?" he grumbled. "Why, they can't even agree among themselves!"

Hit Songs from Broadway shows, 1923:

"Bambalina" (Youmans/Stothart/Harbach/Hammerstein), from **Wildflower**
"Charleston" (Mack/Johnson), from **Runnin' Wild**
"Sunbonnet Sue" (Edwards/Cobb), from **Sunbonnet Sue**

W. C. Fields
started a trend by appearing
in **Poppy**, a book musical that allowed
the development of a consistent comic character in the person of
Professor Eustace McGargle. With him is Madge
Kennedy, heretofore a dramatic
actress.

ROUNDUP

As the best dramatic plays of the year, Burns Mantle selected **You and I**, a light comedy by Philip Barry, with H. B. Warner, Frieda Inescourt, Geoffrey Kerr, Lucile Watson, and Reginald Mason; **Icebound**, by Owen Davis, about New England life, with Edna May Oliver, among others; **Mary the 3d**, Rachel Crothers' play about three generations of Marys, with Ben Lyon; **The Swan**, a mythical-kingdom opus by Ferenc Molnar, with Eva Le Gallienne, Basil Rathbone, and Philip Merivale; **The Changelings**, concerning family relationships, by Lee Wilson Dodd, with Ruth Chatterton, Henry Miller, Laura Hope Crews, and Blanche Bates; **Sun Up**, a mountain-folk play by Lula Vollmer, with Lucille La Verne; **Chicken Feed**, by Guy Bolton, a comedy about wives getting wages, with Leila Bennett; and **Tarnish**, by Gilbert Emery, highlighting American life and its problems, with Ann Harding, Tom Powers, and Fania Marinoff.

The year began gloriously with the opening of the Moscow Art Theatre, led by Constantin Stanislavsky and imported by Morris Gest. The Muscovites, past masters of group acting, began with Tolstoy's **Tsar Fyodor Ivanovitch**, proceeded to Gorki's **The Lower Depths**, Chekhov's **The Cherry Orchard** and **The Three Sisters**, Turgenev's **Lady from the Provinces**, and excerpts from Dostoevski's **The Brothers Karamazov**. One critic said the Russians appealed to "the elite and bon-ton," but a lot of theatregoers turned out to make this non-English-speaking engagement a success. The Players toured to Chicago, then returned to New York for 100 more performances. "No dramatic importation within this generation's memory has created the stir the Muscovites caused, nor the comment," wrote Burns Mantle.

Triumph and tragedy joined in the farewell engagement of Eleonora Duse, who appeared at the huge Century Theatre in repertory including works by Ibsen and D'Annunzio. After profitable weeks in New York, she set out on a tour of major theatrical centers, where her receptions were enthusiastic. In Pittsburgh, near the end of the tour, Duse died. This was also the year death came to Sarah Bernhardt, in Paris.

Other season offerings were Clemence Dane's **Will Shakespeare**, with Otto Kruger as Will and Winifred Lenihan as Anne Hathaway; Ethel Barrymore offered a disappointing **Juliet**, while Jane Cowl triumphed in the same role, with Rollo Peters as her Romeo; Walter Hampden appeared as **Cyrano de Bergerac**, a role he would enact more than a thousand times in a long and distinguished career; **Polly Preferred**, Guy Bolton's lively comedy of the movies, featured Genevieve Tobin; Laurette Taylor failed as a Jewish mother in an adaptation of Fannie Hurst's **Humoresque** but did better in **Sweet Nell of Old Drury**, about Nell Gwynne; Sacha Guitry's **Pasteur** was a failure, with Henry Miller in the title role; the Theatre Guild produced the fabled **The Adding**

Attempting to rival the *Follies* were *George White's Scandals* and *Earl Carroll's Vanities*. *Vanities* relied heavily on nudity (**left**), while *Scandals* girls were cute and peppy as the wild flapper next door (**right**).

Not all plays were worthy. ***Arabesque***, pioneer production
of Norman Bel Geddes, reflected the slipping morals of the Twenties
as a sheik swept a near-naked girl into a torrid embrace.
The girl, Hortense Alden;
Sheik, Bela Lugosi.

Serious drama
flourished in 1923,
though history sees it as a
musical-comedy year. Jane Cowl played Juliet
shortly after Ethel Barrymore opened in the role, and
critics opted enthusiastically for Miss Cowl. Alla Nazimova continued her
distinguished American career in *A Month in the Country*.
In Rostand's **Cyrano de Bergerac**, Walter Hampden
found a role that sustained him
on and off through
his long career.

Nightclubs
were an integral part—or
more—of the Roaring Twenties scene on
Broadway, not only honing talents like Helen Morgan,
Ruby Keeler, and Harry Richman for the musical stage but serving
as late-night playgrounds for hard-working performers.
The eternal queen of Main Stem nightclubs was
raucous Texas Guinan, onetime movie
cowgirl and singer in
Shubert revues.
Present on a routine
night at Tex's El Fay Club
(named for gangster-owner Larry Fay)
were F. P. A., Julia Hoyt, Johnny Dooley, Gallagher
and Shean, Barney Gallant, Avery Hopwood, Hugo Riesenfeld,
Dagmar Godowsky, Ann Pennington, Eddie Cantor, Earl Carroll,
Peggy Hopkins Joyce, Richard Barthelmess,
Mary Hay, Bebe Daniels,
Gloria Swanson,
Harold Lloyd, John Barrymore,
and John Murray Anderson. All sketched
by Wynn, who crouches under table, for **Theatre Magazine**.

Machine, by Elmer Rice; Cyril Maude in Frederick Lonsdale's **Aren't We All?** was a joyous hit; **Zander the Great** had Alice Brady playing a motherly maid servant who adopted a baby and took him across the continent in a flivver.

White Cargo, produced on a $76 shoestring by Earl Carroll, ran the season out and made a mint; J. P. McEvoy unveiled his average family **The Potters** for theatre audiences; Shaw's **St. Joan**, with Winifred Lenihan, proved a solid Theatre Guild hit; Katharine Cornell embellished Pinero's **Enchanted Cottage**; **In Love with Love** had Lynn Fontanne and Henry Hull; **The Whole Town's Talking**, by John Emerson and Anita Loos, provided a hit for Grant Mitchell; **Little Miss Bluebeard** starred accented Irene Bordoni; **What's Your Wife Doing?** had Glenn Anders, Isabel Leighton, and George Spelvin; Maxwell Anderson's **White Desert**, about a blizzard in North Dakota, featured Beth Merrill and George Abbott; Frederick Lonsdale's **Spring Cleaning** starred high-comedian A. E. Matthews; **Meet the Wife** offered Mary Boland, Clifton Webb, and (yes!) Humphrey Bogart; **This Fine-Pretty World** had Aline McMahon.

In the bright field of revue, Earl Carroll introduced his first **Vanities**, starring oft-married Peggy Hopkins Joyce and zany Joe Cook, fresh from vaudeville; **George White's Scandals** featured dancer Tom Patricola and versatile Winnie Lightner; the **Music Box Revue** had Irving Berlin tunes, comic Phil Baker, and Robert Benchley delivering his "Treasurer's Report"; **Greenwich Village Follies**, directed by John Murray Anderson, had Tom Howard, plus the team of Sammy Puck and Eva White; **The Passing Show** boosted Walter Woolf, George Jessel, Flanagan and Morrison, Libby and Sparrow.

Dubious distinction goes to **Artists and Models**, first of a series projected by the Shuberts. This one featured suave Frank Fay, and **Variety** reported that it contained the dirtiest jokes ever heard on the Broadway boards. One comedy sketch burlesqued **Rain**, and a critic called it "the rawest, smuttiest, most shameless misdemeanor ever committed." Far more sedate were **Helen of Troy, N.Y.**, a musical-comedy venture by the redoubtable team of George S. Kaufman and Marc Connelly; and **Little Jessie James**, with hit song "I Love You" and the presence of beauteous Miriam Hopkins.

The operetta **Wildflower** had a memorable score by Vincent Youmans, including the catchy "Bambalina"; **Runnin' Wild**, a Negro musical, starred the team of Miller and Lyles, along with the dance known as the Charleston conceived by George White; **Jack and Jill**, lush song-and-dance show, featured Clifton Webb, Ann Pennington, and Lina Basquette; **Greenwich Village Follies**, moving uptown, added Martha Graham doing a dance described as pretty-pretty interpretive.

Rise of Rosie O'Reilly, a musical by George M. Cohan, included Margaret Dumont, to be chased by Groucho Marx through so many movies to come, and Ruby Keeler, fifteen-year-old alumna of Texas Guinan's nightclub, who got $45 a week for doing what *Variety* called a "fast rhythm tap." New Year's Eve brought the Florenz Ziegfeld production of **Kid Boots**, with Eddie Cantor, a top popular hit of the decade.

SERIOUS PLAYWRIGHTS

What of plays and playwrights as the decade approached midmark?

Eugene O'Neill still towered above the pack, so remote that no one tried to emulate him. Four years had passed since the opening of **Beyond the Horizon**; three since **Anna Christie** brought a second Pulitzer Prize; nearly ten since the gaunt young dramatist walked over the Provincetown sands to greet the Wharf Players. "Who are the American playwrights?" asked Stewart Cheney rhetorically. "Well, chiefly, they are Eugene O'Neill."

The titan was not resting on his laurels but turning out long and short plays (though his short ones were long) on themes both contemporary and universal. As Brooks Atkinson says, playwriting was not so much his profession as his obsession. O'Neill had inherited over $100,000 with the deaths of father, mother, and brother and increased this sum by the considerable royalties of his Broadway hits. Yet he kept laboring.

By now he had also joined with critic Kenneth Macgowan and scenic artist Robert Edmond Jones to run the downtown Provincetown Theatre. The trio worked as effectively as the board of the Theatre Guild, and an admiring profession dubbed them the Triumvirate. In large part because of the success of O'Neill plays, including **The Emperor Jones** and **The Hairy Ape**, the Triumvirate had been able to reach out to take over the larger Greenwich Village Theatre. O'Neill works opened at both these playhouses and on Broadway as well. In four years of the Twenties, twelve new plays from his pen were exposed to the public gaze.

O'Neill's marriage was turning sour, and he still went off on periodic alcoholic binges. Shy and morose in the presence of others, he retained a healthy ego where his writing was involved. "I'm a professional," he liked to state. Or "I'm the first American playwright who isn't a hack." He discouraged interviews, but the few intrepid newshawks to reach him invariably wanted to know why he chose such sordid themes. Once he answered, "There is beauty to me even in ugliness. I don't love life because it's pretty; prettiness is only clothes deep. I am a truer believer than that." Again he said his purpose was to dig deep into the roots of life.

Nineteen twenty-four brought three more O'Neill plays and they boxed the compass of theatres at the playwright's disposal. One opened at the Provincetown, another at the Greenwich Village, and the third on Broadway. Not all O'Neill plays were successes—far from it—and the Broadway effort was typical of those the world has forgotten. Titled **Welded**, it pictured a married couple whose extreme jealousy drove them to get even with each other by seeking extramarital sex. Neither could go through with it. O'Neill, supposedly a confirmed cynic, seemed to be saying, "Real love is failure-proof." One

Eugene O'Neill's
Desire Under the Elms,
with Walter Huston and Mary Morris,
dealt broodingly with incest, greed, and hopelessness
on a New England farm. It brought added stature to an already towering dramatist.

reviewer saw **Welded** as "tense but monotonous"; others were less kind, and the play had a short run. On the record it remains of interest only because its leading lady was the unlikely Doris Keane, a star who had scored a triumph in **Romance**.

The second O'Neill play of the year—at the Provincetown—was **All God's Chillun Got Wings**, featuring Paul Robeson, who had made his debut in a revival of **The Emperor Jones**. **All God's Chillun** offered a theme truly daring for the time: the marriage of a white girl to a black man. This got around, along with word that in one scene the wife kissed the husband's hand. In 1924 such matters caused trouble. Before opening night, letters of protest and threats inundated the Provincetown, and at the premiere police guarded the tiny theatre. Critics thought **All God's Chillun** "heartfelt, but melodramatic, overwritten, and unconvincing."

The third O'Neill offering of the year was **Desire Under the Elms**, first of his so-called masterpiece plays, which opened at the Greenwich Village Theatre, then moved uptown to the Earl Carroll. Here was a grim saga of 1850 New England, where the Cabot family eked out a bare living on a rocky farm. Ephriam Cabot, having worn out two wives, returned home with a third. Ephriam was portrayed by Walter Huston, who had scored his first big-time success in Zona Gale's **Mr. Pitt** earlier in the season.

Ephriam's two sons by his first wife left for California as their father arrived with his bride. Eben, offspring of wife number two, remained to covet the farm that killed his mother, determined to hate Abbie, his new stepmother. But sensual Abbie lusts for Eben and in time seduces him. So the child she bears is not old Ephriam's, though of course he thinks it is. Abbie, who really loves Eben, smothers the child to death, because it will prevent her lover from inheriting the farm. Eben is at first horrified and runs for the sheriff. But as he and the law return, his own love rekindles. After declaring that part of the responsibility for the child's death is his, he and Abbie are led away to jail. This leaves Ephriam alone on the farm. He has always vowed to live to be a hundred and sets about doing so. "God is hard," he often says. But he is hard, too.

Such was O'Neill's first masterpiece play—by no means topical but a tragedy in the eternal sense. It added greatly to the stature of a man who loomed large already.

O'Neill's plays, probing so deep into the recesses of men's souls, should have influenced other dramatists of the time. Some thought they did. Critic Charles Edward Metzger wrote, "There has emerged on Broadway a new group of playwrights. Young men with strange and morbid views of life. Men, not so young, who dream of Freud and Nietszche. Girls and grown women brooding on birth control. Weird psychoanalysts and would-be cynics."

Yet scrutiny of other playwrights fails to justify a viewing-with-alarm. Aside from O'Neill's plays, the theatregoer of these early Twenties was almost certain to have a happy ending under his belt on leaving a theatre. A few experimental or impressionistic dramas faulted the social system—John Howard Lawson's **Roger Bloomer**, Elmer Rice's **The Adding Machine**, and even the Kaufman-Connelly **Beggar on Horseback**. But few more. Playwrights of the era believed the patterns of the prewar past had been tossed overboard, but the heavy hand of Teen dramaturgy still lay on much of the theatre.

The extent of it can only increase admiration for both O'Neill and the Theatre Guild. The Guild was not afraid to offer plays by foreigners with unpronounceable names, turgid of theme and gloomy of ending. "The Theatre Guild brought the New York theatre into the twentieth century," playwright S. N. Behrman believes. He could be right.

This is not to say that contemporary dramatists made no effort to interpret the American scene in theatrical terms. The younger generation of the nation was in the process of rebelling against parents and the customs of the past, with glossy haired sheiks and short-skirted shebas petting in parked cars and drinking bootleg hooch from hip flasks. The revolt of Flaming Youth agitated the entire country. So did the flaunting of Prohibition, with its violation of the law of the land.

Highbrow thinkers, along with the younger generation, also questioned the noble institution of marriage and devoured Count Herman Keyserling's downbeat book on the subject. People were just discovering Freud and Havelock Ellis, starting to talk openly of psychoanalysis and sexual behavior. It added up to what an observer called "the lawless philosophy of the Twenties." Dramatists could see this as well (or better) than anyone else, but the patterns of the past still vitiated part of their efforts at dramatization.

Then, in the fall of 1924, two unusual plays hurtled across the footlights. Not exactly contemporary, they scored because of total realism. They were **What Price Glory?** by Laurence Stallings and Maxwell Anderson, and **They Knew What They Wanted**, by Sidney Howard. It is possible to call them the first plays truly of the Twenties—proceeding in lifelike fashion without apparent nudges, shoves, or manipulation by the authors.

Stallings and Anderson were employed by the New York **World**. The former had lost a leg as a Marine at Belleau Wood and liked to regale his co-worker with war experiences. Finally the two decided to write a play. Anderson roughed out the scenes; Stallings went over the script, adding pungent, realistic dialogue.

The result was a gripping war-is-hell drama; the program said "A play of war as it is, not as it has been presented theatrically for thousands of years." Yet there were steady guffaws amidst the starkness, filth, and bestiality of war, for the play told of the lusty rivalry between Captain

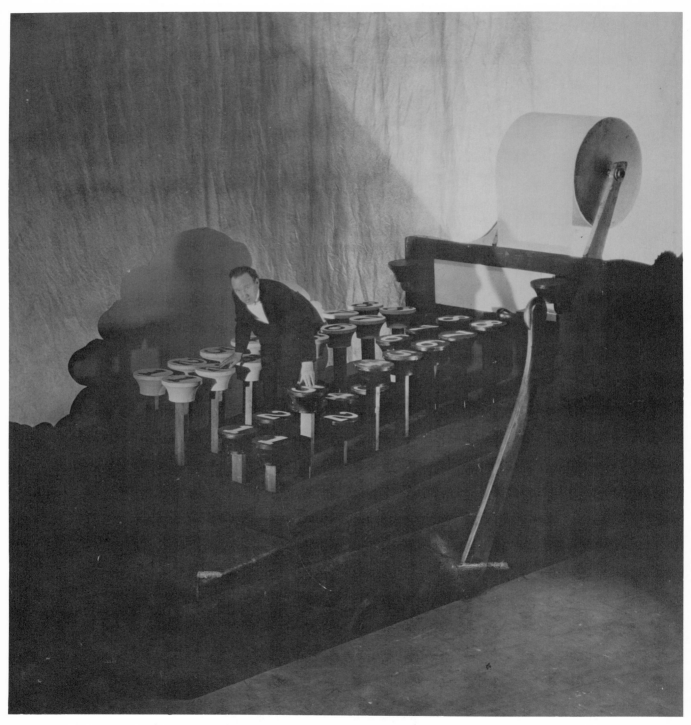

In retrospect, Elmer Rice's **The Adding Machine** stands out as the most
successful of the Theatre Guild's impressionistic
plays. Here Dudley Digges as Mr. Zero operates the oddly
prophetic adder.

Flagg (Louis Wolheim) and Sergeant Quirt (William Boyd), who had long known and hated each other.

If nothing else, **What Price Glory?** emancipated profanity in the drama, for "Christs" and "goddams" embellished nearly every sentence. A few worthy souls objected to this, among them the commandant of the Third Naval District, who declared that Marines did not swear that much. But for the most part audiences accepted the cursing, while the public relished the joke about a young man who took his maiden aunt to see the show. At the end she began hunting for something on the floor. "What's the matter, auntie?" he asks. "I've lost my goddam program," she replied.

Through Flagg, Quirt, and their fellows (among them Brian Donlevy's Corporal Gowdy), war was presented as an ugly business, without heroism or point. "What price glory now?" shouts one soldier as a dying buddy is brought in from no man's land. "Why in God's name can't we all go home? Who gives a damn for this stinking little town but the poor French devils who live here?" Robbed of all dignity, members of an unfeeling military machine, the men grab at any pleasure. In rest periods behind the lines they drink, wench, decorate every utterance with profanity.

What Price Glory? was not so much playwriting as reporting; it had almost no plot, much less formula tricks. Nothing in the play was resolved by courage or patriotism; the men carried out orders like sleepwalkers. Nor was there a happy ending. An exhausted Captain Flagg, promised a behind-the-lines rest with his weary men, is ordered back to the trenches immediately after arrival at the billet. Sergeant Quirt, slightly wounded in the leg, does not have to go; he can stay behind and make time with the trollop Charmaine, over whose lush charms the two men have battled from the rise of the curtain.

But as Flagg leads his stumbling men back to the trenches, Quirt gives the girl a quick kiss and tells her, "Jeez, what a lot of goddam fools it takes to make a war." Then he runs limping after the troops, shouting, "Hey, Flagg, wait for baby!" Heywood Broun wrote, "This is certainly the best use the theatre has yet made of the war, and it is entirely possible that it is the best American play about anything."

Sidney Howard's **They Knew What They Wanted**, a Theatre Guild offering and Pulitzer Prize winner, was not so topical a play. Except for a few references to bootlegging, it might have taken place anytime. This character-comedy, as a reviewer dubbed it, recounted the story of Tony (Richard Bennett), a middle-aged Italian-American who grew grapes on a farm in California's Napa Valley. Tony had always planned to marry as soon as financially able, and now bootleggers were paying high prices for his grapes. On a trip to San Francisco he saw a pleasant-looking young waitress in an Italian restaurant. Learning her name, he began sending her ardent letters. Because he

What Price Glory?,
by Laurence Stallings and Maxwell Anderson,
hit Broadway like the blow of a giant fist. Profane, irreverent, gutsy
as war itself, it proved a dramatic milestone, so powerful that
censorship forces left it alone. Above, James Boyd and
Louis Wolheim, as Quirt and Flagg,
exchange sweaty epithets.

Sidney Howard's **They Knew What They Wanted** proved a milestone like **What Price Glory?** Meaty and vibrant, it dealt with love in grown-up fashion. The scene was California's Napa Valley. In the cast were Glenn Anders, Richard Bennett, and Pauline Lord.

could not write, it was necessary to enlist the help of Joe, his handsome hired hand, in composing the letters. Because he was not good-looking, Tony also enclosed a snapshot of Joe.

A proposal of marriage brings Amy (Pauline Lord) to the farm. On the way to meet her Joe has an accident that breaks both his legs. Arriving alone, Amy gradually realizes that it is not handsome Joe but old, homely Tony who sent for her. It is a shattering shock, but she decides to stay and make the best of the bargain. On the first night (only) she and handsome Joe bed down. The result is a pregnancy that nearly drives Tony out of his mind. But when passions cool, he begs Amy to stay. He still wants a wife; they have come to love and respect each other; Joe's child can be brought up as his own.

A happy ending but not maudlin or dishonest. Love in this case meant a mature adjustment on the part of man and woman; there was no divine lightning of love at first sight. Sidney Howard's skill and compassion for his characters brought believable life.

SHORT TAKE

Q. In 1924, the highly successful British import **Andre Charlot's Revue** made both Beatrice Lillie and Gertrude Lawrence famous over-night. Who were the other members of the cast?
A. Jack Buchanan, Marjorie Brooks, Dorothy Dolman, Fred Leslie, Robert Hobbs, Ronald Ward, and Herbert Mundin. Plus a small but select chorus of long-stemmed English beauties, among them Jessie Matthews and Constance Carpenter.

The intimate **Charlot Revues** had been delighting London for nearly a decade, and during much of this time Gertrude Lawrence served as Beatrice Lillie's understudy. The revues were produced, Miss Lawrence once said, with exquisite economy—ultrasophisticated sketches along with clever songs, dances, and comedy against attractive but unambitious backgrounds, usually draperies.

The **Charlot's Revue** New York went mad over in 1924 contained some of the best bits of past years, among them Bea Lillie draped in an English flag singing "March with Me" and Gertrude Lawrence singing "Limehouse Blues."

There was also material written in London by Noël Coward, of whose sketches it was said, "They glorified not the English girl but the English joke."

"THE THEATRE IS A SEWER!"

No matter how they seem today, the dramas and satires of the first part of the decade represented progress, and often progress is accompanied by protest. The profanity in **What Price Glory?**, the seduction in **Desire Under the Elms** (a woman the aggressor), a long-drawn-out kiss in Edwin Justus Mayer's **Firebrand**, play-titles like **A Good Bad Woman**—these and other infractions of morals inevitably aroused the local forces of virtue. Preachers in pulpits warned that the drama was corrupting the populace, while vice crusaders planned legal means of closing offensive shows. "The theatre is a sewer!" raged John S. Sumner, head of the ever-vigilant Society for the Suppression of Vice.

Matters came to a head in 1924—and would again in 1927. First offender was **All God's Chillun Got Wings**, with its theme of miscegenation. District Attorney Joab S. Banton, born in the South, reputedly favored cracking down on this drama before it opened, but no legal means existed. Still, he did have a weapon of harassment. In the first act a group of white and black children played happily together. Banton could—and did—prevent the appearance of these underage actors. Through the run of the play the stage manager read the children's parts to the audience.

The District Attorney had other headaches. **Spring Cleaning**, an innocent-sounding high comedy by England's Frederick Lonsdale, concerned a novelist who found his bored wife seeking degenerate company. One night, as the wife entertained jaded friends, he turned up with a prostitute on his arm. When the others objected, he professed astonishment. "I have never heard of an amateur billiard player refusing to meet a professional," he said blandly.

The play that finally triggered action was Milton Herbert Gropper's **Ladies of the Evening**, presented by David Belasco, the Bishop of Broadway. In this, three young men sat in the window of their club, idly discussing streetwalkers. Artist Jerry Strong expressed the belief that such girls were victims of circumstance who had souls like anyone else. His unbelieving companions bet $500 that he could not redeem a prostitute in the course of a year.

That night Jerry picks up pretty Kay Beatty on a street corner. In her room she urges him to hurry, to make way for her next customer. Gradually his message gets through to her: Professing to be struck by her beauty, he is offering her a respectable job as his model. She accepts and in a few months not only refines her speech and manners but falls madly in love with Jerry. Then she learns about the bet and runs off to rejoin her old streetwalking colleague Dot. She can't go through with it, however, and takes a job as a waitress. Jerry finds her and proposes marriage.

The course
of American musical
comedy was changed by the arrival
of two bright, intimate revues from abroad.
First came Russia's ***Chauve-Souris***, then England's
Charlot's Revue. Above, the famed Celebrity Curtain drawn for the ***Chauve-Souris*** by
caricaturist Ralph Barton—everyone who was anybody was there.

Curtain by Ralph Barton for Balieff's *Chauve Souris*

This was a popular revue from Russia produced by Morris Gest in 1922. Balieff is shown facing a typical first-night audience of the 1920s

From left to right

Front row:
Al Jolson, John Emerson, Anita Loos, Irving Berlin, David Belasco, Lenore Ulric, John Barrymore, Michael Strange, Lucrezia Bori, Madame Alda

Second row:
Anna Pavlova, Josef Hofman, Reina Belasco Gest, John Drew, Theodore Roosevelt, Marie Jeritza, Giulio Gatti-Casazza, Geraldine Farrar, Mary Garden, Feodor Chaliapin

Third row:
Elsie de Wolfe, Arthur Brisbane, Mrs. William Randolph Hearst, Henry Blackman Sell, Conde Nast, Irene Castle, Frank Crowninshield, Mrs. H. Payne Whitney, Kenneth MacGowan, Alan Dale, Ray Long

Fourth row:
Sam Bernard, Marilyn Miller, Ed Wynn, Mrs. J. Borden Harriman, Charles Dana Gibson, Alexander Woollcott, Mrs. Lydig Hoyt, Franklin P. Adams, Neysa McMein, Heywood Broun, Doris Keane, Percy Hammond

Fifth row:
Moranzoni, Ann Morgan, Burns Mantle, Mrs. W. K. Vanderbilt, Willard Huntington Wright, S. Jay Kaufman, Herbert Swope, Walter Catlett, Sophie Braslau, Dorothy Gish, David W. Griffith, Lillian Gish, Elizabeth Marbury, Leon Errol, Zoe Akins

Sixth row:
Adolf Zukor, Robert G. Welsh, Fay Bainter, Lawrence Reamer, Gertrude Hoffman, Walter Damrosch, Mary Nash, Wilhelm Mengelberg, Charles Darnton, Otto H. Kahn, Frank A. Munsey,

Flo Ziegfeld, Arturo Bodansky, Adolph Ochs, John Rumsey

Seventh row:
Ludwig Lewisohn, George S. Kaufman, Lynn Fontanne, Marc Connelly, Geo. M. Cohan, John MacMahon, Henry Krehbiel, Mrs. Enrico Caruso, Ben-Ami, Dorothy Dalton, David Warfield, Robert C. Benchley

Eighth row:
Karl Kitchen, Antonio Scotti, Fannie Hurst, Hugo Reisenfeld, Vera Fokina, Michel Fokine, Avery Hopwood, Constance Talmadge, Anna Fitziu, Reginald Vanderbilt, Dr. Frank Crane, Jascha Heifetz

Ninth row:
Eugene O'Neill, Prof. Roerich, Joseph Urban, Arthur Hornblow, Paul Meyer, Elsie Janis, Paul Block, John Farrar, Sergei Rachmaninoff, Herbert Hoover, John Golden, Winchell Smith, Jay Gould

Left upper box:
Maude Adams, John McCormack, Charles Chaplin, Marechal Joffre

Right upper box:
Laurette Taylor, Frances Starr, Clare Sheridan, Hartley Manners

Foyer S. R. O.:
A. D. Lasker, Samuel L. Rothapfel, Nicholas Murray Butler, Ralph Barton, Jesse Lasky, Edward Ziegler, William Guard, Louis Untermeyer, J. J. Shubert, Lee Shubert, F. Ray Comstock, Morris Gest, Oliver Sayler, Boris Anisfeld, Robert Edmond Jones, Ring Lardner, Stephen Rathbun, Armand Veszy, Andreas de Segurola, Papi, Raymond Hitchcock

Preparing to conquer the New World in *Charlot's Revue*,
Beatrice Lillie and Gertrude Lawrence
sip a final cup of tea
at Claridge's.

Beth Merrill played a hurry-up prostitute in the daring *Ladies of the Evening*.
The seamy, specific shocker was produced by none other than
David Belasco, the Bishop of Broadway.

One reviewer thought that **Ladies of the Evening** was written in "the language of the gutter . . . it is cheap, tawdry, and sensational." Others were astounded that the Bishop of Broadway had a hand in it. Two scenes in particular upset the virtuous. One was the hurry-up scene in Kay's cheap bedroom. The other came after the girl left Jerry and joined Dot in a hotel where they began hustling customers over the house phone.

Strange to say, Actors' Equity allied with the reformers in advocating censorship; the union believed producers hurt the theatre by offering daring material. But opponents of censorship included many important people in the theatre and out. District Attorney Banton, in a bind, saved himself by an elaborate compromise.

The offending plays boiled down to **Desire Under the Elms**, **The Firebrand**, and **Ladies of the Evening**. **Spring Cleaning** had gone on tour, and objections to the swearing in **What Price Glory?** subsided. Banton impaneled so-called citizens' juries, composed of representatives of the church, reform forces, and Equity. Separate juries were to scrutinize the three plays under question, rendering a verdict on the extent of immorality. The juries did their duty and recommended that the kiss in **The Firebrand** be shortened, the hurry-up scene in **Ladies of the Evening** be transferred to the sidewalk, and the seduction in **Desire Under the Elms** be toned down or eliminated.

The producers of the first two plays hastily acceded. Jones and Green, Broadway entrepreneurs who had brought **Desire Under the Elms** uptown, sat tight. Nothing ever happened. It should be noted, though, that ticket sales of **Desire Under the Elms** soared upward after the public denunciation. Altogether, the O'Neill drama ran 208 performances; it might not have happened otherwise.

In the tumult over censorship, few could understand why **Artists and Models** never got raided. For in this revue girls danced and took part in sketches with bosoms exposed.

Two versions of this breast-baring appear on the record. In one, J. C. Huffman, director of the revue, strove through arduous days of rehearsal to make something impressive out of an opening chorus. Everything about it annoyed him, especially the lackluster costumes, which were fluffy what-nots of tulle without distinctive color or cut. Unable to contain himself any more, Huffman exploded in a temperamental rampage and rushed down the line of girls tearing the bodice from each. As the girls stood bare to the waist both Huffman and J. J. Shubert, who observed from the sidelines, shouted simultaneously, "Let's leave it that way." Says the account, "And so it came to pass that New York was shocked by a chorus of nakedness."

Jerry Stagg, biographer of the brothers Shubert, gives terrifying, lecherous J. J. Shubert sole credit for the bodice-snatching. According to Stagg, Mr. J. J. felt as disgusted as Huffman with the drab costumes and charged down the aisle of the theatre to rip the blouse off one girl.

122

Artists and Models of 1924,
produced by J. J. Shubert, remains the nudest
show ever visible on the Main Stem.
Not only were the girls beautifully bare, but you saw
more beautifully bare girls than ever before or since. No one in
officialdom rose to protest or order a raid.
Why not? Could it have been the power
of the brothers Shubert?

Liking the effect, he instantly decreed that girls in this and other numbers appear naked from the waist up. When one girl protested, he shouted, "No broad that won't show her tits can work in this show—and that's final!"

Artists and Models never got raided. Yet the bare bosoms did make it hard for others in the cast. Fred Allen, following two of these naked numbers, found that when he stepped through the curtain women in the audience were still gasping with shock, while men were bemused. His precious jokes fell flat.

LONG TAKE—"I AM GOING TO LIVE!"

Yes, times were changing! A year or two earlier, ***Dancing Mothers***, a 1924 smash, would have been a fluffy farce with a happy ending. But this four-act play by Edgar Selwyn and Edmund Goulding made a somewhat serious try at delineating the plight of a wife whose husband and daughter had succumbed to the Jazz Age.

Edith (Mrs. Hugh) Westcourt had been an actress but retired to become a well-heeled suburban wife and mother. Twenty years later she thought herself content, though husband Hugh took a surprising number of overnight business trips to Philadelphia and daughter Kittens (Helen Hayes) was a cocktail-happy flapper who seldom stayed home.

Trouble began as Edith's friend Zola Massarene convinced her that the frequent Philadelphia trips meant Hugh had a mistress. She also passed along the tidbit that Kittens was wildly enamored of the carefree older bachelor, Jerry Naughton.

As Mrs. Massarene departs, Hugh enters to announce another overnight trip to Philly. Kittens, still loopy from afternoon drinks, also leaves for an unknown destination. Edith simmers awhile, then phones Zola. The two women decide on a visit to a Manhattan cabaret oft mentioned by Hugh and Kittens.

It hardly comes as a surprise that father and daughter also turn up at the cabaret. Hugh is accompanied by his latest mistress, Kittens by Naughton. Hugh is infuriated to see his daughter in such company and roughly takes her home. When Naughton and Edith meet, she affects a French accent and tells him her name is Yvonne de Cresac, one of her old stage parts. Naughton is smitten by her picturesque accent and mature charms.

Weeks go by, and one afternoon Kittens passes out after cocktails in Naughton's apartment. Reviving, she finds her boy friend whispering amorous nothings to a fascinating French lady—***her mother***!

In *Dancing Mothers*, Helen Hayes played the flapper Kittens, who enjoyed cocktails
for lunch. Edmund Goulding and Arch Selwyn wrote this play about
a modern mother who stole her own daughter's boy friend.
Clara Bow—who else?—was Kittens
on the screen.

The result is a blow-up at home, with Hugh branding his wife a wanton and Kittens sobbing convulsively. Edith moves in with Zola Massarene, telling Hugh, "I am going to *live*." When she returns home for her possessions, Hugh and Kittens beg her to stay, but her freedom has been enjoyable. She also feels drawn to Jerry Naughton. Husband and daughter have hurt her once too often, she declares. "For a moment you almost tempted me," she tells Kittens, "but I mustn't give in. If I did, everything would be the same again."

Song Hits from Broadway Shows, 1924:

"All Alone," "What'll I Do?" (Berlin), from **Music Box Revue**
"California, Here I Come" (De Sylva/Meyer/Jolson), from **Bombo** (return engagement)
"Indian Love Call," "The Mounties," "Rose Marie, I Love You" "Totem Tom-Tom" (Friml/Stothart/Harbach/Hammerstein II), from **Rose Marie**
"Fascinating Rhythm," "Oh, Lady Be Good," "The Man I Love" (Gershwin/Gershwin), from **Lady, Be Good**
"Limehouse Blues" (Braham/Furber), from **Charlot's Revue**
"Somebody Loves Me" (Gershwin/De Sylva/MacDonald), from **George White's Scandals**
"I'm in Love Again" (Porter), from **Greenwich Village Follies**
"Deep in My Heart, Dear," "Golden Days," "Student Life" (Romberg/Donnelly), from **The Student Prince**
"Tea for Two," "I Want to Be Happy" (Youmans/Caesar), from **No, No, Nanette**

ROUNDUP

As the year's best plays Burns Mantle selected ***The Show Off***, the story of a relentless egoist, by George Kelly, with Louis John Bartels in the lead role and Lee Tracy in a smaller but vital part; ***Hell Bent fer Heaven***, Hatcher Hughes' study of Blue Ridge Mountain folk; ***Outward Bound***, by Sutton Vane, an eerie fantasy of a shipload of folk who discover they are dead and bound for Eternity, with Alfred Lunt, Leslie Howard, and Margalo Gillmore; ***The Goose Hangs High***, by Lewis Beach, the conflict between parents and Flaming Youth; ***Beggar on Horseback***, the satire by George S. Kaufman and Marc Connelly, with Roland Young, Osgood Perkins, Spring Byington, and George Barbier; ***What Price Glory?***, the Stallings-Anderson sensation about the seamy and sexual sides of war; ***They Knew What They Wanted***, Sidney Howard's mature treatment of love in the Napa Valley of California; ***The Firebrand***, by Edwin Justus Mayer, a clever romance about Benvenuto Cellini, with Joseph Schildkraut looking almost as handsome as John Barrymore in doublet and tights; ***Desire Under the Elms***, one of Eugene O'Neill's finest plays; ***Dancing Mothers***, by Edgar Selwyn and Edmund Goulding wherein a wife dances away from home and kin; ***Minick***, by George S. Kaufman and Edna Ferber, a sentimental tale based on one of Miss Ferber's short stories; and ***The Youngest***, by Philip Barry, in which the junior member of a family turns out to be the smartest, with Henry Hull and Genevieve Tobin.

By far the most remarkable production of the year was Max Reinhardt's ***The Miracle***, brought from Germany by the master himself, which told in elaborate pantomine the story of an erring nun who deserted her duties in the cathedral to go into the world and taste its pleasures. When she does this, a compassionate Madonna steps down from her pedestal and takes the nun's place.

The Miracle was colossal—no less!—in conception. Playgoers who entered the Century Theatre found it transformed by the young scenic designer Norman Bel Geddes into what appeared to be a real cathedral, with solid pillars, a nave, and stained-glass windows. Seven hundred supers milled around in mob scenes; no curtain fell between scenes and acts, but a "non-irritating smoke screen" hid the stage, adding mystery and atmosphere. ***Theatre Magazine*** called the whole "the most impressive and richly colorful stage spectacle this or any generation of American theatregoers has witnessed." The wanton nun was played by lovely Rosamond Pinchot, daughter of the Governor of Pennsylvania, who won praise in her first role on any stage. The Madonna was the international beauty Lady Diana Manners, who, among other things, stood immovable for three quarters of an hour on a pedestal.

Next in importance during the year was the appearance of Alfred Lunt and Lynn Fontanne in ***The Guardsman***. It was the first time this inspired

George S. Kaufman (**left**) and Marc Connelly (**right**) introduced satire to
Broadway—this despite Kaufman's oft quoted wisecrack,
"Satire on the stage is what closes on Saturday
night." Beginning happily with
Dulcy (Lynn Fontanne)
in 1921, they also provided
To the Ladies (Helen Hayes, Otto Kruger),
Merton of the Movies (Glenn Hunter), and *Beggar on Horseback*.
Along with these they collaborated on three forgotten epics, a satirical
Deep Tangled Wildwood (James Gleason) and the musical comedies
Helen of Troy, N.Y. and *Be Yourself* (Jack Donahue,
Queenie Smith). The pair went
their separate ways after 1924, Kaufman
to become a top collaborator with others and the foremost
all-around theatre artisan of the day, Connelly
to achieve immortality with *Green Pastures* in 1930.
No two names better evoke the mood of the early
Twenties—Kaufman and Connelly,
sweet nostalgia!

Romantic
Joseph Schildkraut
portrayed Benvenuto Cellini in
The Firebrand, by Edwin Justus Mayer,
one of the plays (along with *Desire Under the Elms*) to
arouse the ire of moral crusaders. In this case, the length of a kiss between
Schildkraut and Eden Gray caused a crack-down. The actor was
the male heart throb of the
season—for obvious
reasons.

Another scorching kiss of the time was in *White Cargo*, produced
by Earl Carroll for an all-time low of $67. The sexy sizzler caught on and
earned a fortune. Here Annette Margules and
Richard Stevenson light their fire.

Norman Bel Geddes
designed ultra-spectacular sets
for Max Reinhardt's **The Miracle**. Despite a religious theme,
this spectacle had its share of sex and sadism. At one
point Rosamond Pinchot placed her lovely neck on the block for the Inquisition Scene.

George Kaufman and Marc Connelly
turned impressionistic in **Beggar on Horseback**,
with dream sequences satirizing big business and go-getterism. The stellar cast
(not all pictured here) included Roland Young, Osgood Perkins,
Spring Byington, George Barbier, Kay Johnson,
Greta Nissen. Music for the dream
ballet was by Deems Taylor.

As the unsinkable Aubrey Piper in *The Show-Off*,
Louis Jean Bartels gave one of the top comic performances of the decade. Sadly, he
never found another role as good.

couple had appeared opposite each other as a team, and the play was perfect for the deft interplay of their comedy. Those with long memories will recall that it told of a Viennese actor and actress, wed for six months. Seldom had the actress stayed faithful to one man for so long, and the actor is worried. To test his wife, he sends her love missives and flowers in the name of a Russian guardsman. At a rendezvous he impersonates the guardsman; as she is about to yield her body to him, he reveals his identity. She laughingly insists that she knew him all along. Did she?

Proof that good actors and actresses were kept busy in this era is to be found in the activities of Helen Hayes and Katharine Cornell. During 1924—spring, summer, fall, and winter—Miss Hayes appeared in **We Moderns**, **Dancing Mothers**, and **Quarantine**. Miss Cornell adorned **The Way Things Happen**, **The Outsider**, and **Tiger Cats**, a Belasco production about an "erotic wife." In December she starred in a revival of **Candida**, with Pedro de Cordoba, breaking all records for the run of this thirty-year-old Shaw play.

George Arliss appeared in Galsworthy's **Old English**, about an eighty-year-old man; Ethel Barrymore revived Pinero's **The Second Mrs. Tanqueray**, with Henry Daniell; Marilyn Miller essayed **Peter Pan**, but even the critics who adored the Sunshine Girl had to admit she looked too sophisticated as Peter; Lionel Barrymore suffered three flops in a row; **Pigs**, with Wallace Ford and Nydia Westman, was a simple but hilarious comedy appealing to advocates of clean theatre; Leo Carrillo and Maria Ouspenskaya (what a combination!) were in Stark Young's **The Saint**; equally odd was the joint authorship of **Close Harmony**, by Dorothy Parker and Elmer Rice, which ran only twenty-four performances.

The year 1924 was one of the best America has ever known in the field of musical comedy, revue, and operetta. Brightest success was **Charlot's Revue**, a one-set production from England that featured Jack Buchanan, Gertrude Lawrence, and Beatrice Lillie. A first-night audience that expected a routine show from overseas found itself enjoying one of the most delightful evenings the theatre has ever known. For months New Yorkers paid tribute by quoting an anonymous versifier:

> Lillie and Lawrence,
> Lawrence and Lillie,
> If you haven't seen them,
> You're perfectly silly

Equally felicitous was the domestic musical comedy **Lady, Be Good**, with Fred and Adele Astaire, comedian Walter Catlett, and songs by George and Ira Gershwin. This was the first time the brothers Gershwin collaborated on a show, and the fields of musical comedy and song writing were never the same again. "George Gershwin has made an honest woman of jazz," cracked Samuel Chotzinoff.

Cerebral shockers
came from playwrights who attacked the role of women in a
changing world. In *Craig's Wife*, George Kelly (uncle of Princess Grace)
skewered women who sublimate problems into fanatical
housekeeping. Involved were Josephine Hull
and Chrystal Herne.

England's John van Druten
achieved prominence as the author of **Young Woodley**,
wherein a schoolboy fell in love with his headmaster's wife.
Helen Gahagan and Glenn Hunter emoted.

For those who doted on operettas, the year provided two immortals. First came **The Student Prince**, with Howard Marsh and Ilse Marenga, and one of Sigmund Romberg's best scores. After its highly successful run in New York, the Shuberts toured it into nearly every nook and cranny of the nation; it may be playing somewhere today! Similarly popular was **Rose Marie**, with Dennis King singing the superior music of Rudolf Friml. The full name of the heroine here was Rose-Marie La Flamme; a critic called the whole evening "genuinely magnificent." "Indian Love Call" was outstanding among its songs.

Billie Burke returned to the musical theatre in **Annie Dear**, with Ernest Truex; Ruth Chatterton, hitherto a dramatic actress, embellished the operetta **Magnolia Lady** with husband Ralph Forbes; the Duncan Sisters played **Topsy and Eva**, a musical version of **Uncle Tom's Cabin**, which had Little Eva warbling "I Never Had a Mammy"; the Dolly Sisters, slender and svelte as the girls of today, lit up **Greenwich Village Follies**, along with Moran and Mack, the Vincent Lopez Orchestra, words and music by sophisticated Cole Porter. Inconspicuous in the chorus of the last named was Elsbeth Holman, who later in the decade emerged as deep-voiced Libby.

Ed Wynn starred himself in his own **Grab Bag**; Grace Moore of the soaring voice finally achieved recognition in Irving Berlin's final **Music Box Revue**, where she sang "What'll I Do?"; Joe Cook and Sophie Tucker enlivened Earl Carroll's **Vanities**; the chorus of **George White's Scandals** included the dark-banged beauty Louise Brooks.

One musical offering deserves special mention—**I'll Say She Is**, the first Broadway appearance of the Marx Brothers, up to now vaudeville headliners. It was produced on a shoestring, and one observer commented wryly on its "twenty-four dollars worth of scenery." **I'll Say She Is** was an instant winner, with the mad foursome (in those days) hailed as kings of low comedy. The brothers had not yet adopted their nicknames and were solemnly listed in the program as Julius H. Marx, Leonard Marx, Arthur Marx, and Herbert Marx—in order, Groucho, Chico, Harpo, and Zeppo.

New York gloried in many newspapers during the Twenties, with several drama
critics on each for nights when more than one play opened.
In mid-decade, John Decker caricatured lucky aisle-sitters for **Theatre Magazine**.
Top row:
Robert Benchley (**Life**),
E. W. Osborn (**Evening World**), Stark Young (**Times**).
Second row: George S. Kaufman (**Times**), S. Jay Kaufman (**Mail**), Heywood Broun
(**World**), John Anderson (**Post**). Third row: Alexander Woollcott
(**Evening Sun**), Gilbert W. Gabriel (**Evening Telegram**).
Bottom row: George Jean Nathan
(**American Mercury**),
Charles Belmont Davis (**Herald-Tribune**),
Alan Dale (**American**), Percy Hammond (**Herald-Tribune**).
In the wings awaited such younger talents as J. Brooks
Atkinson, John Mason Brown,
and Richard Watts, Jr.

JEANNE

Consider the outstanding dramatic actresses of the Twenties—Katharine Cornell, Lynn Fontanne, Lenore Ulric, Jane Cowl, Judith Anderson, Francine Larrimore, Pauline Lord, Margalo Gillmore, Helen Hayes, Alice Brady, and others. None shone in 1925 like the forgotten star Jeanne Eagels. Thinking back on her from the vantage point of today, Marc Connelly says, "She had a three-dimensional quality." In his autobiography, Noël Coward wrote, "Of all the actresses I have ever seen, there was never one quite like Jeanne Eagels." Critic Brooks Atkinson recalls "tense, vivid, and smoldering performances." John Colton, co-author of her great success **Rain**, paid tribute to "her beautiful and unearthly genius, which gave a thousand new dimensions to a character that a base touch could so easily make . . . commonplace, perhaps even tawdry."

Many factors combined to make Jeanne Eagels the most conspicuous actress of her time, and not all of them were happy. For one thing, the reckless self-destruction of her life made her appear more *of* the hectic Twenties than any other actress. "If I have thirty cents when I die," she liked to say, "it will be thirty cents too many." More than other performers along Broadway she seemed determined to burn herself out, a moth beating against brilliant flame. It was no illusion. When the Twenties exploded in the stock-market crash of October 1929, Jeanne Eagels, wracked by dissipation, frustration, and illness, had been dead three weeks.

Few in the theatrical profession liked Jeanne Eagels. She was indifferent or hostile to actors in her supporting casts (though nice to stagehands), capable of prodigies of temper and temperament, and madly jealous of Ethel Barrymore and others who rivaled her eminence. She particularly disliked Maxine Elliott, an actress important enough to have a theatre named for her. Jeanne named her dog Maxine — "After the theatre, you know," she'd say.

Yet actors had to admire this tormented woman. Jeanne Eagels, actress, was somehow the quintessence of her craft, displaying all the virtues and faults to be found in the theatrical *persona*. Edward Doherty, her biographer, thinks that from age fourteen she believed herself the greatest actress in the world. It could be. But she was also proud just to be an actress and dared put into words what most thespians thought of their chosen profession: "We are glorious, unearthly people, set above all others because of our genius, our capacity to sway others, to make them laugh and cry, or make them live a romance we but play."

What actor could resent a person who said such things?

The profession also took pride in Jeanne Eagels' fierce integrity. Here was a woman who lived only to act but still refused to compromise by

Jeanne Eagels was the most flamboyant actress of the Twenties
and some say the best. Here a sketch from life by
Janet Dexter at the time of *Her Cardboard Lover*.

The role of Sadie Thompson in **Rain**
made Jeanne Eagels famous but possibly destroyed her in the end. Here she
cavorts before admiring Marines—the behavior
Reverend Davidson disapproved of.

accepting roles in which she would not do her absolute best. Once playwright Channing Pollock came to her with a play, authorized to offer $600 a week if she would appear in it. He found her in near squalor. "I have never seen a room more depressing or eloquent of poverty," he wrote. In this atmosphere he read the script aloud. At the end she said, "You can see I need the money, but I don't like the play. I've got to believe that if I wait my chance will come. I can't afford to compromise with what could only be an opportunity to do my second best." Pollock considered her reaction either folly or genius.

Actors also admired Jeanne because she had risen the hard way. The publicized hardships of Minnie Maddern Fiske and Laurette Taylor were no greater than hers. Born Amelia Jean Eagles in Kansas City in 1890, she was a willful, dreamy child who baffled a Pennsylvania Dutch father and Irish mother.

Later, Jeanne liked to tell interviewers that she had received only a year and a half of formal schooling and had been home for Christmas only once since age seven. This was an exaggeration, but not much. Life began for her at eleven, when a New York actress arrived in Kansas City to open a dramatic school. Determined to begin with a flourish, the woman announced a performance of *A Midsummer Night's Dream* and issued a call for children to appear in it. Jeanne got the role of Puck and never again was the same. Soon she quit school and talked herself into the sanctum of the Dubinsky Brothers, who produced shows in tents and ramshackle theatres over a circuit of five Midwestern states. Their bills were a mixture of the corny and (at the time) classic: *For Home and Honor*, *The Octoroon*, *Little Lord Fauntleroy*, *The Two Orphans*, *Camille*, *Romeo and Juliet*, *King of the Cowboys*, *Under Two Flags*, and *Uncle Tom's Cabin*.

For six years Jeanne played the Dubinsky circuit. "In many ways it was a dog's life, those years I spent with the barnstorming shows," she once told a reporter. "But it didn't seem so to me then. I was free; I was seeing the world; I was an actress." At approximately fifteen she wed a Dubinsky and produced a male child, given out for adoption.

However, she was too ambitious to stay in the hinterlands. Jeanne was close to eighteen when the path of her troupe crossed that of *Jumping Jupiter*, a touring New York musical starring Richard Carle and Edna Wallace Hopper. One member of the cast was Ina Clair, just about Jeanne's age; in the chorus was quick-witted Helen Broderick. When the show resumed its travels, Jeanne was in the chorus, too.

Jumping Jupiter wound up its tour in New York, and Jeanne was ecstatic. But nobody seemed to care about her six years of diversified roles with the tent show; she was pegged as a chorus girl because of *Jumping Jupiter*. In a chorus-line job with Billie Burke's *Mind the Paint Girl*, she stood out from the others well enough for a critic to write, "The girl with the red heels on her shoes has personality." Jeanne was underwhelmed. "He doesn't know the girl with the red heels has played Camille," she said bitterly.

She talked the same way to startled producers. "I'm a dramatic actress, not a chorus girl," she told them. "I was a leading lady at twelve. I played Juliet at fourteen. I've played everything Sarah Bernhardt played. I want to *act*." Someone who heard this christened her the Bernhardt of the Sticks. The name amused people, but to Jeanne it was just right.

At times she was too broke to eat anything but crackers and milk. She got a touring job playing Elsie Ferguson's role in **The Outcast**. She made a movie in New Rochelle, New York, where a fledgling film company set up. Finished, she again commenced the rounds of producing offices.

One intrigued by her was David Belasco, the Bishop of Broadway, who liked to talk to her from the thronelike chair in his rococo office. "She was a timid girl who feared no man," he later pontificated. "She had been whipped by adversity until she cringed, but faced me with hard, ambitious eyes, a girl in shabby clothes, with the air of a Duse, the voice of an earl's daughter, and the mien of an alley cat . . . I asked her why she wanted to be an actress, and she said that something inside her would never let her be anything else."

When Jeanne met Belasco she told him, "All I have left is my ambition—and my virtue." The Bishop did nothing about her ambition but did assail her virtue. Belasco was a lecher with a fourposter bed tucked away behind his office in the theatre bearing his name. Immediately he began a campaign to seduce Jeanne, who did not wish to be seduced; she liked younger, clean-cut, collegiate types. Late one afternoon as the two talked in his sanctum, Belasco asked her to leave because a group of fellow producers waited downstairs. Then, surprisingly, he darted into his bedroom. Jeanne applied eye to keyhole and saw the Bishop vigorously rumpling the sheets of his fourposter. Plainly, he was going to display the messy bed to his visitors and claim her as a conquest. The indignant girl flung open the door and ordered him to stop. Tight-lipped, she waited until his guests arrived, then flounced off.

The popular female impersonator Julian Eltinge put her in **Crinoline Girl** over the protests of producer Al Woods, who watched a rehearsal and declared, "She looks like a dish of raspberries to me." Eltinge supported her, saying, "She can't rehearse; she has to have an audience in front of her." He was right.

Following **Crinoline Girl**, Jeanne had another no-food period and because of it got the part that established her on Broadway. The fine English actor George Arliss was rehearsing **The Professor's Love Story**, by James M. Barrie, a play requiring him to carry his leading lady across the stage. Arliss, a slight man, issued a call for girls light in weight if not in ability. Jeanne, who had been starving, proved lightest.

The two came to respect each other, and Arliss cast her in **Alexander Hamilton**, in which she played Maria Reynolds, a winsome minx who vamped the first Secretary of the Treasury; history takes a harsh view of this young lady. Critics were entranced by Jeanne. One spoke of her "not too retiring young charms," while another raved that her hair "resembled the golden honey of Hymettus—or, as you might say, molasses candy in the pulling." In all, she stole the play from Arliss, and it is a measure of the man that he did not mind.

Jeanne's triumph as Maria Reynolds made her big on Broadway. She was twenty-seven but looked ten years younger, a girl with a high forehead, prominent cheekbones, silken skin, uptilted nose, wide mouth, and eyes that changed color with her many moods. Of her Ruth Gordon says, "Jeanne Eagels was the most beautiful person I ever saw, and if you ever saw her, she was the most beautiful *you* ever saw." She photographed well, and her thin figure exactly fit incoming styles. She increased her Broadway fame by appearing in **Vogue** and **Harper's Bazaar** wearing the latest Paris creations.

Her years with Arliss were the first in which Jeanne made money. Having made it, she greedily set out to make more by resuming relations with the New Rochelle movie company. While in **Alexander Hamilton** she lived in New Rochelle, filming in the daytime and driving to and from the theatre at night. In all, she worked fourteen or sixteen hours on non-matinee days and began taking sedatives to sleep at night and stimulants to stay awake. A frail body resented this. Her chest was weak, with an ever-present threat of tuberculosis. She also contracted sinusitis, an ailment doctors then did not understand.

Success evoked a call from David Belasco. The Bishop wanted her for **Daddies**, a play about five carefree New York bachelors who decided to adopt French war orphans. In moments of companionship these hearty fellows flung arms around one another and bellowed:

> A Bachelor bunch all got a hunch
> To form a Bachelor's Club,
> And every one was a son-of-a-gun,
> But never one was a dub.
> And so they'd meet to toast their feet,
> And pass the time away,
> From far and near they'd come to cheer
> Hurrah! For the Bachelor's Day.

Again Jeanne scored a hit, with critics calling her the fourth jewel in the diadem of Belasco's brilliant leading ladies, already featuring Frances Starr, Lenore Ulric, and Ina Claire. She called Belasco "Mr. David," while she was "Miss Jeannie," but working for him was not as rewarding as expected. His tireless and ingenious attempts at seduction continued, to her annoyance. In Miss Jeannie, Mr. David found a worthy opponent. The Bishop adored opening nights, when his stars took their bows, then stepped to the wings to lead him out to deliver a supposedly spontaneous curtain speech. At the opening of **Daddies**, Jeanne took her bows all right but danced off the opposite side of the stage without pulling Mr. David forward. He never forgave her.

During the run of **Daddies** her health worsened. She collapsed several times, causing a doctor to hover protectively in the wings. Or so it appeared on the surface. One of the Daddies was George Abbott, who would become an outstanding playwright, collaborator, director, and all-around theatre hand. Like others of the **Daddies** cast he was unable to figure out whether Jeanne was actually ill or malingering in order to break her contract. If so, this was one of her better performances, for the sharp-eyed actors could never arrive at an answer. Ultimately, Mr. David let her go; the reason given was poor health.

The years between 1919–1922 were rough on Jeanne; during them Channing Pollock visited her. She was under contract to Sam H. Harris and appeared without notable success in **A Young Man's Fancy**, **Night Watch**, and **A Gentleman's Mother**. She walked out on rehearsals of the other Harris plays and altogether behaved the stormy petrel. Yet the producer retained faith in her.

Into the Harris office came the script of **Rain**, by John Colton and Miss Clemence Randolph. It was based on the short story "Miss Thompson," by Somerset Maugham, so daring in theme that no popular magazine would publish it. Finally Maugham gave it to **Smart Set**, which paid more in prestige than pelf. Maugham and Colton were traveling together when the latter read "Miss Thompson" and immediately visualized it as a play. Maugham, no mean playwright himself, was incredulous. Returning to New York, Colton collaborated with Miss Randolph on the script.

Rain told the story (Maugham had observed its outlines in real life) of Sadie Thompson, a prostitute tossed out of Honolulu in a vice clean-up. Sadie was stranded on the South Seas island of Pago Pago, along with fellow passengers from a ship temporarily broken down. Among them was the Reverend Alfred Davidson, a fanatical missionary who professed to despise Sadie but claimed to hear a heavenly call to save her soul; in reality, he lusted for her body. Sadie at first dismissed him as a sin-buster, then weakened and began to think of expiating her sins with his spiritual aid. When he exposed his interest in her flesh, she became the ultimate victor. Davidson killed himself, and the girl bounced back as the old, raucous Sadie.

Producer Sam Harris thought Jeanne would be good as Sadie and offered her a minimal $350 a week. She herself lit up like a sunburst on reading the script. Here, at last, was a role to make her recognized as a dramatic actress. "You're playing a girl who thinks Christ is a swear word," director Sam Forrest told her, but Jeanne needed no such assistance. She viewed Sadie as a victim of life whose only sin was wanting a good time.

Jeanne combed the secondhand shops of the city in search of the proper costume for a jaunty harlot. She finally chose a sleazy red dress, short lace coat, and broad-brimmed hat with a feather that waved defiance at the world. On her feet she wore a pair of white-topped high-button shoes; she carried a bedraggled parasol; and around her neck slung a scarf and costume jewelry. She also practiced talking tough. Meantime, the production staff had created an amazing rain machine that dumped tons of water onstage in simulation of the tropical rains of Pago Pago. For Jeanne, with her sinus trouble, these were unhealthy work conditions. When it was not raining, Sadie's phonograph ground out "Wabash Blues."

Rehearsals went well, but the first tryout night in Philadelphia was a disaster. First-string critics went to the opening of Doris Keane in **The Czarina**, leaving second-stringers to cover **Rain**. They didn't like it, nor did members of the audience. Playwright Samuel Shipman, who owned 10 percent of the production, sold his share after the second act; it would have brought him $100,000. Producer John D. Williams controlled 25 percent and tried to sell but could find no taker. Veteran playwright Eugene Walter arrived from New York as play doctor, but he and Colton quarreled bitterly. Finally, at a desperate post-performance conference, Sam Forrest rewrote a few speeches and the play jelled.

Rain opened in New York on November 7, 1922, an event called by theatre-buff Ward Morehouse "an emotional demonstration never exceeded in this country and century." During the second act Sadie castigated the Reverend Davidson by screaming, "You! You! I know your kind, you dirty, two-faced mutt. I'll bet when you were a kid you caught flies and pulled their wings off! . . . . You'd tear the heart out of your grandmother if she didn't think your way, and tell her you were saving her soul. You—you—you psalm-singing son of a —" The last word was supposedly lost in a shriek of rage, but Jeanne managed to convey it. The audience roared approval.

The third act brought more electricity. With Davidson dead and her own spirits revived, Sadie embarked for Australia. "I'm sorry for everybody in the world," she declared. "Life's a quaint present from Somebody, there's no doubt about that . . . . Maybe it will be easier in Sydney." The curtain dropped, and the audience leaped up, demanding curtain calls. Then, instead of leaving through the exits, the people moved en masse toward the stage and stood still in quiet tribute.

That night it had been "**Rain**, with Jeanne Eagels." Next day electric lights went up to spell "Jeanne Eagels in **Rain**." Her salary also rose, going from $350 a week to $500, to $600, and finally $3,500, with a percentage of the gross.

Jeanne Eagels played **Rain** for 648 performances on Broadway and then took off for more than a year on a tour of major cities. Did it hurt her to play four years in such an intense, demanding role, performing night after night, plus matinees, over and over in the same part?

She didn't think so. Sadie Thompson was her possession, the role that had made her truly famous. She held onto it compulsively, even fighting the idea of having an understudy. She played the part when ill, through hangovers, and after an automobile accident. She missed only twenty-eight performances in four years, those because of an operation. She never let down, and it's possible her last performance was superior to her first.

To others, though, the long run spelled tragedy. Alexander Woollcott, for one, has written, "After four years' imprisonment in the success of **Rain**, the madness of the caged came upon poor Jeanne Eagels, and in a sense she died of that madness." So the question arises, Would she have done the same things if not trapped by the triumph of **Rain**? For nearly everything she did after that opening night seemed wrong.

For one thing, she married. Her husband was Ted Coy, fortyish, considered the greatest football player the game had ever known. Married and the father of two children when he met Jeanne, Coy was discussing divorce with his wife. But according to Edward Doherty, Jeanne's biographer, he was still living in the past days of his sports glory at Yale. He had never before known an actress or mingled with theatre folk.

The two wed in 1925, and from the beginning the union was a mess. Coy worked halfheartedly as a stockbroker but for the most part let his hours match Jeanne's. She found it easy to dominate the handsome hunk of man and despised him for it. She had never been much of a drinker (and never smoked until the part of Sadie demanded it), but now she began drinking to annoy her husband. He retaliated by getting drunker than she did, trying to show her how badly drunks behaved. She humiliated and nagged him in public and at times slapped his face.

When Jeanne drank she became a spoiler—"Destruction enchanted her," thinks Ruth Gordon. She invited people to her country home in Westchester County, then turned on them to scream, "Get out of here, all of you!" She planned a grand Saturday-night party, for which she bought new furniture. To it she invited Holbrook Blinn, Leslie Howard, and others she admired. A few arrived early, and Coy served drinks. Jeanne finally drove up in the limousine she used after shows; she had been nipping at bottles of champagne held under each arm. Seeing the drinks in the hands of her guests, she screeched, "What the hell is this? I told you not to open the liquor until I arrived." Then she behaved so badly that her guests left.

Some friends, like Clifton Webb and his mother, stuck by her. "She is nothing but nerves, overworked, raw nerves," one explained. Occasionally she was pathetic, as when she said, "The most perfect gift of God is simplicity of soul. But it doesn't come to many of us though, does it?"

She toured in **Rain**, with the tons of water falling around her, in Chicago, San Francisco, and other big cities. Her drinking continued, with Ted Coy trying to stop it. Once she got into a railroad compartment with six bottles of whiskey. Coy couldn't stand it and threw the bottles out the window. She started out the door to get more from her maid. He pulled her back, and she fell and fractured her jaw so badly that a painful steel plate had to be inserted in her mouth. She claimed Coy hit her with his fist and divorced him.

Rain came back to New York for a return engagement. When finally it closed, Jeanne was at liberty after four long years. She didn't like the feeling and avidly began reading scripts. She rehearsed one, walked out, then settled on **The Cardboard Lover**, a bit of Gallic fluff adapted from the French of Jacques Deval by Valerie Wyngate. It told of a sophisticated Frenchwoman who hired a charming man to make love to her so she won't be tempted to return to her husband. The play had been tried out the year before with Laurette Taylor starring and Leslie Howard featured. Producer Gilbert Miller decided on a new star and additional work. As play doctor, he called in P. G. Wodehouse, who added brilliant lines for the male lead but did little to improve the female part.

Jeanne's first move was to demand that the title be changed to **Her Cardboard Lover**. Then she nervously began rehearsals, finding the role of a sparkling French lady a disconcerting switch from rowdy Sadie Thompson. Again the leading man was Leslie Howard, who up to now had appeared in **Aren't We All**, **The Green Hat**, and other plays to good but never spectacular notices.

Howard, a composed, relaxed actor was wary of his temperamental star. This proved wise, for Jeanne began firing other members of the cast, calling their vibrations wrong. Yet she treated Howard with courtesy. As rehearsals progressed he began to feel sorry for her. Like many others, he did not agree with Jeanne that her varied roles as a child-barnstormer had molded her into a rounded actress, nor had her infrequent roles on Broadway brought real experience. In other words, Jeanne Eagels had remained more of a personality than an actress.

The opening night of **Her Cardboard Lover** at the Empire Theatre on the night of March 21,1927,became an ironic event. Jeanne was gowned beautifully and looked lovely—"a pink and gold confection." But the lines P. G. Wodehouse wrote for the male lead sounded in Leslie Howard's clipped accent as if the actor were creating them himself. The audience responded, knowing it was seeing the birth of a male star whose name would be in lights thereafter. The final curtain fell, to trigger one of the most embarrassing moments in theatre history. By the hallowed star system, the star took the final bows of the evening, standing alone onstage, bathed in a golden glow. On this night Jeanne stepped out for the last bow to face an audience chanting, "Howard, Howard, Howard!"

Was it anger, or did she fail to comprehend? Whichever, every time the curtain rose, Jeanne tripped out to accept the applause and cheers meant for Leslie Howard. The stage manager, aware of tradition and terrified of his star, kept ringing the curtain up and down as long as the applause lasted. It became an endurance contest between Jeanne and the crowd. She won, for finally an annoyed audience gave up

Jeanne Eagels'
antics onstage during performances
of **Her Cardboard Lover** were often more exciting than those written in the
script. Young leading man Leslie Howard was often driven to distraction.

Leslie Howard arrived on Broadway from London at the beginning of the decade but was not taken seriously as an actor until the opening night of *Her Cardboard Lover*, with Jeanne Eagels.

and went home. Next morning Percy Hammond wrote, "Mr. Leslie Howard, in one of the richer roles of the season, rather kidnaped the play from its rightful proprietor."

One would expect Jeanne to be seething with fury, but she still treated her leading man with consideration. Aware that her first-night performance left much to be desired, she kept working on her characterization and within a month it had improved. Yet her temperament never abated. After one matinee she summoned the house manager to say, "I read the other day that Marilyn Miller has a red carpet stretching from the dressing room to curb every night." "Is that so?" the man asked. "Yes, it is," snapped Jeanne, "and if there isn't a red carpet for me tomorrow night, I don't show up."

In *Her Cardboard Lover*, physical ailments became apparent. Her throat swelled so that on some nights it was nearly impossible for her to speak. She also had what were diagnosed as ulcers of the eyes and required an operation. Her chest was still bad, sinus trouble worse.

Yet she kept on drinking and, having mastered her characterization, began to let down onstage. Because of liquor or illness—it was hard to tell which—she began misbehaving. In Act II she had to sink into bed and finish the scene from there. Several times she passed out as the comfort of the bed enveloped her. After Leslie Howard tried vainly to rouse her, the curtain came down, and the audience lined up at the box office for its money.

One night, as Howard approached the bed, she said in a loud voice, "I want a glass of water"—a line not in the script. Howard stopped, stunned. She repeated louder, "I said I would like a glass of water." Howard walked offstage to his dressing room and slammed the door. Again the curtain fell. Actors' Equity, responsible for the good behavior of its members, began to take a dim view of Miss Jeanne Eagels.

Her name still drew the public, and when *Her Cardboard Lover* moved to Chicago the theatre was full. Jeanne, says Edward Doherty, was enjoying a love affair with one of the young actors in the cast. Nightly he stopped at her dressing room and the two went out on the town. One night, after a lovers' quarrel, he failed to appear. She began to drink and next day hurled bottles at those who tried to enter her hotel room. Show time came and went. She had committed the unforgivable theatrical sin: The show didn't go on! It was March 1928, and never again did she set foot on a legitimate stage.

Jeanne was brought up on charges before a hostile Equity and forbidden to act for the next eighteen months. Yet she could appear in vaudeville doing bits of *Rain* and *Her Cardboard Lover.* Also, Hollywood dangled a $200,000 contract for three talking pictures.

Her throat infection grew worse, her chest weaker; she had neuralgia, kidney trouble, sinus, and needed the eye operation. She took quantities of drugs and maybe dope for endless aches and pains. After playing in vaudeville she went to Hollywood to make *The Letter*, another Maugham opus. (**Rain** had been bought for Gloria Swanson.) It was one of the first big talkie hits, but her temperament in Hollywood set record highs. She hated the routine of picture-making—the early rising, long waits, meticulous direction. After **The Letter** she starred in **Jealousy** with Fredric March. Her behavior became so outrageous that the studio gladly bought back her contract.

She returned to New York ill but charged with dramatic energy. At times she screamed, "Nobody loves me! Nobody cares if I live or die—and I hate everybody as much as everybody hates me!" Yet a mother and sister were still devoted, as were the Webbs. Lamenting her career, she wailed, "I am the greatest actress in the world, and the greatest failure, and nobody gives a God damn!"

She went through the eye operation, spent nineteen days in a hospital, and suffered a serious convulsion. She rallied when released, but other ailments nagged. She still had the country place in Westchester and an apartment at 38 West 59th Street, alternating between both. With premonitions of death, she scrawled on a piece of paper, "When I am dead from dying, then I shall cease to be—But while I am still living I never want to be **dead**."

On October 3, 1929, she paid a routine visit to her doctor. She collapsed in his anteroom and died a few minutes later.

No other actress has been able to give a worthwhile performance as Sadie Thompson in **Rain**. This may be the greatest tribute to Jeanne Eagels.

Tallulah Bankhead yearned over fifteen years to play the part and when she did turned out to be wooden and uninspired. Lenore Ulric did Sadie adequately (but no more) on the subway circuit around New York City and Sally Rand (no comment) in summer stock. Gloria Swanson, Joan Crawford, and Rita Hayworth essayed Sadie in films without winning hosannahs. June Havoc tried her in a short-lived musical version. In 1972 **Rain** was revived off Broadway in New York. The play was hailed as surprisingly durable, but Madeleine le Roux, as Sadie, got mixed notices.

No one has ever been able to ignite this great role like Jeanne Eagels. It's as if it were forever jinxed.

SOUND OF MUSIC

In 1925, musical comedies, revues, and operettas carried almost as much weight as drama. The bounce, breeziness, and occasional melancholy of their music, together with the mood-evoking words by lyricists, appeared to typify the restless beat of the Tumultuous Twenties. True, these songs brought escape, but it was an escape that quickened the mind and tickled the toes. Of the decade a commentator has said, "People wanted their pleasures to be easy-come, easy-go, swift, and full of kicks, like jazz music and bootleg gin."

The year 1925 stands out as a midway point in a Golden Age of Musical Comedy, with revues and operettas only a hot breath behind. Already the public was familiar with the melodies of Irving Berlin, Jerome Kern, George Gershwin, Vincent Youmans, and Sigmund Romberg, with words by skilled lyricists like Ira Gershwin, Otto Harbach, Irving Caesar, and B. G. De Sylva. Now composers like Richard Rodgers (with immortal lyrics by Lorenz Hart), Cole Porter, and De Sylva, Brown, and Henderson were beginning to caress the contemporary ear.

From here on, hit songs from Broadway shows would be more popular than ever before, since radio was just coming into its own. "The best things in life are free," ran the words of one of the best of show tunes; now it was true of music. Heretofore people had bought the sheet music or phonograph records of the songs from shows. Because of radio they could hear them for nothing, played by outstanding orchestra leaders like Paul Whiteman, Vincent Lopez, and Leo Reisman.

They were something, those show songs of the Twenties! Fifty years later—right now—young and old still cherish them. "Someone to Watch over Me," "Thou Swell," and "What Is This Thing Called Love?" are as fresh as ever. For evoking an upbeat mood, no tunes have ever replaced "Fascinatin' Rhythm," "Hallelujah," or "Who Stole My Heart Away?" For downbeat blues, no one has improved on "What'll I Do?," "Can't Help Lovin' That Man," or "Moanin' Low."

One reason for the number of mid-Twenties musical shows was the cost of show production, which had not yet increased in proportion to the rising expenses of living. Writes musicologist Cecil Smith, "For one mad, magical decade, Broadway could afford to produce as many musicals as it wanted to and market them at box office prices any audience could pay without feeling any pinch."

A better reason, though, was the sudden profusion of songwriters and lyricists on Broadway. The end result was great jazz, with the blues, ragtime, and syncopation from the suffering souls of black people merging with ethnic-inspired melodies stirring in the minds of young composers of European background, in whose ears the laments of cantors still rang. Cole Porter, of course, was the exception who supposedly proved the rule.

Sad to report, few Negro composers or wordsmiths were to be found in the gold rush of musical talent. Eubie Blake (music) and Noble Sissle (words), who wrote "I'm Just Wild about Harry" and other songs for the black musical *Shuffle Along*, were just about the only ones to make an imprint on the Broadway of the day. "After the white composers learned how to write syncopation, they didn't need us and there was no more room for us," said Eubie Blake ruefully on his ninetieth birthday, in 1972.

The overall result was—you might say—discovery of a lost chord, bringing with it an onrush of words and music unsurpassed in our culture. In Noël Coward's brittle phrase, America is a nation that takes its light music seriously. Yet the tunes of the Twenties demanded to be taken seriously; for the first time the country was getting music with what a longhair has called "the fugitive essence and personality that distinguished a song as American."

Alec Wilder, no mean composer himself, has saluted the songwriters and lyricists of the Twenties as the Great Professionals and points out that their show tunes possessed greater sophistication, sinew, and complexity than contemporary Tin Pan Alley hits like "Bye, Bye, Blackbird," "My Blue Heaven," or "Sleepy Time Gal."

The conquest of Broadway by the Great Professionals was speedy and glorious. Suddenly outdated were Victor Herbert and George M. Cohan, as Irving Berlin began writing words and music for *Watch Your Step*, *Ziegfeld Follies*, and his own *Music Box Revues*.

Berlin began it all. "It is difficult to write of Irving Berlin without a certain awe," says Brooks Atkinson. No one has written so many song hits, and probably no one ever will. Born in Russia and transported as a child to New York's lower East Side, he was exposed to little book learning and no musical education. At fourteen he was a singing waiter in saloons like Nigger Mike's and Jimmy Kelly's. After hours he taught himself music on their pianos.

In the late 1920s, during the Harlemania era, Broadwayites who rushed uptown for predawn entertainment were told that as a youth Irving Berlin made a practice of hanging around a Negro musicians' club on West 53rd Street. If so, the composer never labored the fact in his recollections. But with "Alexander's Ragtime Band" (1911) he became the first to take the ragtime of black songwriters like Rosamond and James Weldon Johnson and manipulate it in the direction of jazz.

Berlin's first Broadway show was C. B. Dillingham's *Watch Your Step* (1914), to which he contributed syncopated tunes like "Everybody's Doin' It." At this period and later, songs were often "interpolated" in musical comedies; of course, in the plotless revue everything was interpolated. But if the producer of a book musical liked a song he stuck it in the show, whether or not it fit. If nothing else, this informal practice was a boon to young songwriters.

Berlin songs were interpolated in musicals like *Century Girl* and *Stop, Look, and Listen*. Then he began contributing to *Ziegfeld Follies*,

Irving Berlin
composed his great love
ballads—"Remember," "What'll I Do?",
"All Alone," "Always"—for Broadway shows during his courtship of Ellin Mackay, daughter
of a
multimillionaire Robber Baron. He married her in 1926.
Berlin has never stopped writing hits
for shows, movies, and
Ellin.

where his outstanding effort was "A Pretty Girl Is Like a Melody." For the World War I army show **Yip, Yip, Yaphank**, the composer (then a buck private) wrote "God Bless America." For complex reasons, it was never used. Twenty years later, on the eve of another war, he gave it to Kate Smith, who made it a a second national anthem. For his **Music Box Revues**, Berlin wrote "Say It with Music," "Crinoline Days," and "Lady of the Evening." To the final edition he contributed "All Alone" and "What'll I Do?"

In 1925 Irving Berlin was thirty-seven years old, owner of a music-publishing house and a composer whose every song seemed to be a hit, a fact proven as he wrote "Remember" and "Always." Broadway believed that Berlin, a widower, had embarked on his remarkable series of torch ballads out of his love for Ellin Mackay, an heiress whose father vigorously opposed the match. In 1926 Berlin married his love and celebrated by writing a euphoric "Blue Skies," interpolated into a forgotten musical called **Betsy**, produced by Florenz Ziegfeld, with other songs by Rodgers and Hart. Since then Irving Berlin has written "Puttin' on the Ritz," "Stormy Weather," "There's No Business Like Show Business," and just about every third song you remember.

Jerome Kern's "They Didn't Believe Me," interpolated into **The Girl from Utah**, was almost as much of a milestone as "Alexander's Rag-time Band." Here was the first modern musical-comedy tune. "It towers in an Eiffel way over other songs in the score," **Variety** enthused. Kern was three years older than Berlin and as a musical beginner had been accompanist to Marie Dressler. In London he met P. G. Wodehouse, and this led to collaboration with Wodehouse and Guy Bolton on the Princess Theatre shows that were our first intimate musicals. The score of **Oh Boy** had "Till the Clouds Roll By"; in **Leave It to Jane** "Siren's Song"; in **Very Good Eddie** "Babes in the Wood" and "Ka-lu-a." Kern's 1920 score for **Sally** (lyrics by Anne Caldwell) gave the world "Look for the Silver Lining."

Kern and Oscar Hammerstein II met at Victor Herbert's funeral and quickly became collaborators. Their first joint effort was **Sunny**, with Marilyn Miller (1925), in which hits were the title song and the bouncy "Who?" Two years later their operetta **Show Boat** became the first musical production in which songs advanced rather than delayed the plot. Songs for **Show Boat** included "Ol' Man River," "Why Do I Love You?," and "Can't Help Lovin' That Man." Lyrics for that show's "Bill" were by P. G. Wodehouse; tossed out of **Oh Lady, Lady** and **Sally**, the lament fit perfectly in **Show Boat**. Kern and Hammerstein went on to write **Sweet Adeline**, in which Helen Morgan rendered "Don't Ever Leave Me" and "Why Was I Born?" Later Kern melodies include "Smoke Gets in Your Eyes," "The Way You Look Tonight," and "The Last Time I Saw Paris."

George Gershwin was twenty-seven in 1925, his lyricist brother Ira two years older. A piano prodigy, George became a song plugger in Tin Pan Alley at age fifteen and began contributing songs to Shubert **Passing Shows**. For a brief time he was accompanist to Nora Bayes. It

"George Gershwin made an honest woman out of jazz," said the critic
Samuel Chotzinoff.
The dynamic young Gershwin, twenty-five years old in mid-decade,
had been almost unknown
as the Twenties began but quickly burst forth as a major composer.
Rhapsody in Blue
was only one of his musical accomplishments.

has been said of Gershwin that the public appreciated him because he matured before their eyes. In 1919 his *La La Lucille* ran for a respectable 104 performances; produced by Alex A. Aarons, it had the song "There's More to a Kiss Than XXX," lyrics by Irving Caesar. The same year brought the pair's sensational "Swanee." The young collaborators wrote this on order for a stage presentation at the Capitol Theatre, Broadway's latest film cathedral. When it got lost amidst outsize surroundings, they summoned up nerve to approach the great Al Jolson, a fellow ever on the alert for fresh material. Jolie interpolated it in *Sinbad*, and the rest is history. The Jolson phonograph record of "Swanee" sold millions.

From 1920–24 Gershwin wrote the songs for *George White's Scandals*, among them "I'll Build a Stairway to Paradise" and "Somebody Loves Me." The forgotten musical *French Doll* included his interpolated "Do It Again." Brother Ira assisted Buddy De Sylva in writing the words for "Stairway to Paradise," but the Gershwins did not actually begin as a team until 1924, with *Lady, Be Good*. For this bright musical, starring Fred and Adele Astaire, they conceived "Fascinatin' Rhythm," "Oh Lady Be Good," and "The Half-of-it-Dearie Blues," to which Fred Astaire danced his first solo number. "The Man I Love" also began a checkered career in *Lady, Be Good*. Sung by Adele in the Philadelphia tryout of the show, it was yanked out at the whim of the producer. Later it was tossed out of *Rosalie* at the whim of Marilyn Miller. Then it turned up briefly in the tryouts of *Strike Up the Band*. Finally, a song without a show, "The Man I Love" made its way alone.

In 1925 the Gershwin brothers were proud authors of *Tip Toes*, with Queenie Smith and the songs "Looking for a Boy," "Sweet and Low Down," and "That Certain Feeling." *Oh Kay* (1926) had a superior score in "Clap Yo' Hands," "Do-Do-Do," "Maybe," and "Someone to Watch Over Me," sung by Gertrude Lawrence to a rag doll. That year "Sunny Disposish" was interpolated in the revue *Americana*.

Funny Face (1927) featured the title song, "S'Wonderful," "Let's Kiss and Make Up," and "My One and Only," to which Fred Astaire tapped soft-shoe variations. *Treasure Girl* (1928) had Gertrude Lawrence, along with Clifton Webb and the song "I've Got a Crush on You, Sweetie Pie." *Rosalie* (1929) offered Marilyn Miller and "How Long Has This Been Going On?" *Show Girl* (1929) had Ruby Keeler and the tune "Liza"; *Strike Up the Band* had "Soon."

In 1924 George Gershwin's "Rhapsody in Blue" was played at Aeolian Hall by the Paul Whiteman Orchestra. Four years later the New York Philharmonic performed his "American in Paris," which also served as background music for a Harriett Hoctor ballet in *Show Girl*. At the time of *Oh, Kay*, the composer read the novel *Porgy* by Dorothy and Du Bose Heyward and began gestating the opera *Porgy and Bess*. Gershwin's show music (and all else) was notable for its aggressive pace and rhythmic energy. Of it, Fred Astaire said, "He writes for *feet*."

In 1925 the music spotlight also bathed twenty-seven-year-old Vincent Youmans because of **No, No, Nanette**, with its "Tea for Two" and "I Want to be Happy," lyrics by Irving Caesar and Otto Harbach. Son of wealthy parents, Youmans served a Broadway apprenticeship as personal aide to Victor Herbert. He first made his mark with the airy operetta **Wildflower** in 1923. Next he was hired by tough-minded H. H. Frazee to write the music for **Nanette**, adapted from a non-musical farce. Youmans developed such a hatred for the producer that when "Tea for Two" surfaced in his fertile brain, he tried to keep it to himself. One day Frazee made an unexpected appearance and heard the composer playing the tune for a bevy of chorus girls. From then on it was in the show.

A year later Youmans contributed "I Know That You Know" to **Oh, Please**, Beatrice Lillie's first American show. In 1927 an appreciative public responded to "Hallelujah," "Sometimes I'm Happy," and "Keepin' Myself for You," from **Hit the Deck**. In 1929 he offered **Great Day**, with its title song, "More Than You Know," and "Without a Song." His **Smiling Through** had "Drums in My Heart." Later he joined with B. G. De Sylva to write the music for the musical comedy **Take a Chance**, with "Rise and Shine" and "Eadie Was a Lady," sung by Ethel Merman. He also did the score for **Flying Down to Rio**, the first Astaire–Rogers movie musical. An obsessive desire to produce his own shows weakened a frail man, and Youmans spent the rest of his life a tubercular invalid.

Richard Rodgers and Lorenz Hart—it is impossible to mention one without the other, or the Twenties without both—were just reaching their stride in 1925. Rodgers was twenty-three, Hart thirty. After **Poor Little Ritz Girl** in 1920 came a hiatus until the first **Garrick Gaieties**, with "Manhattan" and "Sentimental Me." Of these songs **Variety** wrote, "They clicked like a colonel's heels at attention." "Mountain Greenery" was heard in the second **Garrick Gaieties**. In 1925 the team was successful with **Dearest Enemy**, a musical about the American Revolution, book by Herbert Fields. Its hit song was "Here in My Arms It's Adorable"—Lorenz Hart's lyrics, along with Cole Porter's, are the most quotable ever.

In 1926, the Rodgers–Hart **The Girl Friend** provided the title tune, plus "Blue Room"; **Peggy Ann**, a year later, had "Where's That Rainbow?" and "A Little Birdie Told Me So"; **A Connecticut Yankee** featured "Thou Swell," "I Feel at Home with You," and "My Heart Stood Still"; **Present Arms** had "You Took Advantage of Me"; and **Spring Is Here** (1929) the title song, "Yours Sincerely," "Baby's Awake Now," and "With a Song in My Heart." When Lorenz Hart died, Rodgers allied himself with Oscar Hammerstein II in a second notable career. Their **Oklahoma!** was the first thoroughly modern musical with a truly mature book.

Cole Porter became the golden boy of American music. Born wealthy, he attended Yale and Harvard Law School and married well. At age thirty-four, in 1925, he seemed to be frittering away his talents on the

George White,
compulsive tough guy,
had a huge influence on dancing
in the Twenties. First, he got chorus girls
from the Harlem musical **Shuffle Along** to teach girls in
George White's Scandals how to dance to jazz. Later, he created the Charleston,
the Black Bottom, and other steps redolent of the Jazz Age.

No one typified the Main Stem better than Ann Pennington, christened by her press
agent the "girl with the dimpled knees."
George White's partner in *Follies*,
she went on with him to create the ***Scandals***.
Long on jazzy personality, she stood forth as Little Miss Broadway.

Throaty Harry Richman,
for whom Irving Berlin wrote ''Puttin' on the Ritz.''
A **Scandals** perennial, his most famous song there was ''Birth of the Blues.''
This Beau Broadway achieved stardom straight from
Club Richman, his nightclub–speakeasy. He called it
''an upholstered sewer.''

French Riviera. True, he had written the short-lived musical **See America First** in 1916 and contributed "An Old-Fashioned Garden" to **Hitchy-Koo** in 1919, as well as "I'm in Love Again" and other tunes to the **Greenwich Village Follies of 1924**. But not until 1928 did Porter's genius really flare, with "Let's Do It," "Let's Misbehave," and "I've Got Quelque Chose," in Irene Bordoni's **Paris**. In 1929 his songs for **Fifty Million Frenchmen** included "You've Got That Thing," "You Do Something to Me," "Find Me a Primitive Man," and "Tale of an Oyster." Over the next three decades Cole Porter wrote words and music for **Anything Goes**, **Kiss Me, Kate**, and other memorable productions. His lyrics added a new dimension to the word **rhyme**.

De Sylva, Brown, and Henderson—Buddy, Lew, and Ray—were experts at providing melodies and musical-comedy plots reflecting the era. In the first five years of the decade B. G. De Sylva wrote lyrics for George Gershwin, Victor Herbert, and others; Ray Henderson, with lyricist Mort Dixon, did "Bye, Bye, Blackbird." In 1925, these two combined with Lew Brown—from here on it was hard to know who did what—to write "It All Depends on You" for Al Jolson's **Big Boy**. Next they inherited George Gershwin's job as songwriter for **George White's Scandals**, and their score for the 1926 edition is considered a musical summit; it contained "Black Bottom" (danced wildly by Ann Pennington), "Birth of the Blues," and "Lucky Day," both rendered by Harry Richman.

Good News (1927) had a timely college theme and the title song, "The Best Things in Life Are Free," "Varsity Drag," and "Lucky in Love." **Follow Thru** dealt with golf and contained "Button Up Your Overcoat" (danced by Eleanor Powell) along with "You Are My Lucky Star." **Hold Everything** (1929) burlesqued prizefighting, using Bert Lahr and the song "You're the Cream in My Coffee." De Sylva, Brown, and Henderson jokingly called themselves the Big Three, but to Broadway this was no joke.

In the field of operetta, Rudolf Friml and Sigmund Romberg supplied the best semiclassical music of the Twenties. Despite the advancing sophistication of the times, a solid public remained for this old-worldish musical form. "I like songs with charm in them," Friml explained, and many echoed him.

Rudolf Friml scored his first success with **Firefly** (1912). In the Twenties, he offered **Rose Marie** (1924), with the title tune, the lyricless "Indian Love Call," and "Totem Tom-Tom"; book and lyrics for this were by Harbach and Hammerstein, with Dennis King and Mary Ellis in leading roles. **The Vagabond King**, also with Dennis King, had the rousing "Song of the Vagabonds" and "Only a Rose." **The Three Musketeers**, still with Dennis King, was produced by Ziegfeld and featured the songs "March of the Musketeers" and "Ma Belle."

Sigmund Romberg broke into show business as staff composer for the Winter Garden, writing Tin Pan Alley tunes for **Passing Shows** and Jolson musicals. He never lost his touch for breezy composing and in the Twenties contributed with Rodgers and Hart to **Poor Little Ritz Girl** and with the Gershwins to **Rosalie**. Still, he was most appreciated by a melody-loving public. His **Blossom Time** (1921) was a musical biography of Franz Schubert, leaning heavily on popularizations of the master's work; **The Student Prince** (1925) was a superior effort, book and lyrics by Dorothy Donnelly; **The Desert Song** had the title song, "One Alone," "The Riff Song," and seven other instant hits; **My Maryland** had "Your Land Is My Land"; and **New Moon** (1928) was a smash with "Lover, Come Back to Me," "One Kiss," and "Stouthearted Men," book and lyrics by Oscar Hammerstein II.

The composers and lyricists who were Great Professionals never worked in ivory towers or soundproof rooms. Rather, they occupied the front line of show business. They were tunesmiths in the best sense of the word, able to move without apparent effort from musical comedy to revue to operetta. Their creating was usually done during hectic nights in hotel suites (or rooms). Arthur Schwartz, a future Great Pro, has recalled how often the management requested them to change rooms because of complaints from other guests about piano music. "No one ever complains about the sound of the words," quipped lyricist Howard Dietz during one of these forced moves.

Once their songs were completed, the composing teams—or words-and-music men like Berlin and Porter—moved into the arena of rehearsals, doing their damnedest to improve on songs already written or provide new ones dictated by changes of plot or sudden inspiration. Here they had to cope with the tin ears of producers and backers, as well as the rampant egos of stars, soubrettes, and juvenile leads.

Arguments, jealous quarrels, and shrill temperament filled the sweaty air of rehearsals; in the background were the constant sound of off-key rehearsal pianos and the staccato rap of tap shoes as weary chorus girls practiced onstage. During the madness of one rehearsal, the usually mild Jerome Kern lost his cool to shout at a producer, "Some people say I'm difficult to work with, and I **am**!" This fierce threat failed to impress, and the madness went on.

Such fine contemporary music should have provoked the slickest of plots as framework, but such was not the case. Revues of course, had no plots whatsoever; operettas demanded a story line that made sense in a lightweight way. But the books—or plots—of musical comedies were something of a joke, never to be taken seriously. "If you are going in for [musical] books," Robert Benchley wrote, "you might as well sit home and tell stories."

Not until **Of Thee I Sing**, in 1931, did the plot of a musical comedy rate remembering. Even 1924's **Lady, Be Good** was silly, though the show seemed modern because of Gershwin's music. In it Fred and Adele Astaire played a hard-up brother and sister act (surprise!) who lost their last cent and moved to the sidewalk, hanging a "Home, Sweet Home" sign on the nearest lamppost.

After 1925 matters improved a little, with the Gershwins' **Oh, Kay** dealing lightly with bootlegging and **Hold Everything** debunking prizefighting. With **Strike Up the Band** (1930) the Gershwins presented a forerunner of **Of Thee I Sing**. This was, believe it or not, an antiwar musical, with a song titled "Whoops! What a Wonderful War."

In the Twenties the book of an average musical had a boy-loves-girl theme on which everything was hung, including such scenes as sunsets in Timbuktu introduced as dream sequences. Boy and girl sang love duets and danced discreetly while so doing. Meanwhile, our heroine had a girl friend and the hero a pal who did the more energetic dancing and sang the blues of unrequited love. An older person or persons—father, mother, uncle, or employer—usually provided the comedy.

Despite the simplicity (or idiocy) of such plots no little skill was needed in concocting them. Guy Bolton, Oscar Hammerstein II, Otto Harbach, and William Anthony McGuire were top book writers on Broadway and usually did lyrics for the songs. The plots devised by such men emerged in a series of "block" scenes of substance, tied together by the thin string of the plot.

"You don't derive the scenes from the plot," Guy Bolton explained. "You see what good scenes you've got and use the plot as a bright ribbon to wrap them together."

Recurrent gripes about the books of musicals were heard. "When there was so much money to be spent," one critic growled about an expensive musical, "they might have set some aside to dream up a good plot."

FUNNY ONES—II

Those brisk, fast-stepping musicals and revues of the second half of the Twenties produced their own crop of younger comedians. Or perhaps new comedians were due anyway.

Beatrice Lillie stuck around New York after **Charlot's Revue** to appear in **She's My Baby** and other musicals, Noël Coward's **This Year of Grace**, and altogether establish herself as one of the funniest women in the world . . . . Gertrude Lawrence pointed herself toward high comedy, musical and non-musical. Fred Allen, popping up in various revues and musicals, finally scored his triumph in **The Little Show** in the last year of the decade . . . . Victor Moore, vaudeville veteran resurrected from oblivion by Guy Bolton and P. G. Wodehouse for **Funny Face**, went on to immortality as Vice President Throttlebottom in **Of Thee I Sing** . . . . Joe E. Brown rose to stardom in minor musicals like **Twinkle Twinkle** . . . . Walter Catlett brought fast comedy to musicals with the Astaires and others . . . . Bert Lahr, after an apprenticeship in burlesque and vaudeville, made his debut in **Delmar's Revels**, then won fame in **Hold Everything** . . . . Charles Butterworth offered low-key laughs in **Americana** . . . . Joe Frisco stuttered amusingly in **Vanities** and elsewhere . . . . Jimmy Savo, of the soulful eyes and tentative gestures, first appeared in a **Greenwich Village Follies** . . . . Tart Helen Broderick, mother of Broderick Crawford, added sophistication to musicals . . . . Jimmy Durante, with raucous partners Lou Clayton and Eddie Jackson, got to Broadway by way of Prohibition-era nightclubs.

After appearing in the shaky **I'll Say She Is**, the Marx Brothers stood on firmer ground with **The Coconuts** in 1925, a show tailored to their charms by none other than George S. Kaufman, with tunes from the piano of Irving Berlin. But as always the brothers loped off on their own, leaving the plot behind. One night Kaufman, standing in the rear of the house, was heard to mutter, "My God! I just heard one of the original lines!"

The Coconuts concerned the Florida land boom, and in one scene, Groucho, as an auctioneer, rallied a crowd of potential purchasers:

> Eight hundred residences will be built right here. They are as good as up. Better! You can have any kind of house you want. You can even get stucco. Oh, how you can get stucco! Now is the time to buy while the boom is on. Remember, a new boom sweeps clean. And don't forget the guarantee. If these lots don't double themselves in a year, I don't know what you can do about it.

Again he chats with brother Chico:

GROUCHO: Do you know what a blueprint is?
CHICO: Sure, oysters.
GROUCHO: We're going to have an auction.
CHICO: I came over here on the Atlantic Auction.
GROUCHO: We have a quota. Do you know what a quota is?
CHICO: Sure, I got a quota (takes a coin out of his pocket and proudly displays it).

But the best Marx Brothers crack of the time involved their real-life wives. "Girls who've made their Marx," the brothers called them.

Roundup

The Burns Mantle best-play selections for the year offered something for everyone.

Highbrows savored **The Dybbuk**, translated from the Yiddish, a folk tale of love in a Hasidic community, offered with such up-to-the-moment Broadway players as Mary Ellis, Albert Carroll, Dorothy Sands, and Paula Trueman. Or Dan Totheroh's **Wild Birds**, moody drama of prairie life. Both might be called off-Broadway productions, since they were done at art theatres away from the bright lights of Times Square.

For those who enjoyed less pretentious drama, critic Mantle included **Craig's Wife**, by George Kelly, in which Mrs. Craig (Chrystal Herne) sublimated her disappointments in life and marriage into impeccable housekeeping; this was no laugh fest like the same playwright's **The Show-Off**, but had dramatic power. **Young Woodley**, by John van Druten, was considered bold because of its suggestions of homosexuality in an English boys' school. Nonetheless, the dramatic high point came when the headmaster's beautiful, understanding wife (Helen Gahagan) was found in the arms of young Woodley (Glenn Hunter). Because of the success of this play, the author decided to quit teaching in favor of full-time playwriting.

For sophisticates, Mr. Mantle's choices provided **The Green Hat**, Michael Arlen's dramatization of his best-selling novel. Critics found the play stilted, but its coverage of nymphomania and the lush life of London's Bright Young People attracted eager audiences. **The Last of Mrs. Cheney**, by Frederick Lonsdale, imposed a crook-play plot on a background of the English aristocracy, including "a woman who calls a spade a bloody spade and means it." Breezily directed by veteran Winchell Smith, its stellar cast included Ina Claire, A. E. Matthews, and Roland Young.

For those fond of wisecracking, Mr. Mantle selected **The Butter and Egg Man**, George S. Kaufman's only venture into solo playwriting, and **The Fall Guy**, by George Abbott and James Gleason, the last-named

Inconspicuous
in the line of a Shubert musical was Joan Crawford, who had
attracted the attention
of Mr. J. J. by accidentally kicking a drink into his lap during her nightclub
act. Soon this vivid child
would be wafted to Hollywood immortality. During her Broadway days she also danced at
Club Richman.

Among discriminating
survivors of Broadway in the Twenties,
the all-time winner among chorus girls
remains dazzling, dark-haired Louise Brooks of *Scandals*. She too went to Hollywood
to become more a footnote than a star.

Nikita Balieff's **Chauve-Souris**, with "Parade of the Wooden Soldiers"
stands out as the first satiric revue.

In ***Charlot's Revue***,
Beatrice Lillie was hilarious as Britannia in
"March with Me," while Gertrude Lawrence shone as Noël Coward's
"Parisian Pierrot."

America's first intimate revue to score was **Garrick Gaieties**, produced
by younger members of the Theatre Guild. It was also the first
show to have a full score by Richard Rodgers and
Lorenz Hart. In it Stella Adler (of all people)
did a burlesque.

Editions of **Americana**,
by J. P. McEvoy, carried on the tradition of satiric revue.
In one, Charles Butterworth, hired for his resemblance to Robert Benchley, did his
"After-Dinner Speech."

Debonair
Fred Astaire makes a **Funny Face** point to Betty Compton
(the girl who wed Mayor Walker), sister Adele, and an enraptured Gertrude McDonald.

Beatrice Lillie
typified comedy at its highest.
With a barely imperceptible gesture she could send audiences
into roars of laughter. Caricature by Irving Hoffman.

Clifton Webb and Mary Hay
also adorned the musical-comedy scene.
Here they're in **Treasure Girl**, starring
Gertrude Lawrence.

The zany comedy
of the Marx Brothers reached Times Square
stages in 1924 with the musical *I'll Say She Is*.
Here Herbert, Julius, Leo, and Arthur Marx—as
then billed—collectively woo
lucky Lotta Miles.

Like W. C. Fields,
Groucho Marx evolved a comic character, not the least of attributes
being lechery.

Hard-working Fred Allen
began in *Greenwich Village Follies*, worked obscurely in other revues until
The Little Show in 1929 brought lasting fame.

Clayton, Jackson, and Durante
polished madhouse routines in the murky
atmosphere of nightclubs. Their Broadway debut came
in Ziegfeld's **Show Girl**. Always the prominent member of the trio,
Jimmy mugged as Well-Dressed Man.

Bert Lahr burst from burlesque and vaudeville in the late Twenties.
With Alice Boulden, he shadow-boxed in *Hold Everything*,
a musical milestone on the fight racket.

Katharine Cornell
starred in **The Green Hat**, a dramatization
of the sensational Michael Arlen novel. With her in the cast were
Leslie Howard and Margalo Gillmore. Caricature by Rawls.

Osgood Perkins, father of today's Tony, was one of the busiest and most applauded actors of the decade. His roles ran the gamut from urbane to rowdy.

De Mirjian

In 1926 Humphrey Bogart
pranced through roles in *Cradle Snatchers* and
Hell's Bells; kissed by him in the latter was Shirley Booth.

Helen Hayes' costume
in the Theatre Guild production of Shaw's
Caesar and Cleopatra made Charles MacArthur do a double-take and
fall in love with her.

Dennis King,
later an admired dramatic actor, achieved fame in the Twenties for swashbuckling
singing roles in **The Vagabond King** (above), **The Three Musketeers**,
and the like.

A large segment of the public yearned for Viennese operettas by Rudolf Friml and Sigmund Romberg. Above, singing chorus in the long-running ***The Student Prince***.

a terse, snappy actor-author who with wife Lucille had worked long and hard to reach Broadway. His play dealt with an out-of-work husband (Ernest Truex) who tried bootlegging and met with adversity.

Finally, Mr. Mantle picked **Mrs. Partridge Presents**, a lightweight treatment of the younger generation, with Blanche Bates, Ruth Gordon, and Sylvia Field; and **The Enemy**, by Channing Pollock.

The Lunts played Shaw's **Arms and the Man** to rave reviews. Basil Sydney brought New York its first modern-dress **Hamlet**. Helen Hayes was triumphant in a revival of Barrie's **What Every Woman Knows**; she also appeared with Lionel Atwill in **Caesar and Cleopatra**, the Shaw play that opened the Guild Theatre (critics thought her performance "flapperish"). David Belasco's glossy production of **The Dove** starred Judith Anderson and Holbrook Blinn. Alfred Savoir's polished **Grand Duchess and the Waiter** boasted Basil Rathbone, Elsie Ferguson, and Alison Skipworth. In addition to **The Green Hat**, Michael Arlen contributed **These Charming People**, another venture into London high life, with Cyril Maude, Edna Best, and Herbert Marshall.

Samson Raphaelson's **The Jazz Singer**, destined to become the first talkie and deal a shattering blow to the legitimate theatre, was a success with George Jessel in the lead, Sam Jaffe in support. A few Theatre Guild subscribers were outraged by John Howard Lawson's **Processional**, billed as a jazz symphony of American life, but it remains a theatre milestone nonetheless. This impressionistic drama dealt with a strike in a West Virginia mining town, while the ominous shadow of the Ku Klux Klan loomed overall. In a large cast were George Abbott, June Walker, and Ben Grauer, with Lee Strasberg, Alvah Bessie, Arthur Sircom, and Sanford Meisner among the supers.

It was a bad year for promising playwrights. Much had been expected of Laurence Stallings and Maxwell Anderson after **What Price Glory?**, but their next two (and final) collaborations failed miserably. However, Anderson redeemed himself with the drama of hobo life, **Outside Looking In**, wherein Charles Bickford got rave notices as Big Red and James Cagney played Little Red, a guy in love with a young prostitute who killed her stepfather seducer. Philip Barry and Sidney Howard did medium well with **In a Garden** and **Lucky Sam McCarver** respectively. Only George Kelly, with **Craig's Wife**, fulfilled 1924 promise.

Comedy abounded. **Is Zat So?**, by James Gleason and Richard Taber, must have been funnier than **The Fall Guy**, for the fast-talking author himself appeared in this one, taking the part of a prizefight manager who joined with his fighter (Robert Armstrong) to become butler and footman of a wealthy household. **The Poor Nut**, with and by J. C. and Elliott Nugent, provided wholesome fun. In **Cradle Snatchers** four bored suburban housewives hired glossy-haired college boys as escorts to arouse the jealousy of husbands; among the cradle snatchers were Mary Boland and Edna May Oliver, among the glossy-haired boys were Humphrey Bogart and Raymond Guion, who became Gene Raymond of films. **Weak Sisters**, a comedy by Lynn Starling, with Osgood Perkins and Spring Byington, was produced by newcomer Jed Harris, who within a year would be the most electrifying figure on Broadway. For the moment, though, his play electrified, since it dealt with the inmates of a bawdy house who for the most part sat around discussing their craft. A critic called it "dirty but diverting."

Other plays, successful or otherwise, were **Twelve Miles Out**, a bootlegging melodrama by the expert William Anthony McGuire; **The Fountain**, a forgotten play by Eugene O'Neill, starred Walter Huston; **Laff That Off** was another about a group of boys adopting a girl, played by Shirley Booth, who had first appeared in **Hell's Bells** with Humphrey Bogart; Edward G. Robinson portrayed Napoleon in Shaw's **Man of Destiny**, which shared a Theatre Guild bill with **Androcles and the Lion**. **Lysistrata** featured beautiful Olga Baclanova; **The Man with a Load of Mischief** had Ruth Chatterton and Ralph Forbes; Ann Harding played the leading role in **Stolen Fruit**; Anne Nichols lost some of her **Abie's Irish Rose** money with **White Collars**, about the taming of a parlor socialist, with Cornelia Otis Skinner; Claudette Colbert was a Montmartre gamine in **Kiss in a Taxi**.

Lionel Barrymore made a sad mistake with Jerome K. Jerome's **Man or Devil**; Lila Lee, dewy-eyed Hollywood star, returned to Broadway in **The Bride Retires**, an adaptation from the French that should have stayed there; Ruth Gordon appeared in **The Fall of Eve**, by John Emerson and Anita Loos, about a flapper wife and marital misunderstanding; **The Book of Charm** had Lee Tracy supporting one Kenneth Dana; Elisha Cook, Jr., was in **The Crooked Friday**; lovely Miriam Hopkins in **The Lovely Lady**, by Jesse Lynch Williams; Ilka Chase in **Antonia**, by Melchior Lengyel; Mischa Auer a butler in **Mortals**; William Gargan could be seen in **Aloma of the South Seas**; Fredric March was visible, though not prominently, in **Puppets**; and Robert Montgomery and an actor with the intriguing name of Pacie Ripple played minor roles in **The Complex**.

In the musical field, **No, No, Nanette** succeeded because of the Youmans/Caesar hit tunes; also involved were Louise Groody and Charles Winninger, with Otto Harbach and Frank Mandel listed as writers of an alleged book. Marilyn Miller starred in **Sunny**, along with music by Jerome Kern and a rare cast, including Jack Donahue, Clifton Webb, Mary Hay, Cliff "Ukulele Ike" Edwards, and Pert Kelton. As star of **Sunny**, Marilyn got $3,000 a week, the highest salary yet for a female in American musical comedy; it remained so until 1941, when Gertrude Lawrence got more for **Lady in the Dark**.

Al Jolson appeared in **Big Boy**, last of his record-breaking string of musical hits, (soon he would be in Hollywood, making **The Jazz Singer**); **Puzzles of 1925**, with Elsie Janis as star, also included Helen Broderick and handsome Walter Pidgeon; **Tip Toes** offered songs by George Gershwin, Queenie Smith in the lead and Jeanette Mac-

Donald in a smaller role; Willie Howard appeared without brother Eugene in **Sky High**; **Tell Me More** had Lou Holtz and Gershwin tunes; **Mercenary Mary** had singer John Boles; Imogene Coca and Wynne Gibson assisted in **When You Smile**; The Ritz Brothers were in **Florida Girl**; Nancy Carroll was obscure in **Wildflower**, starring Joseph Santley and Ivy Sawyer; **City Chap**, produced by Charles Dillingham, had music by Jerome Kern and a cast including Irene Dunne, Richard ''Skeets'' Gallagher, Betty Compton, and dancer George Raft. **Charlot's Revue** came back in a second edition, still with Bea, Gertie, and top-hatted Jack. Balieff's **Chauve Souris** also reappeared in new guise, with the catchy ditty ''I Miss My Swiss (My Swiss Misses Me).''

Broadway rumor said Flo Ziegfeld was bored by **Follies** and planned to concentrate on musicals and operettas. Still, he came up with a 1925 edition with Will Rogers, W. C. Fields, Ann Pennington, and the amazing Tiller Girls, precision dancers from London and forerunners of the Rockettes, who in one number skipped on a dark stage with luminous ropes. The Tillers sparked an immediate battle of dancing girls, for **George White's Scandals** had a line of Albertina Rasch dancers; inevitably a critic spoke of their dancing as ''breaking out in an Albertina Rasch.'' Not to be outdone, **Artists and Models** offered the high-stepping Gertrude Hoffman dancers, who in one daring scene turned into naked girls being broiled on spits over desert fires.

This edition of **Artists and Models**, one of the best, had Phil Baker as master of ceremonies, Aline MacMahon as a fresh young comic, and Jack Oakie dancing in the chorus. After the show Jack usually met with another fresh talent named Joan Crawford, who was hoofing in the chorus of the Shuberts' **Innocent Eyes**. The two discussed futures that did not seem bright.

The play of the decade arrived on the night of September 16, 1926. *Broadway* was its title, and among all else it started producer Jed Harris on a five-year run as the *Wunderkind* of the commercial theatre. Co-authors of the backstage-in-a-nightclub drama were George Abbott and Philip Dunning. The original script had been written by Dunning, a theatre hand who on this opening night dared not abandon his chores as stage manager of Marilyn Miller's *Sunny*.

Abbott had done so much rewriting of the script that his name came first in the credits; he had also directed its fast-paced three acts. *Broadway* brought instant fame to Lee Tracy, an actor who had played a few good parts in the past but never a great one. Ecstatic morning-after reviews told the world that the current theatre had found its hit of hits.

Almost every producer in the business had read and rejected the Dunning original, which had been variously titled *Bright Lights*, *The Roaring Forties*, and *A White Little Guy*. Finally it got to Jed Harris, newcomer to the producing ranks. He read it and immediately thought of Tracy for the leading role, which in turn made him think of George Abbott, an admirer of Tracy's vital, staccato gifts. Abbott read the script and saw possibilities. "It was full of wonderful scenes and characters," he said later. "But it was confused. The trick was to give it order."

Abbott and Dunning worked together getting the show into shape. On the eve of its first out-of-town tryout, Jed Harris summoned the collaborators and declared that the script contained too many cheap vaudeville-type jokes. He ordered them sliced out, leaving only wisecracks germane to the plot. In one of these Tracy told a chorus girl, "Believe me, it pays for a girl to be good." To which she replied, "Sure, but not much."

The action of *Broadway*—and there was plenty—took place in the backstage regions of the Paradise Club, a sleazy Prohibition-era cabaret off Times Square. Hoofer Roy Lane (Tracy), with a quart of ego and ounce of talent, headed up the nightly show, which also included a middle-aged female singer and a line of six young chorus girls. "It ain't only I can dance," Roy liked to say of his gifts, "I got personality, personality plus . . . . There's nothing swelled head about me. I coulda been that way a long time ago if I'd wanted to."

Backstage also functioned as headquarters for the bootlegging activities of suave Steve Crandall, a gangster protected at all times by two sinister bodyguards. Ambitious Steve had begun to muscle in on the uptown territory of rival "Scar" Edwards. Just a few nights before he had hijacked a couple of Scar's liquor-laden trucks.

Both Roy and Steve were attracted to Billie Moore (Sylvia Field), a winsome dancer in the chorus who had not been in show business long

Roy Lane & Co.
Vaudeville lay dying,
but peppy Roy Lane (Lee Tracy) of ***Broadway***
still dreamed of a two-a-day dancing act with a girl partner (Sylvia Field).

enough to grow hard-boiled. "A mighty nifty little chick," Roy called her. He had not yet proposed marriage, but the two were preparing a vaudeville act. "I and she are doing a lot of practicing together," he told people. The name of the act, the egotist added, would be Roy Lane and Company.

Steve Crandall's intentions toward Billie were reasonably honorable. He might conceivably marry her, but in the meantime he wanted to get her into bed as fast as possible. Roy, on the other hand, was the type of guy who'd wait for the marriage vows.

As the play opens five of the chorus girls practice routines with Roy. Only Billie is missing. Nick Vernis, owner of the club, feels angry enough to fire her, but when she comes in with Steve Crandall he doesn't dare. Steve is planning an after-hours party at the club for visiting Chicago hoodlums and pressures Billie and the other girls to stay for it. To Roy's jealous fury, she agrees. Music from the orchestra outside warns of show time, and the performers rush upstairs to balcony dressing rooms.

Enter Scar Edwards in search of a showdown. An angry argument ensues, ending as one of Steve's bodyguards shoots Scar in the back. Roy and Billie, exiting simultaneously from the dressing rooms, watch the bodyguards drag a limp, drunken-looking, scarfaced man out the stage door. The show goes on, with Roy and chorus girls prancing in and out, girls running upstairs to don scanty costumes that transform them from pirates to South Sea islanders to cutie-pies.

Soon Dan McCord, homicide detective, wanders in. Scar's body has been found in the back of a truck parked down the street, and he is curious. As the chorus girls line up, the detective recognizes one as Pearl, Scar Edwards' girl. Obviously, she has been planted in the club.

McCord begins asking questions and finds discrepancies in the stories of the two bodyguards. Steve has given Billie a bracelet, which she proudly puts on, to Roy's rage. She takes it off, though, when the other girls start making dirty cracks. The party is about to begin, and Steve tears six hundred-dollar bills in two, giving halves to each girl, the other to be redeemed at party's end. One of the Chicago hoodlums makes a pass at Billie, who rushes to Steve for protection. He is pleased to comfort her—too pleased. "Make your hands behave," she warns him sharply.

The sight of Billie in Steve's arms sets Roy aflame. He rushes at Steve and the two tussle, the gangster drawing a gun. With his hoofer's agility, Roy knocks it to the floor. McCord walks in, and Steve says the gun belongs to Roy. "Ever heard of the Sullivan Act?" the detective asks. "Where's it playing?" the vaudeville-oriented Roy wants to know. A protesting Roy is hauled off to the station house, on the suspicion that the gun is the one that killed Scar Edwards.

Next night a few hungover girls wander about in show costumes. Roy returns for his clothes and props. He is mad at the world and especially at Billie, who has denied seeing an apparently drunken man being hauled out the backstage door. He plans to quit, but owner Nick reminds him that a true artist thinks of his public first. That's enough for cocky Roy; he'll stay.

The woman singer is too sick to show up, which gives Roy and Billie a chance to do their act before a live audience. Each is delighted but tries not to show it. "We might as well try it," says Billie, "now that we've rehearsed so much, even if you don't love me any more." Says he, "It isn't a question of loving you, but when I get a throw-down like last night, I get wise to myself." She replies, "A couple can be in the same act without being crazy about each other." They run upstairs to change.

Enter Crandall, who takes off his hat and looks fearfully at a bullet hole in the crown: the Scar Edwards mob is out to kill him. As he starts for the safety of Nick's office, Pearl appears behind him, pistol with silencer in hand. "Turn around, rat," she snarls. "I don't want to give it to you like you did him—in the back. Whine, you rat, I knew you would." There is a **whoosh** of the silencer and Steve falls dead. Pearl hastens upstairs.

Roy and Billie fail to note the body as they excitedly reappear, exiting outside to do their act. McCord finds it, though, and bends down for an examination. Pearl slowly descends the stairs and, seeing her, he says gently, "Pull yourself together, kid," the only indication he knows she did the killing. He rises to declare Steve a suicide. Roy and Billie hoof back, their act done. It was so bad that the girls who went outside to watch are snickering. Yet Roy gets a note from a booking agent in the audience saying, "I can offer you and partner Chambersburg and Pottsville next week." Roy and Billie embrace—love at last!

The show must go on, and Roy has an ear tuned to the music outside. Suddenly he shouts, "There's the gong, kids. All ready! Come on, Pearl. Gee, I'm happy! Our names will be in bright lights soon—Roy Lane and Company! Remember, you're artists. Here we go . . . here we go . . ."

What made *Broadway* so great?

Certainly there was nothing cerebral about this play of the decade. Authors like Eugene O'Neill, Sidney Howard, and Maxwell Anderson might be probing character and trying to fathom the meaning of life. Yet *Broadway* merely raced across the surface, its message, if any, lying in the fact that the sophistication of its sharpie characters was only skin deep.

But it added up to dramatic theatre, and perhaps the reason is to be found in the words *realism* and *immediacy*. Not only was *Broadway* staged with the utmost realism, but it possessed a double-barreled kind of reality in that everything happening onstage might be going on next door. All around Broadway gangsters were being shot and girls tempted, while hoofers hoofed, nightclubs dispensed illegal hooch, and detectives failed to do their duty.

Top hit of the decade,
Broadway got its impact from super-realism.
Prohibition-era audiences knew gangsters
could be rubbed out
backstage in any nightclub around Times Square.
Broadway boasted two killings, one by a girl,
and a thumping fist fight.

The play **Broadway** was simply an extension of a scene audiences knew, either at first hand or from newspaper headlines. More, it was presented at the Broadhurst with the kind of excitement only Americans seem able to provide in the theatre. Direction and pace were inspired. Where the average play had only fifty entrances and exits, this one offered 130. With split-second timing, actors dashed in, spoke lines, and exited, bringing an almost unbearable tension to the action. Nothing had been overlooked. When the headwaiter rushed up the stairs to the dressing rooms, the audience heard the coins jangling in his pocket. And with all the excitement and realism, it was a happy play, as Brooks Atkinson has pointed out. Actors and audience seemed to conspire to have a good time. Thousands of backstage plays, movies, and TV dramas since the premiere of **Broadway** have inured us to this genre, but here was the daddy of them all, and it brought sensation.

A startling background also combined with a trenchant handling of the bootleg-gangster scene, another innovation. Lean, hard dialogue made full use of up-to-the-second expressions like "sugar daddy" and "gold digger." Crandall called Roy a "waxed-floor bum," and Roy replied with a timely "Banana oil!" Roy called Billie's infatuation for the mobster "just a buggy ride." Steve's bodyguards were labeled "a couple of gorillas." Tough guys addressed each other as "sweetheart," with no friendship intended.

There were also examples of the fine art of hoofing, hair-pulling fights between cute chorus girls, the tough talk (but no profanity) of the profession, and the acrid smoke of gangland guns. In the second act Roy changed his pants and walked about in his shorts, even proposing to Billie that way. Such informality was fresh and stimulating.

As a play **Broadway** exemplified a new kind of repertorial playwriting. Reflecting tumultuous times, it was as exciting as tomorrow's tabloids. **Broadway** started a trend of journalistic drama that remains alive to this day.

Wrote Alexander Woollcott, "Of all the scores of plays that shuffled in endless procession along Broadway . . . the one which most forcibly caught the accent of the city's voice was this one named after the great Midway itself, this taut and telling cartoon, produced with uncommon imagination and resource."

THE SHANGHAI GESTURE

Let us cherish the plot of **The Shanghai Gesture**, written by John Colton, co-author of **Rain**, and presented to the world in February 1926.

Billed as a melodrama, **The Shanghai Gesture** recounted the saga of Mother Goddam, madam of a gilded Shanghai whorehouse and gambling den. She won the odd name because of the harsh treatment accorded the inmates of her establishment. At first they called her Mother God-damn, but it became shortened by use to Mother Goddam. Florence Reed played this rich part.

Twenty years before, Mother Goddam had been a sweet Manchu princess, madly in love with Guy Charteris (McKay Morris), handsome executive of the British-China Tea Company. Despite his aristocratic looks, however, Charteris was a rotter who turned ugly when his princess got pregnant. Cruelly, he sold her down the Yangtze into a life of prostitution, then returned to his pregnant wife. But after her girl-child was born the Manchu beauty miraculously managed to have her own baby substituted for the newborn daughter of the haughty Englishman.

Twenty years elapse, and Mother Goddam has reached the crest of her profession, presiding over a bordello whose prurient promise no red-blooded male can resist. Along with other Shanghai notables Charteris—now Sir Guy and chief of British-China—is invited to a New Year's Eve celebration at the brothel. During a preliminary banquet Mother Goddam reveals her true identity and denounces her onetime lover. With throbbing passion, she recalls the ugly tortures used by the whoremasters to break her spirit and turn her into a harlot. After each evil example she shrieks at Charteris, "Yet I survived!"

The other guests leave during this impolite display, but Charteris is told to remain by her henchmen. Taken into a sumptuous room, he finds a half-naked white girl in a gilded cage. Mother Goddam tells Sir Guy he will be forced to watch as this girl is sold into whoredom, just as she had been twenty years ago. Then she informs him the helpless girl is in reality his own legitimate daughter. Summoning the Oriental buyers, she cries, "Look at her, Mr. Shu Ki. This is a white girl, not a yellow one. What am I bid? Think of your hairy chest against her lovely young breasts. Think of your mouth against her soft red lips. What am I bid?" A crushed and helpless Charteris watches as his cringing child is disposed of to the sex brokers.

Sir Guy might be down but not out. A constant patron of Mother Goddam's is Poppy (Mary Duncan), a lovely, dissolute English girl in search of drink, opium, and the embraces of degrading men. Sir Guy now tells Mother Goddam that for over twenty years he has considered Poppy his legitimate child, but now, obviously, she must be Mother Goddam's daughter.

Florence Reed
played the sinister Mother Goddam in
The Shanghai Gesture.

The auction of a cowering white girl to Chinese whoremongers.

As he concludes, Poppy emerges, reeling drunk, from a bedroom where she has enjoyed a bout of nympho love with a Japanese. In a fury of love, hate, and contempt, Mother Goddam decides her only recourse is to kill this ill-starred daughter. Making a grab for the girl's throat, she misses and begins chasing her up a long stairway. Trying to escape, the drunken Poppy trips and falls down the stairs, breaking her neck.

Most critics scoffed at the obvious theatrics and blatant sex of **The Shanghai Gesture**; one thought it "a foul play." A few praised it as lusty, gutsy theatre. That ultimate critic, the public, embraced the second view and turned it into one of the hits of the decade.

Produced by Al Woods, the play was directed by Guthrie McClintic. Apparently sensitive over his involvement in such lecherous hokum, McClintic said, "If you think the plot sounds a bit unreal, or funny, remind me sometime to tell you the story of Medea."

NOTES ON PLAYWRITING

Ina Claire, who began as a child impressionist in the **Follies**, developed from an excellent actress to a brilliant one as the Twenties unfolded. Perhaps her most notable successes were in plays by S. N. Behrman.

Playwrights expend great effort in scripts in describing the appearances and nuances of characters as they make an initial entrance. At one point Miss Claire said to Behrman, "Don't put it all in the stage directions, Sam. You fool yourself doing that, but you don't fool me. Get it into the dialogue."

Again, she stopped a rehearsal that seemed to be losing direction. "Sam," she said, "this play's about me, isn't it? So what do *I* do next?"

ROUNDUP

Inevitably, the Harris-Abbott-Dunning **Broadway** headed the list of Burns Mantle's best plays of the year. Right behind (it premiered on the last night of the year) came Maureen Watkins' **Chicago**, with Francine Larrimore and Charles Bickford. A sharp satire, it told of a tough, pretty Windy City murderess who became a court-acquitted angel because of tabloid journalism. At first Roxie Hart (Miss Larrimore) admitted, "I killed him." Replied the sardonic reporter Jake (Bickford), "What if you did? Ain't this Chicago?" It was—and how!

Eugene O'Neill's perplexing **The Great God Brown** rated highest among the Mantle selections of serious dramas; here the ever-questing author, who used tom-toms for effect in **The Emperor Jones**, employed modernized Greek masks to hide and reveal the true feelings of his actors. Paul Green's **In Abraham's Bosom**, a study of Southern Negro life, moved uptown from the Provincetown after its surprise grab of the Pulitzer Prize.

The Bride of the Lamb, by William J. Hurlbut, fingered the thin line between religious frenzy and sexual frustration; in it Alice Brady acted a dentist's seething wife easily victimized by a predatory evangelist (Crane Wilbur). George Kelly's **Daisy Mayme**, about incessant family bickering, was picked by Mantle, but critics liked it least of the playwright's works to date. Sidney Howard's **The Silver Cord**, a devastating look at mother love, was produced successfully by the Theatre Guild, with Margalo Gillmore, Earle Larrimore, and Laura Hope Crews.

Mr. Mantles' selections continued with the smooth sophistication of Ferenc Molnar's **The Play's the Thing**, adapted by the one and only P. G. Wodehouse with Holbrook Blinn, Reginald Owen, and Catherine Dale Owen; it told of a cynical playwright forcing a frolicsome actress to act out (before the eyes of her love) an amorous caper of the night before. In Somerset Maugham's **The Constant Wife**, Ethel Barrymore abandoned mannerisms and throaty tones to sink herself into the part of an English doctor's wife who waited years to get even with a philandering husband. Finally, Marc Connelly's **The Wisdom Tooth** provided Thomas Mitchell with his first major role as a humble clerk who called on the shades of his ancestors to bring him courage; they materialize and do. Others in the cast were Kate Mayhew and Hugh O'Connell.

So ended the Mantle selections, but there was more, much more. Sean O'Casey's **Juno and the Paycock** got its first overseas production, with Augustin Duncan at the head of a large cast. Down on 14th Street, Eva Le Gallienne began her Civic Repertory Theatre, which ran eight years; initial productions were by Benavente and Ibsen. Distinguished Walter Hampden scored in **Caponsacchi**, based on Browning's **The Ring and the Book**. Sacha Guitry and ethereal wife Yvonne Printemps were imported by tough-minded Al Woods, while the Habima Players of Moscow presented the original **The Dybbuk** in Hebrew and other classics.

208

Noël Coward's
second visit to the United States
was far more successful than his first. This time
(1925) his bitter play **The Vortex** conquered the town, and
inevitably the boy wonder posed for a new photo-portrait. Money cares gone,
he leased an ornate apartment
and set out to live the
good life.

Already represented by **The Vortex**, Coward also contributed **Fallen Angels**,
Hay Fever, and **Easy Virtue** to the same season. Only **Hay Fever**
flopped. Above, Estelle Winwood and Fay Bainter
tippled in **Fallen Angels.**

Beatrice Lillie
sang "World Weary" in the Noël Coward revue **This Year of Grace**.
As the Jazz Age whirled
on, young folk danced madly to his "A Room with a View,"
"Dance, Little Lady,"
and "Poor Little Rich Girl." Older folk waltzed to
"I'll See You Again" from **Bitter Sweet.**

Ethel Barrymore,
First Lady of the Theatre,
played a multitude of roles during the Twenties.
Among them were *The Constant Wife*, *The Kingdom of God*, and the revivals *The Second Mrs. Tanqueray*,
School for Scandal, and *The Merchant of Venice*.
Here she is seen at the time of
The Kingdom of God.

Sex was the name of the risky game played by producers and authors who tested how much eroticism could be injected in scripts. Directors played the game, too. In **The Squall**, half-dressed, half-caste Nubi demonstrated her interest in slinking into men's beds rather than into their hearts.

In **Lulu Belle**, the swivel-hipped, gutter-tongued Harlem whore moves from male to male until she reaches Paris, where a lover strangles her. In a huge cast were nineteen white actors and ninety-three blacks, most of them used by David Belasco to create vivid Harlem street scenes.

Mae West presented herself in **Sex**, a drama of her own devising, with Barry O'Neill and Pacie Ripple. Mae recounted the machinations—if that's the word—of Margie LaMont, prostitute and fleet-follower, as she revenged herself on a haughty society dowager by seducing the woman's son and threatening to marry him.

Sex plays marched on as, in **The Half-Caste**, Fredric March portrayed a young man retracing his father's travel footsteps who found himself making ardent love to a half-sister; in **Kongo**, Walter Huston was Dead-leg Flint, who drove his daughter into harlotry, then helped redeem her; in **The Woman Disputed**, Ann Harding (supported by Robert Cummings, Lowell Sherman, and Crane Wilbur) was a wartime French streetwalker who slept with a German officer to save her Yankee doughboy.

In **The Captive**, the Gallic playwright Edouard Bourdet dealt sensitively with the premise that once a lesbian always a lesbian; in **The Pearl of Great Price**, the pearl was the virginity of a character played by Claudette Colbert; **Gertie**, with Pat O'Brien, Elisha Cook, Jr., and Constance McKay, dealt with a girl who tried to sell herself to an older man but couldn't; in **Night Duel**, Marjorie Rambeau bargained her body for money stolen by her spouse; in **The Virgin**, a Holy Roller girl was accepted by her sect as a reincarnation of the Virgin Mary until found in the hot embrace of a man; **The Blonde Sinner** and **Kept** were not as sexy as titles indicated.

Such plays evoked outrage from press and pulpit, with the normally tolerant **Theatre Magazine** lashing out at what it called theatrical filth. Ranted its editor, "Our stage can go no lower in theatrical degradation. All the ordures of brutal concupiscence, the noisome scoopings of the sexual garbage can, the shameless, abandoned jargon of the brothel, raucous ribaldry, rape, debauchery, lewdness, the whole gamut of depravity and lechery—this is the putrescent drama served today."

On a purer plane, the Theatre Guild had a notable season. It presented **Ned McCobb's Daughter**, by Sidney Howard, with Alfred Lunt as a rumrunner from New York loose in New England; his notices in this play were excellent, better than he got in **Juarez and Maximilian**, a previous Guild offering of the year. Lynn Fontanne won rapturous re-

Lulu Belle,
with Lenore Ulric as a brown-skinned
harlot, did as much as *The Shanghai Gesture* to arouse forces of theatre censorship.
It was another daring
Belasco production, written by Charles MacArthur
and Edward Sheldon.

Barbara Stanwyck,
lifted from a nightclub chorus, made a hit in **The Noose**, with Rex Cherryman
and Wilfred Lucas.

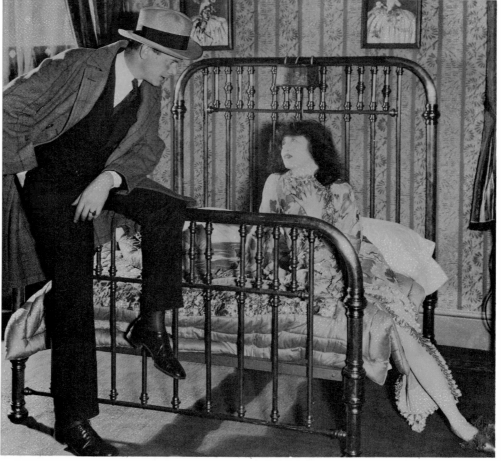

Cynical reporter (Charles Bickford)
needled Jazz Age murderess Roxie Hart (Francine Larrimore) in **Chicago**,
a satire on tabloid mentality.

Strange Stagefellows! Carlotta Monterey, who became the wife and widow
of Eugene O'Neill; Peggy Hopkins Joyce, oft-married
alumna of **Follies**; and Lucile Watson, who went
on to portray acid dowagers on
stage and screen,
appearing in the forgotten epic **A Sleepless Night**.

views in Shaw's *Pygmalion*, where she played Eliza to Reginald Mason's Dr. Higgins. Franz Werfel's *Goat Song*, another Guild effort, had an unbelievable cast, including the Lunts, Blanche Yurka, Edward G. Robinson, Zita Johann, and House Jameson; it dealt with a man-beast born to an aristocratic Serbian family and kidnaped by rebellious peasants. In an innocently titled *At Mrs. Beam's*, by C. K. Munro, the Lunts played a pair of crooks holed up in a respectable London boarding-house.

The Great Gatsby, dramatized by Owen Davis, is considered by old-timers to be the best adaptation ever made of the Fitzgerald novel, either stage or screen; in it were James Rennie (Gatsby), Florence Eldridge, Eliot Cabot, Porter Hall, and Gladys Feldman. Fitzgerald was living in Paris at this time and never got to see the play, but his friend Ernest Hemingway, in New York for a quick visit, reported to him.

Even more successful was the Patrick Kearney dramatization of Theodore Dreiser's *An American Tragedy*, with Morgan Farley and Miriam Hopkins. Watching it, novelist Dreiser kept muttering, ``The poor boy, the poor boy!''

John Howard Lawson followed *Processional* with *Nirvana*, a short-lived effort with Crane Wilbur and Elise Bartlett, about a girl driven to suicide by Jazz Age pressures. John Dos Passos' *The Moon Is a Gong* was another episodic treatment of Jazz Age evils; in one scene mourners did a Charleston around a coffin. Philip Barry's *White Wings*, a fantastic satire, focused on a family of proud street cleaners and their predicament after the horseless carriage.

Fannie Brice essayed the non-musical stage in *Fanny*, about Yiddish flapper Fanny Feibaum who vamped a robber into returning his loot; it ran sixty-three performances, then Fannie returned to the *Follies*. The cast of *Yellow*, a low-life drama doctored and presented by George M. Cohan, included Chester Morris and Spencer Tracy, in that order of importance; *The Noose*, underworld melodrama by Williard Mack, marked the debut of Barbara Stanwyck, playing a nightclub girl; Thelma Ritter appeared with Lee Patrick, Frances Starr, Arthur Byron, and Donald Meek in *The Shelf*; Paul Robeson was a prizefighter in Jim Tully's *Black Boy*; Shirley Booth was in *Buy, Buy Baby*, with Alison Skipworth and Laura Hope Crews; Muni Weisenfrend (Paul Muni to be) attracted attention in *We Americans*.

The celebrated actor-producer Henry Miller had only two months to live when he opened in *Embers*, with Ilka Chase; Claudette Colbert played in *Ghost Train*, with Eric Blore; Pauline Lord was in *Sandalwood*, by Owen Davis and Fulton Oursler; Francine Larrimore, A. E. Matthews, Auriol Lee, and Nigel Bruce appeared in Noël Coward's *This Was a Man*, about the infidelity of both husband and wife; Glenn Anders played the role created by Coward abroad in *The Constant Nymph*.

Gentlemen Prefer Blondes, an adaptation by author Anita Loos of her runaway best seller, was a hit with June Walker, Edna Hibbard, and Frank Morgan; Sessue Hayakawa of the flicks and Catherine Dale Owen, soon to be there, appeared in *The Love City*; *Love 'Em and Leave 'Em*, a comedy about love in department stores, by George Abbott and John V. A. Weaver, was presented by Jed Harris six months ahead of *Broadway*; *Don Q. Jr.*, had tennis ace William T. Tilden and George Spelvin, Jr., talented offspring of the busiest bit actor in show biz; *Hush Money* had Cora Witherspoon and Justine Johnstone, onetime *Follies* queen.

Honors in the musical field went to Winthrop Ames for his presentations of Gilbert and Sullivan, still remembered as the most beautiful and tasteful ever; the year before Ames had offered *Iolanthe*, this time *The Pirates of Penzance*, with more to come.

Also exceptional was the appearance of Spanish-born Raquel Meller, music-hall favorite of Paris, who sang accompanied by members of the New York Philharmonic. On her opening night impresario E. Ray Goetz charged $25 for orchestra seats. He got away with it, and ever-sharp George White was emboldened to charge $50 for the premiere of his next *Scandals*.

The operetta *Countess Maritza* featured Odette Myrtil, who accompanied herself on the violin as she sang "Play Gypsies, Dance Gypsies"; Bea Lillie's first American musical, *Oh, Please!*, had Charles Winninger, Helen Broderick, Nick Long, Jr., Charles Purcell, and Dorothie Bigelow; *Honeymoon Lane* had experienced Eddie Dowling and pristine Kate Smith; John Boles and Dorothy Dilley adorned *Kitty's Kisses*; *Nic-Nax of 1926* featured the ditty "We Are the Broads of Broadway." *Betsy*, the Ziegfeld-Rodgers-Hart show in which Irving Berlin's "Blue Skies" was interpolated, proved a $150,000 disaster.

Musicals also tested sex barriers, pushing purple jokes, daring blackout sketches, and lovely nudity. In midsummer the arm of the law reached out to close the revue *Bunk of 1926* because showgirl-dancer Beryl Halley showed too much of herself, despite repeated warnings. The elaborate revue *Great Temptations*, with Jack Benny midway down its roster of talent, got shuttered because of off-color material and a dance in which the chorus girls waved bare *derrieres* at patrons. Yet *Bare Facts of 1926* was left alone to enjoy a run of 106 performances.

ALTERNATING REPERTORY

"One of the great American dreams is the theatrical repertory that will satisfy everybody, bringing joy to sophisticate and Rotarian alike," writes drama critic Jack Kroll.

In 1927 Eva Le Gallienne, with her Civic Repertory Theatre on 14th Street, was striving to accomplish this. Starting the year before, the Civic Repertory had survived a disastrous premiere to present superior productions at prices ranging from 35 cents to $1.50. "We drew people who really loved the theatre to those Fourteenth Street plays," Miss Le Gallienne has recalled. "We had audiences such as you might find waiting for hours trying to get into Carnegie Hall or the Metropolitan Opera—and there are ever so many such people in New York and all over America."

Assisting Miss Le Gallienne at the Civic were such notable talents as Alla Nazimova, Josephine Hutchinson, Joseph Schildkraut, Jacob Ben-Ami, and J. Edward Bromberg. Her favored playwrights were Chekhov, Ibsen, Barrie, Schnitzler, Goldoni, and Hauptmann; the best productions *The Cherry Orchard*, *Romeo and Juliet*, *Peter Pan*, *Hedda Gabler*, and *Alice in Wonderland*. Thousands, especially the young, were introduced to drama by way of the Civic Repertory, which ran for five years, closed for a sabbatical, and opened for three more. Sad to say, though, the Civic Repertory operated at a loss. Philanthropists like Otto Kahn and Mrs. Edward Bok made up annual deficits.

Even as the Civic Repertory made an initial impression, a far more ambitious repertory was beginning uptown at the Theatre Guild. Over the years the Guild had flourished, becoming more than ever a Broadway miracle. Alfred Lunt and Lynn Fontanne now acted under the Guild banner; indeed, *The Guardsman*, the first play in which this glorious pair really acted together, had been the Guild's first walloping financial success. Other producers, impressed at last, began considering the Guild a formidable rival. Thanks to the Lunts, the Guild had even captured a fresh audience. In addition to artistic folk with liberal leanings, it attracted dowagers and suburban club ladies of the type immortalized by artist Helen Hokinson. The fact that the Lunts were man and wife made the difference here. After spicy onstage banter, one lady supposedly whispered to another, "Isn't it nice to know they're really married."

With the Guild an indisputable success, the minds of its six board members began hatching what seemed impossible dreams. Having opened the fine Guild Theatre on West 52nd Street, they inaugurated a Guild School of Acting and began a monthly Theatre Guild magazine. The Guild brass also began to think of touring plays so that all the country would be their stage, not just Manhattan. They also discussed the possibility of making Chicago a theatrical hub, with an occasional premiere there to make the Windy City feel important.

While the Theatre Guild drove actors like field slaves, Eva Le Gallienne
offered a more relaxed repertory on 14th Street.
Here she listens to Josephine Hutchinson in
Sir James Barrie's **Peter Pan**.

No longer the laugh-hungry comedians
of **Clarence** and **Dulcy** days, the Lunts had become the smoothest of sophisticates, on
and offstage. Loving acting, they willingly bent their backs for
Theatre Guild masters in an incredible assortment of repertory roles.

SHORT TAKE—HOW DO ACTORS ACT?

> In every man are the potentialities of many men. One quality is a little more stressed in this one, another in that one—here is the only difference.
>
> Playing a part is like playing the piano, one key stressed in this passage, another in another. Acting is simply stressing one characteristic more than others; at bottom all characters are alike.
>
> And so are the parts we play. The difference is only in weight of emphasis, the hard or the soft pedal on characteristics.
>
> —Edward G. Robinson

The Guild's soaring dreams included the long-cherished possibility of repertory similar to the Moscow Art Theatre, which gave a different play every night, its actors drawn from a permanent company. Supposedly repertory kept the public interested; gave actors a showcase for versatility and prevented them from turning stale; and lengthened the runs of plays, with the strong supporting the weak. Deciding to proceed, the Guild assembled a company of some thirty actors, including Helen Westley (a Guild director), Lunt and Fontanne, Margalo Gillmore, Edward G. Robinson, Claude Rains, Dudley Digges, and Henry Travers.

Repertory usually meant a different play each night, as was the case with Miss Le Gallienne's company. To the Theatre Guild, however, a modified repertory of changing plays each week seemed better. Alternating Repertory, this was called, and it meant running one play for a week, using the same actors in a different part for the next week, then back to the first. Meantime, the actors rehearsed new plays to be substituted for those sufficiently seen by Guild subscribers and public. A second theatre was needed for all this, and the Guild rented the John Golden, on East 58th Street.

The Guild's Alternating Repertory supposedly began with **Juarez and Maximilian**, featuring Alfred Lunt as the Archduke and Edward G. Robinson as Porfirio Diaz. But this ambitious effort got poor reviews and did not have the durability necessary for repertory.

Accordingly, the project actually started with Lynn Fontanne and Reginald Mason in **Pygmalion**, which got off to a stronger start. As this opened, Alfred Lunt was acting in **Juarez** and rehearsing Sidney Howard's **Ned McCobb's Daughter**, which became the second repertory item.

Next step was to provide two more plays to alternate. This was done by adding Laura Hope Crews to the acting company and casting her in **The Silver Cord**; this second Sidney Howard play alternated week to week with **Ned McCobb's Daughter**. To alternate with **Pygmalion**, the Guild presented **The Brothers Karamazov**, with Lunt and Fontanne, Clare Eames, and Edward G. Robinson. When it failed to grab the

Alfred Lunt was Dubedat in the Guild production of Shaw's **The Doctor's Dilemma**. He also played in **The Brothers Karamazov**, assisted by Edward G. Robinson.

225

public, S. N. Behrman's **The Second Man**, with the Lunts, was offered. Next were Pirandello's **Right You Are If You Think You Are** and a revival of **Mr. Pim Passes By**, to keep Laura Hope Crews busy.

It was all very complex, with certain actors remaining in the same theatre week after week, while others packed makeup kits on alternate weeks and moved. But it worked. In this first season of Guild repertory, Alfred Lunt rehearsed and played five major roles, while Lynn Fontanne did four; two of these were opposite each other.

Having succeeded in this tricky schedule—and deciding to continue it—the Guild essayed another dream. This was the addition of Eugene O'Neill, greatest American playwright, to what the six directors considered the nation's greatest producing organization.

This union was especially dear to the heart of Lawrence Langner, the spark plug of the Guild. Over the years Langner had made several efforts to tie O'Neill to the Guild, but these (believe it or not!) had been sabotaged by fellow board members who did not share Langner's enthusiasm for the playwright.

In the spring of 1927 Langner visited O'Neill in Bermuda, where the dramatist lived. O'Neill was remarkably cordial. The playwright said he had completed two scripts, one **Marco Millions**, which portrayed Marco Polo as a modern businessman, the other **Strange Interlude**, which would require five or six hours to play. In it, actors used spoken "asides" instead of masks to reveal true feelings. Langner gulped at the length but promised to fight for both plays with his recalcitrant board.

Returning to New York, he passed copies around. "Many and varied were the reactions," he has recalled, "and I became frantic." Gradually the members agreed to produce **Marco Millions** but fought hotly over **Strange Interlude**. Finally, it was accepted after O'Neill agreed to cut forty pages, thus reducing playing time to between four and five hours.

The part of Nina Leeds in **Strange Interlude** had been offered to Katharine Cornell, Pauline Lord, and Alice Brady, all of whom refused. Grudgingly it was passed to Lynn Fontanne, who did not like the role either. She found no subtlety in Nina, who started out as a twenty-year-old, tortured because she had held back sexually on her aviator-lover, killed in the war. In nine acts, Nina progressed through discovery of insanity in her husband's family, abortion, a healthy child by a doctor-lover, and finally bitchy motherhood; the play ended in vague happiness for her. Miss Fontanne could see little motivation for the neurotic Nina, but Alfred Lunt persuaded her to take the part. "It's the first Broadway show that has ever been done in nine acts," he argued.

Strange Interlude was scheduled to begin at 5:15 in the afternoon and run until 7:00, when the audience got an hour-and-a-half dinner break. Returning at 8:30, they sat until 11:00. Through rehearsals of this drawn-out opus Miss Fontanne found herself at odds with the playwright, who refused to trim down her lengthy speeches. She re-

Sidney Howard,
in **The Silver Cord**, drew a bead on mother love.
Here the figurative silver cord becomes a real-life telephone wire as
Laura Hope Crews and Margalo Gillmore
tug for possession.

Eugene O'Neill's *Strange Interlude*
was an outstanding hit of the Guild's repertory. In it, Lynn Fontanne appeared with
Glenn Anders and Tom Powers. This drama was so long it ran before and after dinner.

sponded by cutting them herself, an offense the author never discovered. Despite the hazards, she gave a superb performance as Nina, and **Strange Interlude** became the most successful play done by the Guild until the musical **Oklahoma!** in 1943.

SHORT TAKE—WHY DO ACTORS ACT?

"When I'm on a stage, I am the focus of thousands of eyes and it gives me strength. I feel that something, some energy, is flowing from the audience into me. I actually feel stronger because of these waves. [But] when the play's done, the eyes taken away, I feel just as if a circuit's been broken. The power is switched off. I feel all gone and empty inside of me—like a balloon that's been pricked and the air let out."

—Lynn Fontanne

If **Strange Interlude** proved an unexpected triumph, it also brought the first crack in the façade of Guild repertory. It was too long, too complex—and too successful—to alternate with another play. The Guild further compounded the problem by producing Du Bose Heyward's **Porgy** with an all-Negro cast. Nor could this be alternated either, for no other plays contained parts for black actors.

Still, the Guild continued its intricate plan as long as possible. Plays began touring cities like Boston, Philadelphia, and Pittsburgh. In Chicago, the Lunts premiered **The Doctor's Dilemma**, then did **The Guardsman** and **Arms and the Man**. An acting company headed by Fredric March and Florence Eldridge took **The Guardsman** and other plays out on one-night stands. Even **Strange Interlude** went on tour and was forced to play in Quincy, Massachusetts, rather than Boston, because city censors objected to its immorality.

For all the virtues of Alternating Repertory, it was hard on the important actors—at least as practiced by the Theatre Guild.

Notable sufferers were Alfred Lunt and Lynn Fontanne, whose heroic efforts never won real appreciation from the six-member Guild board. With them, as with other thespians, the Guild seemed to proceed on the theory that actors were a necessary nuisance. When the outside praise heaped on the Lunts seemed to be altering this attitude, a member of the organization circulated an impassioned memo that read, "Our only salvation is to remember first, last, always, and all the time that the play's the thing; that up and down, backwards, forwards, and sideways, the play is forever the thing, and that without a sound play, no amount of acting can save you from deserved damnation."

The Lunts had found out in days of **The Guardsman** that they did not have the confidence of the Guild board. At the final dress rehearsal, with the premiere only a night away, the directors gloomily watched, then informed Alfred Lunt that the play was a mess and his own performance a disaster. Lunt calls this the worst moment of his life, the only time in maturity that he broke into tears. Still, it was too late to do anything—as the board well knew—and *The Guardsman* opened the next night to raves, especially for the Lunts.

This brought no vote of confidence from the Guild. After viewing a rehearsal of a frivolous scene in *The Second Man*, the Guild board voted to toss it out. Alfred Lunt strode to the footlights and said bitterly, "Playing light comedy for you is like feeding a soufflé to a horse." Members of the Guild board were the last to learn (if they ever did) that Alfred Lunt and Lynn Fontanne could play anything.

SHORT TAKE

Every dedicated actor supposedly yearns to play repertory, with its challenging variety of roles, as well as the opportunity to display humility by playing small parts after big ones.

An exception was Leslie Howard, one of Broadway's most popular leading men in the Twenties and destined to be a top Hollywood movie star over the next decade. Howard seemed to be one actor who didn't even like to act. When the suggestion of repertory was broached to him, he turned pale and stammered, "You see, I don't really like being an actor, even quite mildly, let alone as violently as all that."

Yet the pair kept performing for the Guild, perhaps because they were eternally stagestruck and loved acting more than anything else. After they had become the most talked-about actors on the American stage, the Guild raised their collective salary from $250 to $750 a week. At this moment Marilyn Miller was getting $3,000 a week in *Rosalie* and Ed Wynn $7,500 in *Manhattan Mary*.

Whatever the play, the Lunts gave their all—and more. For the role of gangster Babe Callahan in *Ned McCobb's Daughter*, Alfred had a front tooth gold-capped and studied the mannerisms of real-life hoodlum Larry Fay; for the part of the roué in *Volpone*, he added fifty pounds to his fit frame. The two always watched for costumes to match their characters onstage and after buying them usually had trouble collecting the money from the Guild. More, the Guild seemed to take perverse pleasure in keeping them apart onstage. Why, for example, couldn't Alfred play Professor Higgins in *Pygmalion*? Finally, the two refused to appear any longer on separate stages and, here, it has been said, Alfred Lunt and Lynn Fontanne truly became the Lunts.

But in the years of Alternating Repertory, the pair worked like coolies. When Lynn was appearing in *Pygmalion* and rehearsing *The Second*

Man, it was decided to send the former play to Philadelphia as a test of out-of-town reaction to Guild shows. After performances of **Pygmalion** in Philadelphia, she took the midnight train to New York, rehearsed the Behrman play all day, and returned to Philadelphia at night. On Wednesdays and Saturdays she played restful matinees.

In 1927 the two began by appearing together in **The Doctor's Dilemma**. When it opened, Alfred rehearsed **Marco Millions** and Lynn **Strange Interlude**. At the opening of **Marco Millions** Lunt was exhausted and acted with what Alexander Woollcott called "an almost hypnotic weariness." Nonetheless, the Guild ordered him into rehearsals of **Volpone**. Learning this Miss Fontanne snapped, "This isn't an art theatre, it's a sweatshop." But she rehearsed and played Nina Leeds until she collapsed after six months.

Others had trouble with the Guild management. Edward G. Robinson, a stalwart of the permanent company, asked for a $25 raise. It was rejected and he quit. Fredric March returned from his tour of small towns in a cold fury, convinced the Guild had tried to obtain the worst possible accommodations. Said he, "The hotels in most of the towns were so bad that, when we did have the opportunity to sleep, the beds and the noise made it impossible to do so."

Still, the real heroes were always Alfred Lunt and Lynn Fontanne. Working under unpleasant pressures, they nevertheless perfected their unique type of team acting. Eight times a week they projected gaiety, skill, and delight at being onstage. In any theatre, the acting Lunts appeared to be enjoying themselves more than anyone else in the house.

Some believe the refusal of the Lunts to appear separately meant the end of Guild repertory. Lawrence Langner gives many reasons and concludes that with the repertory the Guild overreached itself. From **Pygmalion** to **Volpone** the Guild produced an unprecedented string of thirteen hits. When this uncanny run of luck ended, repertory was doomed.

Yet downtown Eva Le Gallienne was still at it.

THE RAIDS

On the night of February 9, 1927, police wagons from the West 47th Street precinct house fanned out to stop before three Broadway theatres, where the cops rudely informed the producers and actors they were under arrest as a menace to public morals. Raided plays were **The Captive**, Edouard Bourdet's delicate treatment of lesbianism, which had racked up 160 performances; Mae West in **Sex**, a forty-eight-week veteran; and **The Virgin Man**, a recent arrival wherein three Broadway babes failed to erase the virginity of an upright Yale boy. Among those arrested were Mae West, Helen Menken, Basil Rathbone, and Pacie Ripple—in all forty-one actors, producers, and authors.

The rolling of these Times Square tumbrils represented sweet victory for the bluenoses who had long been agitating to clean up the Broadway theatre. During the past year plays like **The Shanghai Gesture** and **Lulu Belle** had brought the forces of morality further ammunition; in fact, both these plays had been forced to tone down certain scenes. But this was still not enough—the legions of censorship demanded action.

They got little help from Mayor James J. Walker, a man who could easily be termed a Broadwayite. Walker's rise to political eminence had been accelerated by an anti-censorship speech in the state legislature where he had cried, "Nobody was ever raped by a book." The Mayor obviously did not believe anyone had ever been raped by a play either, but pressure from strait-laced Governor Alfred E. Smith, as well as angry civic groups, finally forced him to unleash the powers of District Attorney Joab H. Banton.

So the tumbrils rolled on this night in February, and the raids triggered the greatest theatrical brouhaha since the Equity strike of 1919. Perhaps it was greater, for a larger number of outsiders got into the act. From Albany, Governor Smith applauded the raids and accused the theatre of going too far in its sexiness. Mayor Walker had conveniently removed himself to Miami; from there he issued a statement approving the raids on the one hand, on the other saying the theatre had a right to police itself. No word came from President Calvin Coolidge.

Distinguished clergymen rose to the occasion. Dr. S. Parkes Cadman, growing popular from his radio sermons, stepped forth to organize a Church and Drama Society. He then joined with Cardinal Hayes, Canon Chase of Boston, and Rabbi Stephen Wise in backing the raids. Rank-and-file preachers in the five boroughs of New York City and elsewhere had made-to-order sermons for this Sunday and many to come.

Theatre folk reacted in interesting ways. The distinguished Winthrop Ames, head of a committee to cleanse the theatre from within, plaintively asked for more time. Actor-playwright Frank Craven put forward the provocative suggestion of a blue-light district for bawdy plays. Did

Raids of 1927
swept into the net ***The Captive***,
a serious play about lesbianism, with Basil Rathbone
and Helen Menken. Intellectuals wept over this closing.

Mae West, whose **Sex** also got raided. Mae served ten days on
Welfare Island and then said farewell
to the warden at the end.

he really mean it? No one knew, for the press paid little heed to his constructive idea.

The Theatre Guild sponsored a high-domed discussion of the Menace of Censorship, with Owen Davis, Frank Crowninshield, and Joseph Wood Krutch viewing with alarm. At another forum Robert E. Sherwood and William A. Brady debated Canon Chase and John S. Sumner, head of the local Society for the Suppression of Vice.

Producer Florenz Ziegfeld garnered publicity by telegraphing the District Attorney his belief that nudity in the *Follies* did not corrupt the public. The DA obligingly played along by sending his snoopers to girl shows and reporting to Ziegfeld that the *Follies* did not exceed bounds, though some nightclubs did. No raids were made on the nightclubs.

Scandals producer George White, apparently miffed by Ziegfeld's coup, issued a pious statement approving the raids. Such words from tough-guy George White, who considered every chorus girl in a *Scandals* his property, caused Broadway to gasp. So did Mae West's remark to a reporter—"You may think I'm kidding, but plays like *The Captive* make me blush."

When Gilbert Miller, producer of *The Captive*, showed signs of closing his play before trial, publisher-producer Horace Liveright began publicized efforts to take over and continue the run. Nonetheless, *The Captive* bowed itself out of existence.

Appeals to the State Supreme Court allowed *Sex* and *The Virgin Man* to keep running, with actors out on bail. At first audiences were large but slowly fell off. *The Virgin Man* expired, then *Sex*. By that time, lawyers had been in and out of court, asking for jury trials, non-jury trials, and dismissals—anything, it would seem, to obscure matters. One judge fell sick; another refused to view the plays at first hand. Finally, the case of *The Virgin Man* went before a jury that found producers and author guilty, with ten days in the workhouse and $250 fines apiece. The cast got sin-no-more suspended sentences.

On April 21 Mae West and her cast endured an identical ordeal. The charge against *Sex* had been switched from public nuisance to obscenity, and again the verdict was guilty. As author and star, Miss West was fined $500 and sentenced to ten days at light labor. The lady showed no visible sorrow, for she was dwelling delightedly in the eye of a hurricane of publicity. Her stay in jail seemed sure to increase this.

In the workhouse, Mae donned a rough cotton dress and languidly dusted the prison's meager supply of books. Outside the crescendo of publicity rose higher. Mae West had become a blend of the famous and infamous—the latest heroine of the Era of Wonderful Nonsense.

Officially, the result of the turmoil was passage of what was called the Wales Padlock Law. Aimed at theatre owners, it ordered that any playhouses showing dubious material be shut down. Like the night clubs of Broadway after a Prohibition raid, they would be padlocked.

Al Jolson got his usual standing ovation on the opening night of
Big Boy in 1925, but soon his mind was on Hollywood,
where he had signed to appear in
The Jazz Singer.
The entertainment world has never been
the same since, on the screen, Jolie
spoke the tinny words, "Come on, Ma, listen to this!"

TALKIES

The talking film *The Jazz Singer* opened at the Warner Theatre on the night of October 6, 1927. So, unexpectedly, at the robust peak of an active year, the theatre was dealt a body blow. Because of it, the legit would soon be called the Fabulous Invalid, a dubious tribute to its ability to survive the successive onslaughts of talkies, radio, and finally television.

Actually, *The Jazz Singer* was not the first sound picture. A year before the pioneering Warner brothers had offered a $5.50 evening of Vitaphone entertainment. This began with a series of shorts featuring the New York Philharmonic and the singing voices of Giovanni Martinelli, Marion Talley, and other stars of the Metropolitan Opera.

The shorts were followed by the world premiere of John Barrymore in *Don Juan*, to which a symphonic sound track had been added. In this film the romantic Barrymore kissed his leading ladies 143 times by press-agent count, a feat overlooked in favor of the music that emanated from a sound track attached to the picture rather than from the usual hard-working pit orchestra. "The sound reached out from a huge, invisible horn behind the screen and wrought its spell on the viewers," a reviewer enthused. At the end of *Don Juan*, the audience rose to its feet and cheered.

People yelled louder at the opening of *The Jazz Singer*. For the great Jolie not only sang three songs but spoke twice. "Come on, Ma, listen to this," he said at one point, seating himself at a piano. After rendering "Dirty Hands, Dirty Face" on the Hollywood sound stage, he had shouted, "Wait a minute! Wait a minute! You ain't heard nothin' yet!" to the assembled sound engineers, cameramen, and café extras. These words were retained on the sound track, and at the Broadway premiere the electric Jolson personality flooded the theatre as he uttered them. Again a Vitaphone audience roared to its feet.

A haze of many tellings shrouds the tale of exactly how Al Jolson got to star in the film version of *The Jazz Singer*. Samson Raphaelson, author of the play, had much trouble getting it on Broadway because a minority-group theme was considered dubious theatre fare. Finally, the multitalented George Jessel, who had begun his career in Gus Edwards' vaudeville acts, agreed to play the lead. Jessel gave a performance sensitive enough to raise the show to the hit class. Reputedly, the proud actor visualized himself playing *The Jazz Singer* off and on for the rest of his life, like David Warfield in *The Music Master*.

Possibly for this reason he opposed the movie version when the Warner brothers bought the play; he may have hoped that without him no film would ever be made. At any rate, he read the film script and professed to find it inferior. After consulting with his friend Eddie Cantor, he continued adamant.

Rejected by Jessel, the Warners began courting the great Jolson—"massaging his ego," an observer called it. The treatment worked, for Jolson not only agreed to do the picture but opted to take his payment in Warner Brothers stock; also he invested some of his own money in a film that ultimately made $3,000,000 in profit. Yet the California climate may have been the deciding factor. Jolson worshipped the sun, and his long months as a Broadway and touring star kept him away from it, except for brief Miami vacations. He may have reasoned hopefully that pictures with sound would let him work and dwell in the land of perpetual sunshine.

There was poetic justice in Jolson's eventual appearance in **The Jazz Singer**, for it had been written with him in mind, though he had been too busy and too successful to consider doing it onstage. Few found Jolson a likable person in his high-riding Broadway days, yet he was capable of occasional, erratic kindness. As Samson Raphaelson, author of **The Jazz Singer**, tells it, "When I was just a kid, I went to see Al Jolson in a show. He made such an impression on me that I went backstage after the performance. He was real swell to me. I don't know why, but he invited me into his dressing room while he changed and told me all about his childhood. He told me about how religious and strict his father had been and how the old man only wanted his son to sing in a synagogue. He added that his father still wasn't enthusiastic about Al's place in the theatre.

"I grew up on the lower East Side of New York and I saw many cases similar to Al's. I felt I knew a little about the reasons behind this and I decided to put it into a short story. This did all right for itself and the story kept haunting me. I guess in the back of my mind I had a dream of maybe seeing Jolson in one of my works. Anyway, I turned it into a play."

So talking pictures arrived, at first seeming no more than an amusing novelty. But technical advances were rapid, and films that offered only intermittent scenes with sound quickly became All-Talking, All-Singing, All-Dancing. The real threat in the new medium rose to the surface when it became apparent that movie theatres did not perceptibly raise prices because of the talkies. At the grand new Paramount Theatre on Times Square, the cost of admission was 65 cents from eleven o'clock in the morning. Then, at the stroke of six, a pair of spankingly uniformed ushers marched out in military precision to change the admission to one dollar.

In smaller theatres across the land the public paid 35 cents or a quarter to see movies that now shaved to a thin line the differences between stage and screen.

THE WEEK THAT WAS

Nineteen-twenty-seven has come down to us as the peak moment of Twenties theatrical production—quantitatively, anyhow. Nearly 275 shows were viewed by critics during the year, and expectation rose high that the next year would be greater.

The great fame of 1927 as a theatrical summit rests in part on the amazing Christmas week of the year, when eighteen shows were presented in the span of six days. Eleven of them opened—as has often been cited—on the night of Monday, December 26. Eighteen plays in a week—eleven in one night! The world will never again experience such a thing again.

Like all statistics, however, these bear scrutiny. There is no doubt that the number of plays is correct, but the matter of their worth is questionable. Of the week's eighteen plays, only four proved worth the effort, with two of the four paying off spectacularly. And of the eleven shows opening on that magical Monday, only two had merit.

On this fabled Monday, city editors corralled movie critics, music critics, ship-news reporters, City Hall regulars, and copy boys to cover the eleven shows. First-stringers opted to attend George Kelly's **Behold the Bridegroom**, about a spoiled, willful rich girl (Judith Anderson) who felt herself too jaded to love when the right man finally came along; ''life-wearied'' was her phrase. Not much happened in this humorless drama—was this the hand that wrote **The Show Off**?—but it was the most distinguished premiere of the night and ended by running eighty-eight performances.

The night's other worthwhile item was **Excess Baggage**, a laugh provoker by John McGowan, with Miriam Hopkins, Frank McHugh, Eric Dressler, Morton Downey, and Frances Goodrich. Eddie (Dressler) and Elsa (Miss Hopkins) were a juggling team in small-time vaudeville, where Eddie had the talent and Elsa the beauty; she was really excess baggage in the act. Matters changed when her good looks won a movie contract; then *he* was excess baggage. The play evolved into a cheery, happy ending and went on 198 times.

Other plays of this December 26 included **Venus**, by the experienced Rachel Crothers, which ran eight performances, and **It Is to Laugh**, by novelist Fannie Hurst, which did little better. Anna Held, Jr., produced another flop of the night, and a revival of **L'Aiglon**, with poetess Michael Strange, the onetime Mrs. John Barrymore, barely limped through the week. The other efforts of the glorious night are best left buried.

Next evening the major critics chose to attend **Paris Bound**, Philip Barry's glib, happy-ending comedy about divorce. It had a long run and can be rated a success, but even so the critics erred in attending. For this was also the opening night of **Show Boat**, one of the masterpieces of the American theatre. **Show _ _at** had such an effect on an opening-night audience that Robert Benchley and Marc Connelly, two of the most sophisticated men about Manhattan, wept tears of delight as it unfolded.

On Wednesday, December 28, everyone attended **The Royal Family**, produced by Jed Harris and written by George S. Kaufman and Edna Ferber. Not only was this a merry romp of a play but it titillated first-nighters by obviously being about the Barrymore family. In fact, Ethel Barrymore heard of the impending production and demanded to read a script. It so infuriated her that she consulted a lawyer who said her brother John was the only family member actually libeled. Determined to stop the play, Miss Barrymore frantically tried to phone her brother in Hollywood. It tells something—but what?—about the real Royal Family of Broadway that John Barrymore was too lazy, too indifferent, or too something else to answer his older sister's urgent calls.

Any statistics of this immortal week must include the musical comedy **Lovely Lady**, with music by Dave Stamper and book by Gladys Unger. Here the part of Folly Watteau was played by Edna Leedom, once of the **Follies**, with Guy Robertson as Paul De Morlaix. A pleasant, unambitious effort, it ran 164 performances.

Such are the facts of the week that was—eighteen plays in six days, eleven in one night, only four of them running as far as Lent.

And over at the Warner Theatre long lines kept forming for **The Jazz Singer**.

SHORT TAKE

What was the funniest moment in a Twenties musical comedy?

Probably it came in George White's **Manhattan Mary**, a good but not legendary 1927 item starring Ed Wynn, with Lou Holtz, Ona Munson, and Harland Dixon. A show within a show, it had the Mary of the title dream of appearing in **George White's Scandals**, which she did in the finale.

Ed Wynn, who reputedly got $7,500 a week for his efforts, played a timid waiter in a speakeasy. One day a gangster appeared and sat down at a table, loudly demanding a menu. A terrified Wynn had no menu but helpfully lisped out suggestions like lady fingers or a jelly roll. The hoodlum erupted in fury. "My God," he yelled, "I'm so hungry I could eat a horse and you mention crap like that!"

Ed Wynn scurried through the swinging doors into the kitchen and returned tugging a live horse.

ROUNDUP

In this lustiest of years, Burns Mantle bestowed his accolade on **Saturday's Children**, by Maxwell Anderson, with Ruth Gordon and Roger Pryor, a young-marriage comedy indicating that not everyone enjoyed prosperity in boom years; **The Road to Rome**, by Robert E. Sherwood, with Jane Cowl and Philip Merivale, posing the notion that a sex urge may have kept Hannibal from marching on Rome; **Cradle Song**, by Martinez Sierra, a Civic Repertory production, with Eva Le Gallienne, Josephine Hutchinson, and Hardie Albright; **The Royal Family**, by Kaufman and Ferber, that lampoon of the Barrymores; **Burlesque**, by George Manker Waters and producer Arthur Hopkins, starring Hal Skelly, calling more attention to Barbara Stanwyck and to Oscar Levant.

Also **Coquette**, a tragic item by George Abbott and Ann Preston Bridgers, produced by Jed Harris, that made the public take Helen Hayes seriously as a dramatic actress; **Porgy**, the non-operatic version of the Dorothy and Du Bose Heyward novel, dramatized by the authors; **Paris Bound**, Philip Barry's comedy about divorce that seemed brilliant then; **Escape**, by John Galsworthy, in which Leslie Howard portrayed a convict on the run; **The Racket**, by Bartlett Cormack, an all-male melodrama about gang-ridden Chicago, with Edward G. Robinson, Hugh O'Connell, and Norman Foster—the first time Robinson played a gangster; **Behold the Bridegroom**, by George Kelly, wherein a rich girl gave up on herself; and **The Plough and the Stars**, performed for the first time in America by the Irish Players, led by Sara Allgood and Arthur Sinclair.

It was a year of commercialism rather than uplift. Yet in the area of culture Max Reinhardt arrived with his repertory company to give elaborate performances of **A Midsummer Night's Dream** (with Teutonic overtones), **Danton's Death**, and **Everyman**, with Alexander Moissi, Germany's Jack Barrymore. Walter Hampden offered a successful **An Enemy of the People**, along with other roles. In addition to **The Plough and the Stars**, the Irish Players revived **Juno and the Paycock**. For fun there was a modern-dress version of **The Taming of the Shrew**, done with gusto by Basil Sydney and Mary Ellis, Maria Ouspenskaya, and C. H. Croker-King; in this the wedding journey took place in a trick flivver.

Notable commercial plays of the year were Kenyon Nicholson's **The Barker**, a play about carnival life, with Walter Huston, that gave Claudette Colbert her first big role as a snake-charming temptress; **Crown Prince**, a version of the Mayerling tragedy, adapted from the Hungarian by Zoë Akins, also with Basil Sydney and Mary Ellis; **The Spider**, by Fulton Oursler and Lowell Brentano, a mystery sensation in which the murder took place in an orchestra seat; **The Second Man**, S. N. Behrman's first play, a happy affair with Alfred Lunt and Lynn

Other Guild actors
worked almost as hard as the Lunts. Above, Claudette Colbert and Eliot Cabot
in Eugene O'Neill's **Dynamo**.

Forever
famed in Broadway
lore is **The Ladder**, a drama financed
by a Texas millionaire who believed in reincarnation.
When the public failed to buy tickets, the Croesus offered free entry to all comers.
Brock Pemberton, respected Broadway figure,
was the nominal producer. In it were young
Irene Purcell and older
Antoinette Perry.

Two girls who made good: Florenz Ziegfeld's **Rio Rita**, lush operetta,
was embellished by Paulette Goddard and Susan Fleming.
Paulette went on to marry Charles Chaplin
and others; Susan became an ever-loving
Mrs. Harpo Marx.

All this and **Show Boat** too!
In the fabled Christmas week of 1927, Otto Kruger,
Haidee Wright, and Ann Andrews opened in the Kaufman–Ferber **Royal Family**

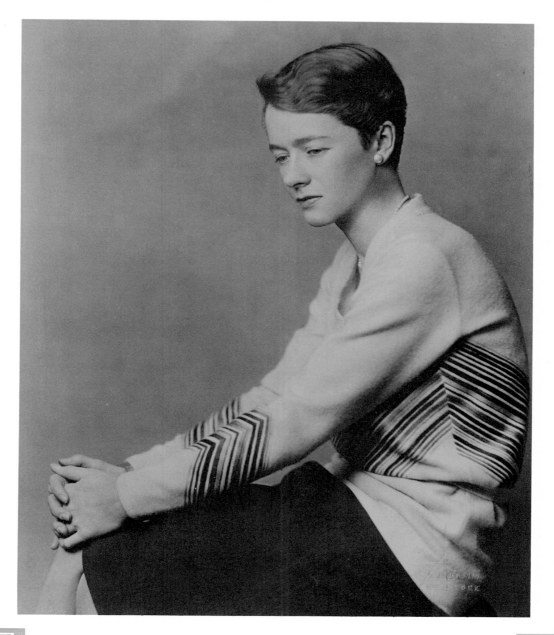

Hope Williams, socialite turned actress,
won notices in Philip Barry's ***Paris Bound***

Judith
Anderson brought distinction to George Kelly's disappointing
Behold the Bridegroom

Miriam Hopkins caught Hollywood's eye in
Excess Baggage

James and Lucille Gleason,
wisecrackers supreme, hit the jackpot with *The
Shannons of Broadway*

Claudette Colbert scored for acting as well as
beauty with Walter Huston in *The Barker*

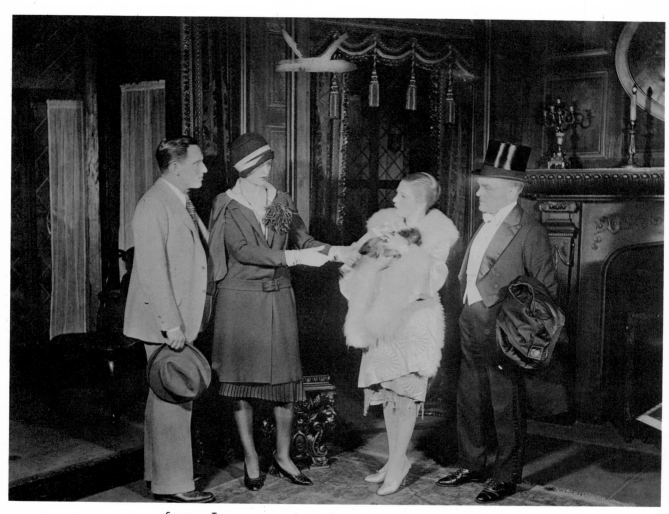

Spencer Tracy appeared with Grant Mitchell in **Baby Cyclone**;
and the Theatre Guild produced the original,
non-operatic **Porgy**, by Dorothy and Du Bose Heyward.

Caricature by IRVING HOFFMANN

Mae West's
brush with the law over **Sex**,
along with the attendant publicity,
aided in finding herself artistically.
During **Sex** she had begun (out of boredom) to burlesque part of the
golden-hearted
prostitute in play. Audiences
roared. Now, as a public figure, Mae resolved
to do more of the same. Simultaneously, an associate suggested that her new
tongue-in-cheek performing suited a Gay Nineties background.
Mae wrote **Diamond Lil**, and on opening night the
vaudeville-trained
actress who had been a Broadway joke
found herself hailed as a rare comic talent.
Glowing Mae reveled in fame. Of Katharine Cornell,
Ina Claire, Ethel Barrymore,
and others, she said, "Sure, they can act, but
can they write their own stuff? They can't. See what I mean?"

Fontanne; ***The Trial of Mary Dugan***, a tingling courtroom drama about a Follies Girl killer, with lovely Ann Harding and handsome Rex Cherryman, an actor who died before the decade ended; ***The Shannons of Broadway***, by and with James Gleason (along with his wife), which told of a stranded vaudeville act fixing up matters in a New England town; and shuddery ***Dracula***, with Bela Lugosi, Nedda Harrigan, and Dorothy Peterson evoking chills.

Despite the potency of the Wales Padlock Law, a few producers tried daring plays. ***Maya***, translated from the French by Ernest Boyd, told of a Marseille prostitute (Aline MacMahon) who seemed a different girl to each customer; police closed it after fifteen performances. In ***Escape***, Leslie Howard was sent to prison for killing a London bobby in a fight to protect a Hyde Park prostitute; in ***The Garden of Eden***, by Avery Hopwood, with Miriam Hopkins, Douglass Montgomery, Alison Skipworth, and T. Wigney Percyval, Toni Lebrun (Miss Hopkins) delightfully stripped down to her step-ins; ***Katy Did***, with Juliette Day, was not as naughty as it sounded; ***A Very Wise Virgin*** had a character uttering the classic line "It's a wise virgin who knows her own boiling point"; in ***Sinner***, by Thompson Buchanan, Cynthia (Claiborne Foster) was a girl of shifting morals who enjoyed a premarital honeymoon with her fiancé but found marriage dull; after catching her playing around, hubby slapped her into obedient adoration as the curtain fell.

After these plays, critics rejoiced at ***Tommy***, by Howard Lindsay and Bertrand Robinson, with Peg Entwistle, Alan Bunce, Sidney Toler, and William Janney. "As clean as a kennel of hounds teeth," an aisle-sitter commented and advised parents to take the kids.

Flotsam and jetsam of the year included ***Spread Eagle***, a Jed Harris follow-up to ***Broadway***, which accused Wall Street of fomenting wars; ***Women Go On Forever***, on boardinghouse life, with Mary Boland, Osgood Perkins, Douglass Montgomery, James Cagney, and Sam Wren; Billie Burke in Noël Coward's ***The Marquise***, another about a fellow who almost married a half-sister; ***Four Walls***, by Dana Burnet and George Abbott, which brought Muni Weisenfrend a step closer to Paul Muni.

In ***Baby Mine***, a disgraced Fatty Arbuckle of Hollywood tried a comeback, with Humphrey Bogart and Lee Patrick; Spencer Tracy appeared in ***Baby Cyclone***, about ownership rights to a Pekinese; ***The Wild Man of Borneo***, by Marc Connelly and Joseph Mankiewicz, lasted two weeks; Franchot Tone was visible in ***The Belt***, by Paul Sifton; ***The Love Nest***, Robert Sherwood's dramatization of the Ring Lardner short story, was an unhappy flop, with June Walker, Albert Carroll, and Paula Trueman.

Musical theatre flourished.

Once again the dignity award went to Winthrop Ames for ***The Mikado***, latest in his stunning Gilbert and Sullivan revivals. The non-dignity award fell to Florenz Ziegfeld and Eddie Cantor, after the Great

Glorifier surprised Broadway by producing another **Follies**, depending heavily on the Cantor skills. Shortly Eddie collapsed from overwork, or so he claimed. Ziegfeld lashed back, accusing the comedian of malingering for more money. The case was taken to Equity, which decided in favor of Ziegfeld. Threats of suits and countersuits filled the air; then suddenly all was harmony, presumably because Cantor got his raise.

Also appearing in this **Follies of 1927** (last of the decade) were Irene Delroy, Claire Luce, and Ruth Etting, who sang up a storm with Irving Berlin's "Shaking the Blues Away."

Flo Ziegfeld also postured before the world as the year's operetta king, in part because of **Rio Rita** but more on account of **Show Boat** and its superscore by Jerome Kern and Oscar Hammerstein II. With Helen Morgan, Charles Winninger, Jules Bledsoe, Eva Puck and Sammy White, Edna May Oliver, Howard Marsh, and Norma Terris, **Show Boat** was among the most rewarding productions of the decade.

Some of the best musical comedies of the Twenties opened in 1927. Tops was De Sylva, Brown and Henderson's **Good News**, with a sis-boom-bah college background, featuring Zelma O'Neal, Inez Courtney, John Price Jones, and George Olsen's music pounding out "Varsity Drag." Equally popular was **Funny Face**, with Fred and Adele Astaire, Betty Compton, Victor Moore, music by the Gershwins, and a plot loosely involving a jewel robbery. **Hit the Deck**, another legendary show, had music by Vincent Youmans, plus the talents of Louise Groody, Stella Mayhew, Charles King, and the Locust Sisters; it was the first musical considered good enough to use the stage of the hallowed Belasco Theatre. **A Connecticut Yankee**, out of Mark Twain by Joseph Fields, had memorable Rodgers and Hart songs, William Gaxton, and Constance Carpenter.

Harry Delmar's **Revels** has grown famous over the years because in it Bert Lahr, veteran of burlesque and vaudeville, made his theatre debut, along with Frank Fay, Winnie Lightner, and Patsy Kelly. This was a busy though not sensational year for Ruby Keeler, who hoofed in **Bye, Bye, Bonnie** and **The Sidewalks of New York**, by and with Eddie Dowling, in which she played two parts. Archie Leach, the Cary Grant to be, appeared in **Golden Dawn**, with Barbara Newberry. Libby Holman, Leonard Sillman, William Collier, and Marie Cahill were in **Merry-Go-Round**, music by Harry Souvaine and Jay Gorney, lyrics by Howard Dietz.

Yes, Yes, Yvette, with Jeanette MacDonald, Charles Winninger, and Jack Whiting, made an unsuccessful attempt to duplicate the success of **No, No, Nanette**; glamorous Hope Hampton, from Hollywood, warbled in **My Princess**, by Edward Sheldon and Dorothy Donnelly; the Shuberts had a solid hit in **My Maryland**, music by Romberg, based on the Barbara Frietchie legend, with Evelyn Herbert as Barbara and James Ellis as Stonewall Jackson.

Finally, Texas Guinan, the Main Stem's most popular nightclub hostess, appeared in **Padlocks of 1927**. She made her entrance as a cowgirl on a large white horse, bellowed her songs, and jollied audiences in thunderous fashion. Lillian Roth, Jay C. Flippin, and glossy-haired George Raft aided her.

Has any other art—or profession or business—ever flaunted a figure like Jed Harris?

At age twenty-seven, he was hailed as the Wonder Boy of Broadway, the single indubitable genius of the commercial theatre. His co-workers in the vineyards of thespis, fascinated alike by his mercurial personality and his feats of theatrical legerdemain, talked of him end-lessly.

Public and profession were so mesmerized by his slight, ominous figure—"the young darkling," a friend called him—that he was es-teemed as a producer of steady hits when the record shows otherwise; as a masterful director of plays, though he employed name directors for the jobs; and as a discoverer and nourisher of talent, despite the fact that he often browbeat actors.

S. N. Behrman, who for a time served as his play reader and press agent, writes that Jed Harris fascinated the theatre for a decade, and so he did. But the first few years were the finest. Then he had four simultaneous hits—**Broadway**, **The Royal Family**, **Coquette**, **The Front Page**—and was well on the way to making a million dollars.

"I was born with this instinct for seeing situations visually, dramatically" is the way he described his rare gifts. The Harris touch, famed on Broad-way, stood for inspired casting, clever direction, impeccable backgrounds, and subtle lighting. Yet he was characteristically ungrate-ful to the theatre that brought him renown. "Broadway is the shell game of the arts," he told a reporter.

Harris was an egotist, a charmer, a demon. "The Gitano," publicist Richard Maney dubbed him. Slight and forward-sloping, he had a large nose, hooded eyes, and perpetual five-o'clock shadow. Some thought him handsome in a brooding way; to others he was a stalking bird of prey. This Cassius had a lean and hungry look—"grasshopper thin," wrote Ben Hecht. At various times in his career Harris was com-pared to Svengali and Rasputin, while his own view of himself included overtones of Disraeli.

Jed Harris spoke in barely audible, hypnotic tones, but the talk was marvelous—"a dazzling cascade of eagle-winged words," a listener decided. His conversation was called creative, for it prodded others into thinking. Even as a young man Harris was a walking encyclopedia of the theatre past and present who not only knew the names, dates, and caliber of bygone performances but could recite scenes of plays and famous vaudeville acts **in toto**. This last endeared him to Alfred Lunt, a vaudeville buff who also doted on burlesque.

With all his facets, Jed Harris excelled in the area of love-into-hate relationships. Recollections and biographies of Broadwayites are stud-ded with instances of those dazzled by Jed Harris at first who soon

Posing for a formal portrait,
Jed Harris might look saintly, but backstage, actors said,
he could be a monster.

found themselves loathing him. This was not done without cooperation from the Boy Wonder, who lifted hostility to a fine art. "I love my enemies and hate my friends," he said once. "Your enemies are steadfast, but with your friends you can't tell what the hell they want out of you."

One whose love went rancid was George Abbott, who co-authored and directed **Broadway**, the first big hit for both. "My early fondness for Jed turned into wholehearted, uncomplicated hatred," he writes. George S. Kaufman traveled the same route and at the end tried to think up the ultimate in insults. Finally he got it: "When I die I want to be cremated and have my ashes thrown into Jed Harris' face."

Harris was born Jacob Horowitz in Vienna and brought to Newark, New Jersey, as a baby. At age three he saw his first play and was stagestruck thereafter. Determined to be a producer, he labored initially as press agent for various unspectacular shows. Even then he was arrogantly sure of himself. When he approached Otto Kahn about financing a project, the philanthropist delivered a few words of wisdom. "I came here for your money, Mr. Kahn," the darkling snapped, "not your advice."

At one point Jed Harris had his fingers on **What Price Glory?** but lost it because of lack of Main Stem status. With **Broadway** he lacked money but made an arrangement with the established producer Crosby Gaige that each would put up half the funds. Gaige, an easygoing soul, did not mind Harris getting sole credit as producer. Yet **Broadway** was done on the Gaige money alone, since Harris never came up with his share. Instead of thanks, Gaige got hatred. "Jed was eaten with resentment that Gaige owned half," writes S. N. Behrman. "The detail that Gaige had financed the entire production constantly escaped him."

The reason for Harris' inability to keep friends may have been a basic insecurity that belied an image of total self-assurance. His frequent black moods probably had the same root. On the surface, though, he lost friends because in dark moods the egotist did not hesitate to tell people his precise opinion of them. At such times his unsparing verbiage slipped easily from sarcasm to sadism. Nobody told off by Jed Harris was likely to forget or forgive. One of his enemies learned The Gitano was to dine with a certain family. "Be careful not to let him bite any of your dogs," he warned the host.

Ina Claire was perhaps the only person to cope with a Harris dark mood. Her real name was Fagan, and during an argument Harris said nastily, "Miss Fagan, you stink." Ina gasped, grabbed his arm, and twisted it with such vim that the producer fell to the floor. She then vented further rage by kicking him in the stomach.

Miss Claire instantly became the heroine of the Times Square love-into-hate set and was constantly asked, "Show what you did to Jed Harris." Nothing loath, she explained, "I grabbed him by the arm, like **this**, and then I **threw** him onto the floor like **this**. And then I **kicked**

262

Delightful Ina Claire, fresh from triumphs in **The Last of Mrs. Cheyney**
and other roles, won kudos in the profession by hurling
Jed Harris to the floor and delivering a well-aimed kick.

The Front Page, by Ben Hecht and Charles MacArthur,
featured Lee Tracy and Osgood Perkins in the hectic
city room of a Chicago newspaper. Times had changed so much that
the final line—"The son of a bitch
stole my watch!"—failed
to shock audiences.

him but good." A brilliant actress in every role, Miss Claire usually succeeded in tossing her listener to the floor and had to be restrained from kicking him, as well.

George Abbott encountered Harris when the latter was press-agenting **Hell Bent fer Heaven**, in which Abbott played a leading role. Harris confided his producing aspirations and discussed with Abbott such vital matters as whether his name should be J. E. D. Harris or plain Jed, a name picked from an old-time melodrama. The two got along famously, with Abbott acting as play-doctor on **Love'Em and Leave'Em**, the first Harris success.

They split over **Broadway**. Abbott gives Harris full credit for removing the cheap vaudeville jokes from the script, but after that came anger as Harris suddenly lost confidence in rapid-fire direction of the play and subjected Abbott to one of his celebrated tell-offs. Only the strong protests of co-author Philip Dunning kept Harris from employing a more conventional director. Then, after the sensational opening, Harris allegedly reneged on a verbal promise to pay Abbott one percent of the gross as director's fee.

In friendly days Harris had agreed to produce **Coquette**, a superior tearjerker by Abbott and Ann Preston Bridgers, in which a deep-South flapper stepped out of her social set to trigger murder and her own suicide. Abbott was to direct and, for the sake of the play, Harris wanted him to. With the full support of Helen Hayes, who played the lead, Abbott agreed so long as Harris did not set foot in the theatre. **Coquette** was another big hit, and so great was the Harris mystique that he not only got credit for direction but for turning Helen Hayes into a first-rate dramatic actress.

The saturnine Harris liked to disconcert visitors to his hotel suite by greeting them in the nude. One day he sat without apparel through a conference over **The Front Page** with Ben Hecht, Charles MacArthur, and George S. Kaufman, who directed the rowdy play. "His hairy and coleopterous nudity stuck in our eyes for an hour," Hecht recalled. It irked all three men, but no one said anything until time to leave. Then Kaufman unfolded his length, to utter Broadway's most cherished wisecrack. "Oh, by the way, Jed," he said, "your fly is open."

His reputation for venom never bothered Harris, who failed to change his winsome ways. "Once an actor, always a son of a bitch," he cracked once. He dared call drama critics "boys" and said, "I've never seen anyone so ill-equipped for their jobs as the boys now reviewing on the New York dailies." He greeted Brooks Atkinson of the **Times**, "My boy, you know next to nothing about the theatre."

Indeed, he seemed to revel in a reputation for evil. On the wall of his outer office hung a sign, "Please don't call Jed Harris a bastard." The checks he signed were stamped, "Local No. 1—S.O.B." Once he called himself "the all-time, All-American, uncompromising megalomaniac." Sidney Skolsky put it another way in an early "Tintype": "It is said that his favorite character in history is Jed Harris."

In 1928 Jed Harris stood supreme on Broadway. Noël Coward had christened him "Destiny's Tot," and Ben Hecht made him the anti-hero of the novel *A Jew in Love*. The magazine *Time* did an unprecedented cover story on him, while authors and play agents gave him top position on lists of desirable producers. Actors courted him, actresses clamored to get into his plays or his bed. Only press agent Richard Maney kept perspective; he saw "symptoms" of genius in Harris, never the real thing.

From this eminence Harris turned himself a figure of the Era of Wonderful Nonsense in the matter of the "Act of God baby." Helen Hayes, star of *Coquette*, married playwright Charles MacArthur and in due time became pregnant. She informed Harris, who paid no attention. *Coquette* went on tour and continued until Miss Hayes' condition prevented further performances. Harris was informed of this and abruptly closed the show without notice. Members of the cast demanded two weeks' pay, which he refused.

According to the Equity contract, "The management (producer) is not responsible for fire, strikes, or an Act of God." Harris branded Miss Hayes' pregnancy an Act of God, though Broadway considered it an act of MacArthur that Harris might have avoided by hiring another star. The producer was adamant and received wide and amused newspaper coverage because of the Act of God baby. Finally, the matter went to Equity councils. At a first meeting the board could not decide; at a second, the voters went against Harris, saying he might have hired a replacement. By that time the name Jed Harris was familiar throughout the land.

With all the brickbats came some genuine tributes. "Every playwright should have Jed Harris once—like the measles," said George S. Kaufman grudgingly. Brooks Atkinson wrote, "If it were not for the Theatre Guild and Jed Harris, the theatre in New York would be lamentably deficient in producers who have both the desire and the ability to preserve the theatre as one of the major arts." S. N. Behrman writes, "Jed was a primal force, an artist. He was not, as so many producers are, an assembler, an exporter-importer; he was an innovator." Others call him Broadway's greatest catalyst.

Destiny's Tot seemed to have burned himself out by 1930, when he produced the first of six successive failures. With *The Green Bay Tree*, in 1933, he regained the Harris touch, though never as handsomely as before. Now he became famed as a director, with *Our Town* and *The Heiress* his major triumphs. The years have not brought mellowness. As recently as 1972 *The New York Times* carried a drama-page story about Jed Harris crashing into the life of a promising young playwright, twisting his script in all directions, then vanishing as rapidly as he came.

Had the young playwright's love turned to hate? He was too stunned to say.

Mr. and Mrs. Charles MacArthur, parents of Act-of-God baby.

LONG TAKE

Back in 1920 Guy Bolton and P. G. Wodehouse, authors of the book of the upcoming musical comedy **Sally**, paid a jittery call on Marilyn Miller, whose first starring show this was to be.

The authors wanted Marilyn to make her first entrance as one of six cotton-clad orphans led into the kitchen for inspection at a restaurant in need of a girl dishwasher. The orphan yanked out of line would be Marilyn, and the audience was supposed to gasp in astonishment and delight.

Would the star go along? Though only nineteen, Marilyn Miller had been on the stage since childhood and was known to hold a justifiably high opinion of her talents. More terrifying was that, despite an angelic appearance, the girl had a temper, plus a vocabulary honed by years backstage.

The writers hesitantly broached this idea of a "cute" entrance rather than the "star" type. When they finished, a beatific smile spread over Marilyn's face. "Swell," she said. "It'll give me a chance to do my eccentric dance."

As expected, audiences at **Sally** gasped, then applauded, as one of the six little urchins turned out to be the star of the show. But this was the only cute entrance Marilyn Miller ever made. After it, she began to lift the star entrance to new dimensions. In 1928, appearing in **Rosalie**, she outdid herself. In his opening-night review, Alexander Woollcott described the magic moment thusly:

> Down in the orchestra pit, the violins chitter with excitement and the brasses blare. The spotlight turns white with expectation. Fifty beautiful girls in simple peasant costumes of satin and chiffon rush pell mell onto the stage, all squealing simple peasant outcries of "Here she comes!" Fifty hussars in fatigue uniforms of ivory white and tomato bisque march on in columns of four and kneel to express an emotion too strong for words. The lights swing to the gateway at the back and settle there. The house holds its breath.
>
> And on walks Marilyn Miller. . . .

In ***Rosalie***,
the fetching Marilyn Miller disguised herself as a West Point cadet.

LOVE, BROADWAY STYLE

During the glorious Twenties—and, indeed, long before—the four-letter word *love* was probably spoken more often on Broadway than anywhere else.

It was evoked in tragedies, exalted in romances, probed in dramas, bandied in comedies, and warbled in musical shows. One smart comedy branded love "the perpetual emotion," while an irreverent musical called it "a flash in the pants." Even the supersophisticated *Little Show* used it to satirize movie theme songs with "Hammacher Schlemmer, I Love You."

The Main Stem not only sang and spoke love but wove it into newspaper sensations as well. One movie called such sagas Broadway Melodies, and in a song lyric they were Lullabies of Broadway. These sentimental, exciting, tragic, or cruel real-life stories added up to show business glamour and heart throb, and the public could never get enough of them.

Of course, Broadway's most tuneful melody was that of Mayor James J. Walker and his deep love for dark-haired Betty Compton of the better musicals. Hizzoner was widely saluted as the gayest man in American public life, his wisecracks as famous as his wasp-waisted suits and debonair sharp-brim hats. Jimmy's love of night life was such that he often stayed up through the small hours, to begin his City Hall days at 5:00 P.M. As a result he was fondly known as the Late Mayor or the Night Mayor of New York. Political cronies protested this playboy image, but he cut them off with the words "It's Jim Walker's life I'm living."

The dapper, flip mayor had been married for twenty years, most of them lackadaisically. He also had his pick of Broadway beauties and at one point dallied with a showgirl. But usually his path was the straight moral line, in part because he was chary of love. Seemingly the most lighthearted of men, the mayor had an unlikely streak of masochism that made him prefer girls who gave him a hard time. Miss Betty Compton was well equipped for this.

Born on the Isle of Wight, raised in Canada, Betty had studied dancing and singing until victory in a beauty contest propelled her into the musical theatre. On Broadway, she had class with a capital C. Her first appearance was in the *Follies*, where Will Rogers used her as a foil. Betty never played star roles but proved a delightful second lead who danced, sang, and quipped in top shows like *Oh, Kay*, *Hold Everything*, and *Fifty Million Frenchmen*. Walker met her on the opening night of *Oh, Kay*, when he went backstage to compliment the cast. It was love at first sight for a man who at forty-six was twice her age.

One critic saw Betty Compton as frisky, but the lovely Dutch-bobbed girl was actually a bed of neuroses. Quick-tempered and insecure, she was terrified of being alone and so fearful of old age that she vowed

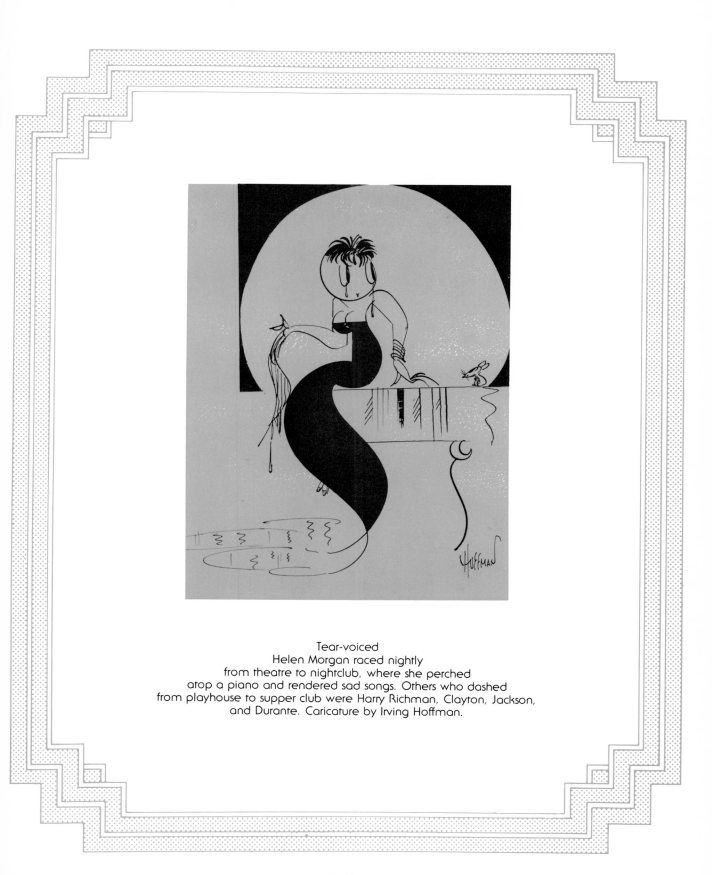

Tear-voiced
Helen Morgan raced nightly
from theatre to nightclub, where she perched
atop a piano and rendered sad songs. Others who dashed
from playhouse to supper club were Harry Richman, Clayton, Jackson,
and Durante. Caricature by Irving Hoffman.

to die by forty. An early marriage, ending in divorce, had not improved her psyche. Still, one part of her was a sensible female person who wanted a home and children. She also knew a love affair, or marriage, with a man in public life would bring problems.

It took time for Jimmy Walker, a fellow with two songs about him in the *1927 Follies*, to win the reluctant heart of Betty Compton. First he left his wife, taking up residence in a smart hotel. Then he romanced Betty through **Oh, Kay** and hovered over rehearsals of **Hold Everything**.

However, Betty did relish nightclubbing with the mayor, though Walker, who looked like a song-and-dance man, hated dancing. He urged members of his entourage to Charleston with frisky Betty but flipped with jealousy if she danced with anyone outside the group. After one public spat a contrite mayor amazingly took her in his arms and fox-trotted to the tune of "To Know You Is to Love You," from **Hold Everything**. With this, the love bug bit her. "There was nothing urbane or sophisticated about him then," she later recalled. "He seemed as wistful as a college boy at a junior prom."

With Betty in love with him, the mayor more than ever desired a place to be alone together. He got it by persuading rich friends to join him in renovating an old restaurant in the middle of Central Park, calling it the Central Park Casino. This would not be a restricted restaurant but an exclusive one where, because of price and atmosphere, only those compatible with the mayor would appear. "The Casino will be *our* place," he told Betty.

The two assisted Joseph Urban of **Follies** fame in spending $140,000 on a decor that embraced rhythm, line, and sensuous color. Kitchens cost another $100,000, and a fountain and stone terrace added more. Walker himself insisted that $22,000 be spent to knock down an interior wall so the view would be better from his favorite table. Leo Reisman's Orchestra played in the Pavillion Room, with Emil Coleman setting the mood in the Black and Gold. Elsewhere two young men tinkled soft pianos. One was Eddy Duchin, the other Nat Brandwynne; when temperamental Leo Reisman quit, Duchin took over his band.

Yet Jimmy and Betty had problems. She nagged him to quit politics and waxed furious over the time he spent as a public figure. As her temper got shorter, demands rose. At one point she made him miserable (the slight fellow actually lost weight when unhappy) by eloping with a younger man but immediately had the union dissolved.

Walker's political star was waning, in no small part because of gossip and the time he lavished on her. He wanted a divorce, but an ingrained Catholicism told him a first wife was forever. No mention of this love affair had been printed in newspapers, largely because everyone was so fond of Jimmy. But by 1929 the whole country seemed to know of it. Unaware of the internecine warfare between the two principals, the public saw in Jimmy Walker, black-haired Betty, and their Central Park Casino the joys of illicit Broadway love...

Behold the bridegroom!
Al Jolson already looked frazzled on his honeymoon
with younger Ruby Keeler.

The romance of Al Jolson and Ruby Keeler started as an item in Walter Winchell's column and advanced to big, black headlines.

It too began with love—or interest—at first sight. One night at Texas Guinan's nightclub Jolson saw Ruby, then a fourteen- or fifteen-year-old hoofer. "Who's the little kid?" he asked Texas, who told him to switch his eyes elsewhere. "She's Johnny Costello's girl," Tex explained. In those raucous days it was customary for the toughest gangsters to protect the youngest nightclub kids on a nobody-touches-her-not-even-me basis. Such, the street understood, was the relationship between Ruby and hoodlum Costello.

Jolson's career zoomed higher, while Ruby's merely rose. Her clear, staccato taps could easily be heard over the din of a supper club or, as she moved into musicals, in the top rows of a balcony. In 1927 the hard-working girl took a first vacation by going to California on a train bearing Fannie Brice. Jolson went to Pasadena to welcome Fannie and spotted Ruby. Again he was smitten, and this time no one told him to lay off. He found her a job in a local night spot and began ardent wooing.

Returning to New York for the opening of his second film, **The Singin' Fool**, Jolson was summoned by Johnny Costello, who demanded to know his intentions toward nineteen-year-old Ruby. The star gulped and said marriage. The wedding took place after the premiere, and Ruby got a glimpse of the future as he took two male pals along on their European honeymoon. It wasn't that Jolie didn't love the girl, but guys were so much easier to talk to.

The story of the young dancer and the great singing star made headlines everywhere; it was just like the plot of a musical comedy or early talkie. Jolson wanted her by his side while making his third film, **Say It with Songs**, and the idea momentarily appealed to a girl who had so far tap-danced her way through life.

Al Jolson's young bride would be an embellishment to any show, and Flo Ziegfeld, casting **Whoopee**, shortly sent out feelers. Already restless as a homebody, Ruby accepted, but Al's telephoned importunings made her leave the show during tryouts. Still unhappy doing nothing, she again listened to Ziegfeld and agreed to play the lead in **Show Girl**. To make an immortal Broadway story, Jolson rose up from an aisle seat on the opening and other nights to sing Gershwin's "Liza" as she danced it onstage.

Jolson's excuse was that Ruby felt nervous and needed his support. Ruby has denied the nerves and—on her heart-warming return for the 1970s' **No, No, Nanette**—stated that Jolson never sang from his seat, though contemporary evidence says he did. Jimmy Durante, who was supposed to rasp "Liza" from the background as Ruby tapped, recalls that he had just opened his mouth to sing on opening night when Jolson's throbbing baritone cut through the ozone. Jimmy never got the chance again.

This marriage set a pattern for contemporary youth-age matings of show business. After quitting **Show Girl** because of appendicitis, Ruby tried housewifery once more. Meanwhile, the Jolson magic was fading. **The Singin' Fool** had been a greater money-maker than **The Jazz Singer**, but at a sneak preview of **Say It with Songs**, Jack Warner declared, "We'll have to make a lot of improvements on this one." "It'll clean up when it hits Broadway," the euphoric Jolson assured him. "You're just like all those acting hams," Warner snapped back. Jolson took this as a personal insult and began fighting with his bosses, who put him in an almost songless **Hallelujah, I'm a Bum**. Al never could act and the result was dismal.

Meanwhile, Ruby had been talked into appearing in the movie **42nd Street**. As his career slipped, hers soared.

News stories rather than headlines greeted the wedding of Frank Fay to Barbara Stanwyck, then appearing opposite Hal Skelly in **Burlesque**. But to Broadway this was a lullaby more redolent of show business than the exciting Jolson–Keeler nuptials. Here you found the classic story of the cute little dancer madly in love with the arrogant star. To heighten it, the love affair uncannily paralleled the plot of **Burlesque**. Frank Fay had grown up in vaudeville, developing an ego second only to that of Al Jolson. He was never kidding when referring to himself as The Great Fay or The King of Broadway. "There's a refreshing lack of modesty about the guy," a wit cracked. After discoursing at length about his personality to a group of friends, Fay once said, "Well, let's change the subject. How did you like my act?" That story has been attributed to many actors but (says theatre authority Maurice Zolotow) the fellow who fondly called himself "Faysie" said it first—and meant it.

There was reason for Fay's conceit, since his rapier wit stood unmatched along the Main Stem. No one ever verbally topped Frank Fay, who tirelessly sharpened his skills in vaudeville, revues, and nightclubs. He was the first master of ceremonies at the Palace and maybe anywhere. At the Palace he introduced and interrupted acts, luring comics onstage for word battles they invariably lost. Once he so infuriated Robert Woolsey that Woolsey slapped his face. Fay was unfazed. "That's what you get for associating with low comedians," he confided to the audience.

Onstage Fay was a figure of total poise and suavity. Handsome in an Irish manner, with reddish hair and very white skin, he liked to stand alone on a bare stage and ramble on cleverly about his favorite subject—Faysie. Once his agent berated him for a misdeed. "You are scolding the man I love," Fay said gently.

Elegant and haughty before audiences, Fay offstage was a drinker, brawler, and wencher. It was part of his image to have a pretty, worshipful chorus kid as part of his life, to be neglected, maybe abused, and intermittently cherished. Young Barbara Stanwyck, a hoofer at Texas Guinan's and other nightclubs, had elected to play this role in Faysie's life, adoring him no matter how he treated her. Fay

Frank Fay, Bad Boy of Broadway, condescendingly wed Barbara Stanwyck
after the adoring young nightclub hoofer
became a top dramatic actress.

Barbara Stanwyck
hit the heights with veteran
Hal Skelly in **Burlesque**, a play with a story line
oddly like her real-life romance with Frank Fay.

cocked an eyebrow in slight surprise when Williard Mack picked Barbara out of a nightclub line to put her in **The Noose**. The eyebrow lifted higher when his ever-loving was cast in **Burlesque** and higher still when she scored a resounding hit.

"She was a dame/In love with a guy," ran the theme song of the movie version of **Burlesque**. This play in which a cute girl adored Skid, an irresponsible comic, had so many overtones of Faysie and Barbara that it might have been borrowed from life. There was no really happy ending in **Burlesque**, even though Skid turned up after a bender to salvage the opening night of his show. But Faysie and his girl played it otherwise. On tour in the Middle West, Fay apparently felt lonesome. Barbara had risen in his esteem by becoming a toast of Broadway, and as she lovingly phoned him in St. Louis, he said, "C'mon out and get married." She did.

Few recall it today, but Frank Fay was one of the first stars of talking pictures, crooning and emoting in **Under the Texas Moon**, in which this child of Broadway played a caballero. But he never made a good picture thereafter. As a wife, Barbara was as restless as Ruby Keeler. One day Fay used his glib gifts to persuade Columbia Pictures to give his wife a movie role. He may have regretted it, for as her career shot up, his sank.

Mellower was the wooing of Helen Hayes and Charles MacArthur, a charmer who was once the Golden Boy of Chicago journalism.

Early in the decade Marc Connelly took young Helen Hayes to an afternoon gathering at Neysa McMein's studio. An actress since childhood, Helen had been overprotected by a stage mother. She felt uneasy among the celebrated wits of the Algonquin Round Table, especially as one of them had just called her performances "fallen archness." Noting her discomfiture, MacArthur elaborately passed her a bowl of peanuts and quipped, "I wish they were emeralds."

Right there, Helen Hayes fell in love. She assured herself that MacArthur detected something special in her. "He saw the woman lurking in the girl," she has said. Could be—but it took a long time for him to prove it. She continued to adore him, but not until MacArthur saw her in her skimpy last-act costume of **Caesar and Cleopatra** did he show interest.

Then he began courting, though the wits of the Algonquin considered her too drab for him—"a case of miscasting," George S. Kaufman said. Her mother also opposed the match, ending tirades with "and he **drinks**!" As for MacArthur, he promised, "I may never be able to give you contentment, but you'll never be bored."

Miss Hayes saw flaws in him but did not care. The two married and produced the child who became the Act-of-God baby. From then on they pursued their careers as Miss Hayes appeared on Broadway (making an occasional movie) and, her husband, with partner Ben Hecht, became a leading Hollywood screenwriter. In a moment of prosperity he dumped a parcel of emeralds in her lap and said, "I wish they were peanuts."

Such was Love, Broadway Style, as the decade ended. It is hardly surprising that stormy weather lay ahead for each of these unions. Jimmy Walker and his Betty finally married and seemed reasonably happy while living abroad, where Walker fled after political disgrace. Returning, they found that New York still loved Jimmy. As he ventured back into public life, she turned brooding and resentful. After a divorce, she married again—and Walker moved in with the newlyweds! Betty Compton, who onstage had class with a capital C, died at age forty, just as she always predicted.

Al Jolson and Ruby Keeler divorced in 1937, when the careers of both appeared over. However, Jolson sprang back to life with World War II and rediscovered his admiring audience in the Army and Navy. No entertainer gave more of himself than Jolie as he sang before troops at home and overseas. After the war Hollywood made two highly successful films based on his singing career. He set out after the troops in the Korean War, and it killed him. Following the death of her second, non-theatre husband, Miss Keeler triumphantly returned to Broadway in the 1971 revival of *No, No, Nanette*.

The marriage of the Frank Fays followed the accepted Hollywood pattern, with Barbara trying to rally a morose husband whose career had vanished. Similarities to *Burlesque* increased as she financed him in a revue and he failed to turn up for the opening night. They were divorced in 1935. Faysie, of course, came back to Broadway in the 1940s to make the hit of his life in *Harvey*.

Only the Hayes–MacArthur match endured, because Miss Hayes had determined it must. More self-destructive than otherwise, Charles MacArthur in many ways proved a problem husband. But the union lasted until his death.

SHORT TAKE—PULITZER PRIZES

1920—*Beyond the Horizon*, by Eugene O'Neill
1921—*Miss Lulu Bett*, by Zona Gale
1922—*Anna Christie*, by Eugene O'Neill
1923—*Icebound*, by Owen Davis
1924—*Hell Bent fer Heaven*, by Hatcher Hughes
1925—*They Knew What They Wanted*, by Sidney Howard
1926—*Craig's Wife*, by George Kelly
1927—*In Abraham's Bosom*, by Paul Green
1928—*Strange Interlude*, by Eugene O'Neill
1929—*Street Scene*, by Elmer Rice

Eugene O'Neill's outsize **Strange Interlude** came first on Burns Mantle's list of the year's best plays. Here Lynn Fontanne won raves for her performance as Nina Leeds, the neurotic girl-into-woman who juggled three men. Close behind in this critic's annual selections was another Guild production, **Wings over Europe**, by Robert Nichols and Maurice Browne, the latter also father of the little-theatre movement in America. A prophetic drama, it told of a young scientist (Alexander Kirkland) who discovered the secret of the atom and expected it to be used for the betterment of mankind. Of course, top-echelon diplomacy and intrigue stood in his way. Action took place in the Prime Minister's residence at 10 Downing Street.

The Front Page, that rousing Hecht–MacArthur play about wild newspaper doings in Chicago, continued the Mantle choices. Lee Tracy, Osgood Perkins, George Barbier, Dorothy Stickney, Allen Jenkins, and Joseph Spurin-Calleia were in the Jed Harris production, directed by George S. Kaufman. Censorship forces, ever on the alert, rose to protest its profanity, exemplified by the famed curtain line, "The son of a bitch stole my watch!" But Jed Harris stood firm, and an unlaundered **The Front Page** was a top hit of the Twenties.

Holiday, by Philip Barry, was on the high-comedy level of the playwright's **Paris Bound**. Written to suit the astringent talents of the young socialite Hope Williams, who had a minor part in the first play, this told of a young man about to marry into a Rockefeller-type family who found he had picked the wrong sister. Naturally, the right one was Miss Williams.

Sophie Treadwell's impressionistic **Machinal**, based on the sordid Snyder–Gray murder case, featured Zita Johann as the young wife bored enough to slay her husband. **Machinal** remains historic because a young Clark Gable played her lover.

The Mantle selections ended with Martinez Sierra's **Kingdom of God**, with Ethel Barrymore as the daughter of a Spanish duke who went into a nunnery and helped the poor; and **Little Accident**, wherein an illegitimate child was rendered legitimate, by Floyd Dell and Thomas Mitchell, with Mr. Mitchell and Katherine Alexander heading the cast.

It was a good year for revivals, though all did not run as long as hoped. George Arliss played **Shylock** in the Winthrop Ames production of **The Merchant of Venice**, with Peggy Wood as Portia; **Merry Wives of Windsor** boasted Otis Skinner, Mrs. Fiske, Will Geer, Henrietta Crosman, and Boyd Zook; **She Stoops to Conquer**, with Glenn Hunter and Mrs. Leslie Carter, was a doleful failure; at the Civic Repertory, Eva Le Gallienne revived **Peter Pan** and **The Cherry Orchard**, the latter with a superb performance by Alla Nazimova; Blanche Yurka and Linda Watkins appeared in **The Wild Duck**; Walter Hampden returned with

Clark Gable won minor attention in his Broadway debut opposite
Zita Johann in **Machinal**, the Sophie Treadwell drama
based on the Snyder–Gray murder case.

Richard Bennett,
still one of most popular
actors of the day, introduced his youngest daughter
Joan in *Jarnegan*, which dealt with dissolute Hollywood.

his familiar **Caponsacchi**; Mr. and Mrs. Charles Coburn revived **The Yellow Jacket**, a Chinese fantasy, and squeezed sixty-nine performances out of it.

The Theatre Guild, approaching its tenth anniversary, had another hyperactive year. In addition to **Strange Interlude** and **Wings over Europe**, it presented **Volpone**, Stefan Zweig's adaptation of Ben Jonson's sardonic farce, with Margalo Gillmore, Albert Van Dekker, Dudley Digges, Ernest Cossart, and Morris Carnovsky; Shaw's **Major Barbara**, with Winifred Lenihan, Gale Sondergaard, Helen Westley, and Eliot Cabot; **Dynamo**, the third O'Neill effort of the year and a failure, though it displayed the beauty and skills of Claudette Colbert; and Sil-Vara's **Caprice**, with the Lunts, Lily Cahill, and Douglass Montgomery, about a man who brought his son into his life, thus allowing his mistress (Miss Fontanne) to seduce the youth. Though **Caprice** sounds like a sexy play, no complaints were heard about it. Instead the Lunts were complimented for the way they "ping-ponged scintillant sentences."

Katharine Cornell had a rewarding run as Countess Olenska in Margaret Ayer Barnes' adaptation of Edith Wharton's **Age of Innocence**, produced by Gilbert Miller, directed by Guthrie McClintic, with Rollo Peters, Stanley Gilkey, and Franchot Tone; Somerset Maugham's **Our Betters**, starring Ina Claire, with Madge Evans, Constance Collier, Hugh Sinclair, and Gordon MacRae, told of an American girl, disgusted with the decadence of British society, who returned to a Yankee love; Robert E. Sherwood's **The Queen's Husband**, with Roland Young and Gladys Henson, dealt lightly with the henpecked king of a mythical island kingdom; **The Bachelor Father** (not to be confused with **Little Accident**), by Edward Childs Carpenter and a Belasco hit, had June Walker, Geoffrey Kerr, and C. Aubrey Smith as an Englishman who decided belatedly to aid his grown-up bastards.

Jarnegan, a raw look at Hollywood, had a death by abortion as crux and boasted Richard Bennett supported by youngest daughter Joan, Wynne Gibson, Beatrice Kay, and Dennie Moore; **Mirrors**, by Milton Herbert Gropper, dealt with flaming youth and blind necking parties, using the talents of Sylvia Sidney, Raymond Guion, and Albert Hackett; John Gielgud came to these shores to play briefly in Gilbert Miller's production of **The Patriot**; **Salvation**, by Sidney Howard and Charles MacArthur, was a failure concerned with a female evangelist who might have been Aimee Semple MacPherson; Patrick Kearney's adaptation of Sinclair Lewis' **Elmer Gantry** did no better; **Gentlemen of the Press**, by theatre columnist Ward Morehouse, with John Cromwell, Helen Flint, Hugh O'Connell, and Millard Mitchell, might have been a hit had it opened before **The Front Page**; Brian Donlevy emoted in **Ringside**, which George Abbott co-authored and directed, along with Suzanne Caubaye, once sensuous Nubi of **The Squall**; ex-heavyweight champion Jack Dempsey and movie-actress wife Estelle Taylor brought realism to **The Big Fight**, by Milton Herbert Gropper and Max Marcin; Ring Lardner's ***Elmer the Great***, produced by George M. Cohan, about a bonehead baseball player in the Three-I League, had Walter Huston, Nan Sunderland, and Katherine Francis, later Kay.

In addition to ***Dynamo***, Claudette Colbert appeared in ***Fast Life***, with Chester Morris and Crane Wilbur, and ***Tin Pan Alley***, with Norman Foster; Robert Montgomery was visible in ***Possession***, by Edgar Selwyn, with Edna Hibbard and Walter Connolly; Dorothy Gish and James Rennie brightened ***Young Love***, by Samson Raphaelson, about trial marriage; Edward G. Robinson performed in ***Man with Red Hair***, adapted from the Hugh Walpole novel by Benn W. Levy; Katharine Hepburn began in ***These Days***, an Arthur Hopkins production, with Mildred McCoy in the lead; Lionel Stander could be spotted in ***The Final Balance*** at the downtown Provincetown.

Flo Ziegfeld offered Marilyn Miller in ***Rosalie***, a blockbuster with book by William Anthony McGuire and Guy Bolton, lyrics by P. G. Wodehouse, music by George Gershwin and Sigmund Romberg. Its complex plot told of Rosalie, princess of Romanza, falling in love with a cadet at a Joseph Urbanized West Point. After a meeting there, he flew the Atlantic Lindbergh-style to woo her. Also involved were Jack Donahue, Frank Morgan, and gladsome Gladys Glad.

Later in the year Ziegfeld gave an appreciative public Eddie Cantor in ***Whoopee***, another musical-comedy sensation; also taking bows here were Ruth Etting, Ethel Shutta, Frances Upton, and Tamara Geva.

Joe Cook, of the wide grin, ingenious stunts, and diversified talents, came along in ***Rain or Shine***, with Dave Chasen, Tom Howard, and the plot of a girl who inherited a circus. The first Negro smash hit on Broadway was Lew Leslie's ***Blackbirds of 1928***, with the great Bill Robinson and Adelaide Hall heading the cast. Mrs. Lew Leslie, who pawned $40,000 in jewels to allow this bright revue to open, got her money back. One ***Blackbirds*** song was "I Can't Give You Anything But Love, Baby," by Jimmy McHugh and Dorothy Fields; this show stopper had been tossed out of ***Delmar's Revels***.

Advertisements for the 1928 ***Vanities*** read **W. C. FIELDS IN EARL CARROLL'S VANITIES**— so anxious was the producer to snare the comedian that he promised topmost billing in a revue that also featured Joe Frisco, Lillian Roth, Dorothy Knapp, Beryl Halley, and Jean Tennyson. C. B. Dillingham went to similar lengths to get Will Rogers for his ***Three Cheers***. After Fred Stone got hurt in a pre-opening accident, Dillingham offered Rogers a signed blank check at the end of each week; the star could fill in his own salary. On that basis, ***Three Cheers*** ran 210 performances. Also included were Dorothy Stone, Patsy Kelly, Andrew Tombes, and Rags Raglund.

Paris, with fetching Irene Bordoni, was naughty Parisian stuff with the first Cole Porter songs to set Broadway atingle; ***Hold Everything***, satire on the fight game, was Bert Lahr's big break, along with Victor Moore, Betty Compton, Ona Munson, Jack Whiting, and Phil Sheridan;

Lenore Ulric continued to shock
audiences in plays offered by David Belasco. She peeled down daringly
in the expensive but unsuccessful *Mima*.

Animal Crackers, by George S. Kaufman and Morrie Ryskind, brought added luster to the Marx Brothers, who depicted Captain Spalding, Emanuel Ravelli, and the Professor (Harpo), all chasing stately Margaret Dumont.

Long-legged Eleanor Powell danced in short-lived ***The Optimists***; Arthur Treacher could be found in ***The Madcap***, along with Mitzi Hajos and Sydney Greenstreet; Jeanette MacDonald and Eric Blore were seen in ***Angela***; Fats Waller was part of an onstage orchestra in Miller and Lyles' ***Keep Shufflin'***; Ben Bernie talked and played the catchy "Crazy Rhythm" in ***Here's Howe***; Rodgers and Hart provided songs for ***Present Arms***, with Charles King, Busby Berkeley, and Flora La Breton; Bob Hope appeared in ***Ups-a-Daisy***, with Luella Gear and Marie Saxon; Helen Kane chirped "I Wanna Be Loved by You" in ***Good Boy***, dances by Busby Berkeley; Fred Waring and Lucy Monroe were visible in ***Hello Yourself***; ***Rainbow***, a romantic musical by Laurence Stallings and Oscar Hammerstein II, had Brian Donlevy, Harland Dixon, and Libby Holman—it attained fame because on the opening night Fanny the Mule was indiscreet onstage.

"TO THE THEATRE"

With the dawn of the final year of the decade it appeared that Broadway's great worries were talking pictures and radio. Few on the Street of Streets bothered to heed the prophets of doom who maintained the stock market had overextended itself, placing the nation in danger of devastating financial collapse.

Yet Broadway's woes were real enough. First talkies, now radio! In a sense, the latter was worse, since families could sit in the comfort of homes and be regaled with entertainment. The *Ziegfeld Follies* of 1922 had included a condescending song titled "Let's Listen to Some Radio," but now the airwaves were offering what the entertainment industry had always feared—fun for free.

Those on the production side of the theatre began feeling like General Custer as the Indians closed in. One evening the distinguished producer Winthrop Ames took his staff to see the talking picture *Bulldog Drummond*, starring Ronald Colman, who ten years before had been a Broadway job hunter.

Afterward, Ames led a mournful procession to the nearest speakeasy. There he ordered a round of drinks and intoned, "Gentlemen, I'm afraid what we've seen tonight is the end. This is what they want. I fear the theatre, as you and I know it, is doomed. It will become small and highly specialized. Gentlemen—"he raised his glass—"*to the theatre!*"

Deeply ironic was the fact that Broadway expatriate John Barrymore had been the one who brought respectability to talking films. Still high on the roster of Warner Brothers stars, the Hamlet of 1922 had allowed himself to be cast in their massive talking-dancing-singing revue *The Show of Shows*, with seventy-five name players surrounded by a thousand—count 'em—chorus girls.

Show of Shows typified the chaos and tastelessness of the early sound era in Hollywood. But in one scene Barrymore stood alone before the cameras to deliver a soliloquy from *Richard III*. He was magnificent, bringing instant maturity to the medium and revealing, in a few crackling words, its vast potential. From then on, the world took talkies seriously.

At first there was jubilation in Broadway producing ranks, for in its desperate need of dramatic material with dialogue Hollywood bought old stage properties with a wild hand. One purchase was the Harris–Abbott–Dunning *Broadway*. In true Hollywood fashion the Paradise nightclub grew so elegant and enormous that the impact of the play got lost. Hollywood also depended heavily on the Main Stem as background in making musicals like *Broadway Melody*, *Glorifying the American Girl*, and *42nd Street*.

Broadway had
developed a new cast of playwrights
since the beginning of the decade. Of those caricatured
in *Theatre Magazine* by Aline Fruhauf, only Rachel Crothers was active
in 1920. Eugene O'Neill, still the titan,
was about to greet the 1930s with
Mourning Becomes Electra.

Maxwell Anderson achieved theatric fame as co-author of WHAT PRICE GLORY *and later cemented that fame with* SATURDAY'S CHILDREN. *He was not so fortunate with his* GODS OF THE LIGHTNING. *He owns up to Atlantic, Pa., as his birthplace. He snared a B. A. at the North Dakota University and walked off with the pelt of an M. A. at Stanford, California.*

Floyd Dell, modernist novelist, in association with Thomas Mitchell, is responsible for that highly successful American comedy LITTLE ACCIDENT. *This play was preceded by his novels "An Unmarried Father," "This Mad Ideal" and a volume of essays.*

Rachel Crothers, whose breezy little comedy LET US BE GAY, *sponsored by John Golden, is one of the season's outstanding successes, wrote those other well-known plays* MOTHER CAREY'S CHICKENS, ONCE UPON A TIME, EXPRESSING WILLIE *and* OLD LADY 31. *She directs the production of her plays. She was born in Bloomington, Ill., and is not averse to saying so.*

Samuel Nathaniel Behrman is the perpetrator of SERENA BLANDISH, *the "fabulous comedy" based on the novel of the same name "By A Lady of Quality." He is also responsible, with Kenyon Nicholson, for that smart piece of playwriting known as* THE SECOND MAN. *He comes from Worcester, Mass. Next season The Theatre Guild will produce his* METEOR.

HOLIDAY is just another big hit turned out by the nimble typewriter of Philip Barry. His YOU AND I *won the Harvard Prize in 1922. His* PARIS BOUND *was produced in 1927 and ran and ran. He achieved an A. B. at Yale and then rounded out his education at Harvard. Rochester boasts him as a native son.*

Elmer Rice, whose dramatic realism found full expression in STREET SCENE, *is the only playwright in this galaxy native to New York City. He is one of the five alleged living New Yorkers born on Manhattan Island and is shameless in announcing the fact. He wrote* CLOSE HARMONY, THE ADDING MACHINE, ON TRIAL, FOR THE DEFENSE, SUBWAY, *and several other more or less successful plays.*

Broadwayites entrained for Hollywood in droves. Here George White
headed a group aboard the Twentieth Century Limited. Among
them were designer Charles LeMaire, composer Ray
Henderson, Cliff "Ukulele Ike" Edwards,
lyricist Irving Caesar. White never clicked
in Hollywood, LeMaire and Ukulele Ike did. Irving Caesar
quickly returned home to become one of Broadway's busiest figures.

But while profitably selling plays to Hollywood, producers had to note that the commercial theatre was slowing down, with reduced prices, quicker closings, and dark theatres. After the stock market collapsed in late October 1929, trend became awful reality.

Only peak entertainers seemed happy as Hollywood made inroads on the Broadway preserve. Without visible tears of sorrow, Fannie Brice went west to make *My Man*, Eddie Cantor agreed to do *Whoopee*, and Marilyn Miller *Sally*, for which she earned a neat $100,000. Eddie Cantor, currently the most popular comedian of the time, made the best of each world. After completing *Whoopee*, he turned to radio to make $100 a minute on the Eveready Hour. Then the stock market, the great leveler, wiped him out.

It was easy to blame talkies and radio for the miseries of the theatre. But it also seemed that the theatre had harmed itself—or that the era had done something injurious. To some the legitimate drama in 1929 resembled an overripe fruit. Even before the talkies became a major threat, the legit seemed to have paused in its progress, with Burns Mantle using the word "dismal" to describe conditions and writing:

> The theatre season of 1928-9 will probably be remembered, should the occasion arise to remember it at all, as one that started promisingly and faded hopelessly. You can count the outstanding successes on the fingers of two hands, and the collapse of the native drama at the close of the season left theatre gates open for the entrance of imported London hits.

SHORT TAKE

The 1929 hit show *June Moon*, by Ring Lardner and George S. Kaufman, satirized Tin Pan Alley and its popular songs. It provided a few samples supposed to be funny but really not far different from the real thing. The best of them, lyrics by Lardner, was sung by a girl to the man who made her an unwed mother:

> Should a father's carnal sins
> Blight the life of Babykins?
> All I ask is give our child a name
>   (*Not just a first name*).
>
> I don't ask to share your life
> Live with you as man and wife;
> All I ask is give our child a name
>   (*Not just a first name*).

Pundits peering back over the Twenties salute a vigorous era when the theatre, no less than the country, freed itself of old-fashioned constrictions to present plays of ideas as well as cleverness. It was an era when playwrights had much to say, and actors who spoke their lines did so naturally. Also when directors like Philip Moeller and Guthrie McClintic worked to bring the drama closer to reality, and scenic designers like Robert Edmond Jones and Norman Bel Geddes labored to heighten that reality.

Certainly much trash (and more heartbreak) was to be found among the 2,000-plus offerings of the Twenties, but there had also been important American dramas, while the public had been exposed to fine presentations of Shaw, Ibsen, Chekhov, Pirandello, Sierra, and Molnar. Taken all in all—especially in comparison with the past—this had been an exciting time, replete with dramatic life, one which Louis Schaeffer, biographer of O'Neill, calls

> . . . the most exciting [theatrical] decade and one that for sheer vitality has never yet been equaled, much less surpassed. Not the calendar, but **Beyond the Horizon** ushered in that period. Ahead lay **What Price Glory?**, **They Knew What They Wanted**, **Craig's Wife**, **The Silver Cord**, **In Abraham's Bosom**, **Street Scene**, and **The Front Page**, the emergence in short of George Kelly and Sidney Howard, of Maxwell Anderson, S. N. Behrman, and Robert E. Sherwood. But always apart from them and in front of them, pursuing a solitary, unpredictable course, would be O'Neill. Now with tom-toms, now with masks, now with psychological use of "asides," he would set the pace as the most gifted of playwrights.

Yet by the end of the Twenties this marvelous progress—except for O'Neill and a few in other fields—seemed to be over. It was as if the theatre, like the stock market, had gone as far as possible in one direction.

In fact, it seemed that a malaise had settled over the once pulsing theatre. Indicative were the critical hosannahs over Preston Sturges' **Strictly Dishonorable**, a light comedy of 1929 that began in a speakeasy and wound up in a bedroom; its title derived from the fact that the dashing opera singer told the deep-South virgin his intentions toward her were strictly dishonorable. Aside from speakeasy atmosphere, bright lines, and smart acting by Tullio Carminati and Muriel Kirkland, there was little remarkable about this opus. Yet reviews treated it as a masterpiece. "It brought the critics new life," noted Burns Mantle.

Amid the malaise, old hands seemed to lose unerring skills. Jed Harris produced **Serena Blandish**, by S. N. Behrman, a moderate success, and abandoned **The Gaoler's Wench**, by Edwin Justus Mayer, which became a hit as **Children of Darkness**. Flo Ziegfeld, flushed with the triumphs of **Show Boat** and **Whoopee**, produced **Show Girl**, based on the Dixie Dugan stories of J. P. McEvoy, with Ruby Keeler and Clayton, Jackson, and Durante.

Times were changing.
Show Girl, an elaborate, fast-moving
Ziegfeld musical with Ruby Keeler (***above***), and Clayton, Jackson,
and Durante, failed to cause a box-office storm,
despite such excitements as the Gershwin song
"Liza."

Also disappointing was *Serena Blandish*, with Ruth Gordon and Britain's incomparable A. E. Matthews. Lovingly written by S. N. Behrman and produced by Jed Harris, it failed to jell.

Show Girl seemed to have everything in the best Ziegfeld tradition, but the public did not respond. "All dressed up and no place to go," a critic said, and for the first time in history tickets to a Ziegfeld show were available at cut-rates. Ziegfeld turned his genius to *Smiles*, with Marilyn Miller and Fred and Adele Astaire, which turned out to be a worse flop.

Barriers seemed to be crumbling as Earl Carroll offered *Fioretta*, with Fannie Brice and Leon Errol prominent in the cast. Broadway reeled as these two Ziegfeld stars went to work for the master's hated rival. Their presence was highlighted as the financial backers of *Fioretta* loudly sued Carroll for giving the leading role to Dorothy Knapp, his beautiful but not too talented sweetheart.

Even audiences seemed in the grip of the malaise. Apparently restless and seeking more exciting playgoing, people eagerly crossed the Hudson to Hoboken, where essayist Christopher Morley and scenic designer Cleon Throckmorton had combined to lease the old Rialto Theatre and present gaslight melodramas like *After Dark* and *The Black Crook*. Audiences joyously hissed the villain, sang the old songs, drank beer at intermissions, and forgot Broadway altogether.

Yet greatest evidence of the malaise showed in the manner Broadwayites shuffled off to Hollywood.

True, names like Clark Gable, James Cagney, and Bette Davis were still visible on Times Square playbills. But *Variety's* weekly "N.Y. to L.A." list had grown so long and varied that Moss Hart, sitting at home in Brooklyn, needed only to read it to get inspiration for the play *Once in a Lifetime*, telling of a family of vaudevillians who hastened to Hollywood to teach diction to silent stars.

This second California Gold Rush added a fresh dimension to Horace Greeley's "Go west, young man." Not only did musical stars like Cantor and Marilyn Miller participate, but dramatic players like Lionel Barrymore, Ruth Chatterton, and Basil Rathbone quit Broadway. Fredric March departed, as did Ina Claire, who astounded the world by marrying John Gilbert, the silent-screen lover whose high voice made him a number-one talking-picture fatality.

Songwriters took the trip, with Irving Berlin writing "Puttin' on the Ritz" for Harry Richman's first picture and De Sylva, Brown, and Henderson doing "If I Had a Talking Picture of You" and other melodies for *Sunny Side Up*. George Abbott went, and Lawrence Langner felt sorely tempted. The Guild's Rouben Mamoulian directed Helen Morgan in the distinctive *Applause*. P. G. Wodehouse and Guy Bolton found themselves on a transcontinental train, with the assignment of writing a film for W. C. Fields. Also aboard the rattler were Fields himself, Vincent Youmans, Rudolf Friml, and a dozen other theatre names. It was, Wodehouse thought, like one of the great race movements of the Middle Ages.

From all this comes the inescapable conclusion that Broadway had not treated its talents well, and there was truth in it. In every way the legitimate theatre was a gamble offering scant protection to its own. Producers, on whom so much depended, were far from infallible and often arrogant, untrustworthy, and unpleasant as well; the skills of playwrights were uncertain and the public fickle. Thus the theatre offered a precarious living to everyone involved, from Florenz Ziegfeld to George Spelvin, Jr. Any venture ran the risk of possible failure—or, as those involved were inclined to see it, the theatre was at the mercy of the critics. As Brooks Atkinson wrote at the time, "People who love the theatre repeatedly discover that their love is not returned."

By contrast, Hollywood not only seemed to offer larger salaries but greater security, plus a chance to be seen by millions rather than thousands. Said George Abbott, as he gave what appeared to be his last regards to Broadway, "Hollywood pays money for writing services, while the theatre pays royalties. You can be sure of making a certain amount of money, while in the theatre you are likely to starve to death, but always with the hope of making it up with a hit."

With such persuasions in mind, playwrights no less than actors, directors, and songwriters headed west. Abandoning a freedom that seemed vital to their craft, they labored from ten to five in prosaic offices. Actors also worked harder, rising at 5:00 A.M. to be on the set at 7:00. Some Broadway talents stayed, while others (like Abbott) came back. For Hollywood, despite its glittering promise, proved to have its own special brand of frustrations.

Soon the Gables, Bogarts, and Blondells were also there. According to Lee Strasberg, the theatre lost an entire generation of young actors because of the talkies.

Behind them, they left a Fabulous Invalid.

Some believe the irresistible
call of Hollywood robbed Broadway
of a generation of young talents. The soon-to-be-famous
movie actors pictured here were, in varying degrees, embarked on
theatre careers before joining the second
California Gold Rush.
Cary Grant, who on Broadway was Archie Leach (*above*)

Joan Blondell

James Cagney

Paul Muni, seen here in a scene from *Four Walls*, with Jeanne Greene

Bette Davis, who in 1928 appeared
at the Provincetown Playhouse in *The Earth Between*,
with Carl Ashburn

Humphrey Bogart

Fredric March

Spencer Tracy

Clark Gable

ROUNDUP

As the best of the year, Burns Mantle picked **Street Scene**, a panorama of tenement life, by Elmer Rice, produced by William A. Brady, directed by the author, and featuring Erin O'Brien-Moore, Leo Bulgakov, Horace Braham, and Beulah Bondi; **Let Us Be Gay**, Rachel Crothers' comedy about guests at a house party with a moral or two derived from their behavior, with Francine Larrimore and Warren William; **Gypsy**, by Maxwell Anderson, with Claiborne Foster and Louis Calhern, in which an anti-heroine tried to lead her own life and failed; **The Criminal Code**, by Martin Flavin, a grim prison play with Arthur Byron and Russell Hardie; **Strictly Dishonorable**, by Preston Sturges, with Tullio Carminati and Muriel Kirkland, a comedy that did for speakeasy life what **Broadway** had done for nightclubs; and **June Moon**, by Ring Lardner and George S. Kaufman, a satire on Tin Pan Alley, with Jean Dixon, Linda Watkins, Norman Foster, and Harry Rosenthal.

From the many imports of the year Mr. Mantle culled **Journey's End**, a superior war play by R. C. Sherriff, who had gone to World War I at age seventeen, with Leon Quartermain, Derek Williams, Colin Keith-Johnston, and Jack Hawkins; **Berkeley Square**, an into-the-past fantasy with Leslie Howard and Margalo Gillmore; **The First Mrs. Fraser**, a smart comedy by St. John Ervine; **Michael and Mary**, in which a pair grew older, by A. A. Milne; and **Death Takes a Holiday**, in which deaths around the world came to a sudden halt, from the Italian of Alberto Cassella, adapted by Walter Ferris.

Other plays favored during the year were John Drinkwater's **Bird in Hand**, amusing doings at the Bird in Hand Inn in Britain; Basil Sydney and Mary Ellis in **Meet the Prince**, with J. M. Kerrigan and Eric Blore; George M. Cohan in **Gambling**, wherein a gambler solved his daughter's murder; **The Channel Road**, a collaboration of Alexander Woollcott and George S. Kaufman, based on De Maupassant's "Boule de Suite," concerning a whore who mixed in rarefied company, with Anne Forrest and Edgar Stehli; Ethel Barrymore in **The Love Duel**, with Louis Calhern, Henry Stephenson, and Ferdinand Gottschalk, where two mature people fell in love; and **Kibitzer**, by Jo Swerling and Edward G. Robinson, who played the leading role of a newsstand dealer beloved by his neighborhood.

Also Walter Huston in **The Commodore Marries**, its plot loosely based on Smollett's **Peregrine Pickle**; **Rope's End**, a taut English melodrama in which two schoolboys murdered a third and dined off the chest hiding his body; Jane Cowl in **Jenny**, wherein an actress broke up a marriage that needed breaking; **It's a Wise Child**, another about illegitimacy that helped David Belasco recoup the $250,000 lost on an elaborate **Mima** the season before; and **See Naples and Die**, an Elmer Rice change-of-pace, with Claudette Colbert, Roger Pryor, and Pedro de Cordoba.

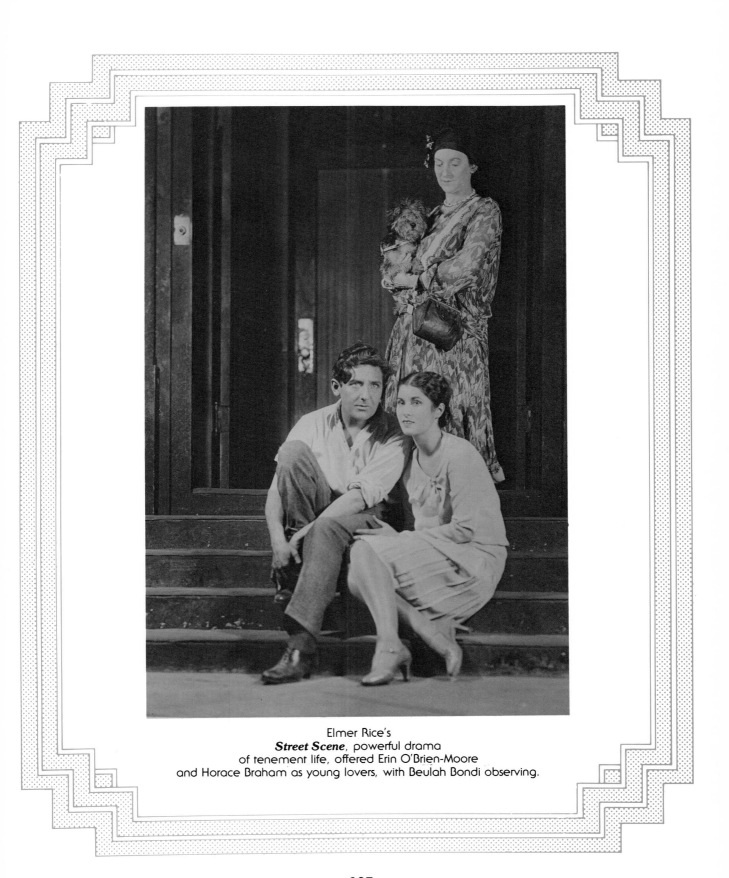

Elmer Rice's
Street Scene, powerful drama
of tenement life, offered Erin O'Brien-Moore
and Horace Braham as young lovers, with Beulah Bondi observing.

The melodramatic **Subway Express** brought tense excitement.

Cross Roads, by the prolific Martin Flavin, concerning a medical student whose girl would neither marry nor bed down, featuring Sylvia Sidney and Franchot Tone; *Broken Dishes*, another Flavin, with Bette Davis and Donald Meek, about a rebellious daughter; *Subway Express*, by Martha Madison and Eva Flint, directed by Chester Erskin, about murder on a subway train; *Houseparty*, by and with Roy Hargrave, in which a murder took place at Williams College; Smith and Dale in *Mendel, Inc.*, which appealed to the *Abie's Irish Rose* public; and *He Walked in Her Sleep*, not as funny as it sounded.

Old-timers returned, among them Otis Skinner in *A Hundred Years Old*; Minnie Maddern Fiske in *Ladies of the Jury*; and William Gillette in a revival of *Sherlock Holmes*. As for newcomers, Samuel Levene had a microscopic part in *Headquarters*, another murder mystery. Down on 14th Street Eva Le Gallienne had a fine season, with *The Cherry Orchard*, *Cradle Song*, *Would-Be Gentleman*, and *The Master Builder*. A lamentable failure was Freiburg's *Passion Play*, imported in its enormity by Morris Gest and presented at the vast Hippodrome. Mei Lan-Fang, China's greatest actor, gave his one-man show for forty nights, accounted a success.

Other plays in a season of sorrow rather than joy were the Jed Harris production of *Serena Blandish*, adapted by S. N. Behrman from Enid Bagnold's novel, with Ruth Gordon, Constance Collier, A. E. Matthews, and Julia Hoyt; *Harlem*, a play about uptown rent parties that caused a mild sensation because of locale and color; *Remote Control*, interesting because of the novelty of its radio-studio scene; and *Candlelight*, adapted from the French by P. G. Wodehouse, with Gertrude Lawrence, who as a ladies' maid impersonating her mistress, spoke the line "Shakespeare! My goodness, is that man still writing?"

Clark Gable played the lead in *Hawk Island*, which lasted twenty-four performances; Laurence Olivier made an initial American appearance in Frank Vosper's *Murder on the Second Floor*, another flop; Spencer Tracy was an aviator who made a poor marriage in *Conflict*, with Edward Arnold; Melvyn Douglas, in *Now-a-Days*, got himself involved in bootlegging and mayhem; Glenda Farrell appeared with Guido Nadzo in *Divided Honors*, about a gin marrage; Ralph Bellamy had a minor role in *Town Boy*, which ran three nights; James Cagney and Joan Blondell played second leads in *Maggie the Magnificent*, by George Kelly; and Raymond Guion (Gene Raymond) emoted opposite Peggy Allenby in *Young Sinners*, about a seventeen-year-old out to get her man.

The musical sphere also had ups and downs. Far up was *The Little Show*, with Clifton Webb, Fred Allen, Libby Holman, Romney Brent, and Portland Hoffa, score by Arthur Schwartz and Howard Dietz, sketches by George S. Kaufman, Fred Allen, and others. "Little but mighty," a critic called this spectacular blend of the sophisticated and hilarious. No other intimate revue of the year, or perhaps the decade, matched the *Little Show*.

While Broadway worried about Hollywood's talking pictures,
English imports took over the season of 1929.
Foremost was the gripping war play **Journey's End**. Sketches by George Shellhase.

The Little Show,
with Clifton Webb and Libby Holman
singing the sultry ''Moanin' Low,'' proved the outstanding revue of the
decade. Fittingly, it came at the era's end.
Fred Allen also clicked in it.

The future of W. C. Fields was cloudy at decade's end, though he was popular enough to see his name placed over that of the producer of *Earl Carroll's Vanities*. Would he stay east or go westward? The great man seemed unconcerned.

Flo Ziegfeld, as noted, laid an egg with **Show Girl**, featuring Ruby Keeler, Clayton, Jackson, and Durante, Eddie Foy, Jr., and Frank McHugh. Tops among musicals were **Follow Thru**, about golf, with Irene Delroy, Zelma O'Neal, and Eleanor Powell; **Spring Is Here**, book by Pulitzer Prize winner Owen Davis, score by Rodgers and Hart, with Glenn Hunter, Inez Courteny, Charles Ruggles, and Joyce Barbour; **Sons o' Guns**, with Jack Donahue and Lily Damita, about a rich fellow who found his valet to be his top sergeant in World War I.

Fifty Million Frenchmen, about a Parisienne named Looloo, had Genevieve Tobin, William Gaxton, Helen Broderick, Evelyn Hoey, and Betty Compton; **Boom-Boom**, music by Werner Janssen, had Jeanette MacDonald, Frank McIntyre, Archie Leach, Stanley Ridges, and the dance team Cortez and Peggy; **Heads Up**, score by Rodgers and Hart, had Ray Bolger, Victor Moore, Betty Starbuck, and Barbara Newberry; **A Wonderful Night** had Mary McCoy and Archie Leach; **Top Speed** had Harland Dixon, Irene Delroy, and Ginger Rogers; and **Polly**, an adaptation of Belasco's hit **Polly with a Past**, starred June Inverclyde and focused attention on Fred Allen, hurtling him into **The Little Show**.

In a class by themselves were **Sweet Adeline**, the Kern–Hammerstein follow-up to **Show Boat**, about Hoboken in the Gay Nineties, with Helen Morgan, Irene Franklin, and Charles Butterworth; and Noël Coward's **Bitter Sweet**, with Evelyn Laye in the lead. Vincent Youmans' ambitious **Great Day** was a failure, lasting only thirty-six performances; lyrics for this were by William Rose, not yet Billy. Gratifying (perhaps) was the unexpected success of eleven Victor Herbert operettas from previous decades offered by the Shuberts.

On the last night of the decade—December 31, 1929—four shows opened on Broadway. One proved a moderate success, two were flops, and one a happy hit. This was **Wake Up and Dream**, an English import with Cole Porter music, plus Jack Buchanan, Jessie Matthews, and Tilly Losch. One of its songs was Porter's "What Is This Thing Called Love?"

And so, on the wings of melancholy song, the Theatrical Twenties floated into the far different days of the Depression Thirties.

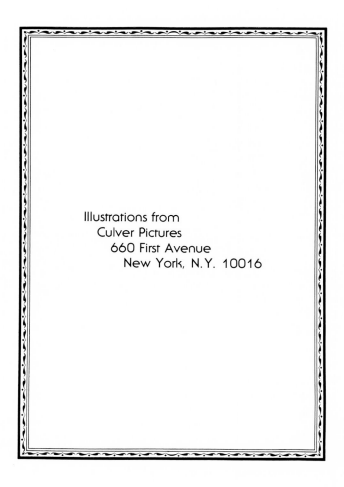

Illustrations from
Culver Pictures
660 First Avenue
New York, N.Y. 10016

BIBLIOGRAPHY

The author is grateful to the Broadwayites who talked to him during the preparation of this volume. Special thanks go to Marc Connelly and Irving Caesar for their time and reminiscences. The following books also yielded nuggets of information about the Theatrical Twenties:

Abbott, George. *Mister Abbott*. New York: Random House, 1963

Adams, Samuel Hopkins. *A. Woollcott*. New York: Reynal & Hitchcock, 1945

Allen, Fred. *Much Ado about Me*. Boston: Little, Brown, 1956

Alpert, Hollis. *The Barrymores*. New York: Dial Press, 1964

Astaire, Fred. *Steps in Time*. New York: Harper & Bros., 1959

Atkinson, Brooks. *Broadway*. New York: Macmillan, 1970

Barrymore, Ethel. *Memories*. London: Hulton Press, 1956

Behrman, S. N. *People in a Diary*. Boston: Little, Brown, 1972

Bishop, Jim. *The Mark Hellinger Story*. New York: Appleton-Century-Crofts, 1952

Blum, Daniel. *A Pictorial History of the American Theatre*. New York: Chilton Company, 1950

Brown, John Mason. *The World of Robert Sherwood*. New York: Harper & Row, 1962

Burke, Billie, with Cameron Shipp. *With a Feather on My Nose*. New York: Appleton-Century-Crofts, 1949

Connelly, Marc. *Voices Offstage*. New York: Holt, Rinehart and Winston, 1968

Coward, Noel. *Present Indicative*. New York: Doubleday Doran, 1937

Doherty, Ed. *Rain Girl, the Life of Jeanne Eagels*. Philadelphia: Macrae Smith, 1930

Dunn, Don. *The Making of No, No, Nanette*. Secaucus, New Jersey: Citadel Press, 1972

Ewen, David. *New Book of American Musical Theatre*. New York: Alfred A. Knopf, 1961

———— *New Book of Popular American Composers*. New York: Holt, Rinehart and Winston, 1970

Farnsworth, Marjorie. *Ziegfeld Follies*. New York: G. P. Putnam, 1956

Ferber, Edna. *A Peculiar Treasure*. New York: Doubleday, 1960

Fowler, Gene. *Beau James, the Life of Jimmy Walker*. New York: Viking Press, 1949

———— *Goodnight, Sweet Prince*. New York: Viking Press, 1944

Gaige, Crosby. *Footlights & Highlights*. New York: E. P. Dutton, 1948

Gordon, Ruth. *Myself among Others*. New York: Atheneum, 1971

Green, Abel, and Joe Laurie, Jr. *Show Biz*. New York: Henry Holt, 1951

Harriman, Margaret Case. *Vicious Circle*. New York: Rinehart & Co., 1954

Hart, Moss. *Act One*. New York: Random House, 1959

Hayes, Helen, and Sandford Dody. *On Reflection*. New York: M. Evans, 1968

Higham, Charles. *Ziegfeld*. Chicago: Henry Regnery, 1972

Howard, Leslie Ruth. *A Quite Remarkable Father*. New York: Harcourt Brace, 1959

Israel, Lee. *Miss Tallulah Bankhead*. New York: G. P. Putnam, 1972

Jablonski, Edward, and Lawrence Stewart. *The Gershwin Years*. New York: Doubleday, 1958

Katkov, Norman. *Fabulous Fanny*. New York: Alfred A. Knopf, 1953

Krutch, Joseph Wood. *American Drama Since 1918*. New York: Random House, 1939

Lahr, John. *Notes on a Cowardly Lion*. New York: Alfred A. Knopf, 1965

Langner, Lawrence. *Magic Curtain*. New York: E. P. Dutton, 1951

Lawrence, Gertrude. *A Star Danced*. New York: Doubleday Doran, 1945

McClintic, Guthrie. *Me and Kit*. Boston: Little, Brown, 1955

Maney, Richard. *Fanfare*. New York: Harper & Bros., 1957

Mantle, Burns. *Best Plays, 1920-30*. New York: Dodd Mead, 1921-1930

Morehouse, Ward. *Matinee Tomorrow*. New York: McGraw-Hill, 1949

Oppenheimer, George (ed.). *The Passionate Playgoer*. New York: Viking Press, 1958

Pollock, Channing. *Harvest of My Years*. Indianapolis: Bobbs-Merrill, 1943

Richman, Harry, and Richard Gehman. *A Hell of a Life*. New York: Duell Sloan & Pearce, 1966

Schaeffer, Louis. *O'Neill, Son and Playwright*. Boston: Little, Brown, 1968

Sieben, Pearl. *The Immortal Jolson*. New York: Frederick Fell, 1962

Smith, Cecil. *Musical Comedy in America*. New York: Theatre Arts Books, 1950

Stagg, Jerry. *The Brothers Shubert*. New York: Ballantine Books, 1968

Taylor, Robert L. *W. C. Fields*. New York: Doubleday & Co., 1945

Teichmann, Howard. *George S. Kaufman*. New York: Atheneum, 1972

Wodehouse, P. G., and Guy Bolton. *Bring On the Girls*. New York: Simon and Schuster, 1953

Wynn, Keenan, and James Brough. *Ed Wynn's Son*. New York: Doubleday & Co., 1959

Yurka, Blanche. *Bohemian Girl*. Athens, Ohio: Ohio University Press, 1970

Ziegfeld, Patricia. *The Ziegfelds' Girl*. Boston: Little, Brown, 1964

Zolotow, Maurice. *No People Like Show People*. New York: Random House, 1951

———— *Stagestruck, the Romance of Alfred Lunt and Lynn Fontanne*. New York: Harcourt Brace & World, 1964

American Society of Composers, Authors, and Publishers (ASCAP). *Forty Years of Show Tunes; Forty Years of Hit Tunes*

Theatre Magazine, 1920-30

Index

MacArthur, Charles, *188*, *213*, *264*, 265-266, *267*, 278, 280, 283
Macbeth, 50
McClintic, Guthrie, 39, *41*, 44, 205, 283, 292
McComas, Carroll, 49
McCoy, Mary, 313
McCoy, Mildred, 284
McCullough, Paul, 96
McDonald, Gertrude, *178*
MacDonald, Jeanette, 192–193, 256, 286, 313
McEvoy, J. P., 105, *177*, 292
McGlynn, Frank, 21
Macgowan, Kenneth, 108, 240
McGuire, William Anthony, 49, 168, 192, 284
Machinal, 280, *281*
McHugh, Frank, 240, 313
McHugh, Jimmy, 284
McIntyre, Frank, 313
Mack, Willard, 216, 278
Mackaill, Dorothy, 81
McKay, Constance, 212
Mackay, Ellin, 158, 159
McMahon, Aline, 105, 193, 255
McMein, Neysa, 278
MacRae, Gordon, 283
Madcap, The, 286
Madison, Martha, 309
Maeterlinck, Maurice, 62
Maggie the Magnificent, 309
Magnolia Lady, 138
Major Barbara, 283
Make It Snappy, 74
Malvaloc, 71
Mama's Affair, 21
Mamoulian, Rouben, 295
Mandel, Frank, 192
Maney, Richard, 260, 266
Manhattan Mary, 230, 241
Mankiewicz, Joseph, 255
Manners, Diana, 127
Manners, J. Hartley, 21
Man of Destiny, 192
Man or Devil, 192
Mansfield, Martha, 84
Mantle, Burns, 21, 49, 71, 99, 127, 170, 191, 207, 242, 280, 291, 292, 306
Manville, Tommy, 84
Man with a Load of Mischief, 192
Man with Red Hair, A, 284
March, Fredric, 155, 192, 212, 229, 231, 295, *303*
Marcin, Max, 284
Marco Millions, 226, 231
Marenga, Ilse, 138
Margules, Annette, *131*
Marie Antoinette, 71
Marinoff, Fania, 99
Marion, George, 49
Marlowe, Julia, 49
Marquis, Don, 71
Marquise, The, 255
Marsh, Howard, 138, 256
Marshall, Herbert, 191
Martinelli, Giovanni, 238
Mary Rose, 49
Mary the 3d, 99
Marx, Groucho, 105, *181*
Marx, Harpo, *245*
Marx Brothers, 138, 169–170, *180*, 286
Mason, Ann, *72*

Mason, Reginald, 99, 216, 223
Master Builder, The, 309
Matthews, A. E., 105, 170, 216, *294*, 309
Matthews, Jessie, 116, 313
Maude, Cyril, 105, 191
Maugham, Somerset, 49, 71, 148, 207, 283
Maxwell, Perriton, *8*
Maya, 255
Mayer, Edwin Justus, 117, 127, *131*, 292
Mayhew, Kate, 207
Mayhew, Stella, 256
Meek, Donald, 216, 309
Meet the Prince, 306
Meet the Wife, 105
Mei Lan-Fang, 309
Meisner, Sanford, 191
Meller, Raquel, 217
Mendel, Inc., 309
Menken, Helen, 60, *61*, 232, *233*
Mercenary Mary, 193
Merchant of Venice, The, 71, *211*, 280
Merivale, Philip, 99, 242
Merman, Ethel, 162
Merrill, Beth, 105, *120*
Merry-Go-Round, 256
Merry Wives of Windsor, 280
Merton of the Movies, 71, *129*
Metzger, Charles Edward, 110
Michael and Mary, 306
Middleton, George, 5, 21
Midnight Frolics, 93
Midsummer Night's Dream, A, 145, 242
Mikado, The, 255
Miles, Lotta, 180
Millay, Edna St. Vincent, 63
Miller, Alice Duer, 49
Miller, Gilbert, 151, 283, 286
Miller, Henry, 21, *22*, 71, 99, 216
Miller, Marilyn, *6*, 24, 76, 85, *86*, 135, 154, 159, 161, 192, 230, 268, *269*, 284, 291, 295
Miller, Rachel Burton, 21
Miller and Lyles, 105
Milne, A. A., 44, 49, 63, 71, 306
Milton, Robert, 49
Mima, 285, 306
Mimic World, The, 50
Mind the Paint Girl, 145
Minick, 127
Miracle, The, 127, *132*
Mirrors, 283
Miss Lulu Bett, 49, 279
Mrs. Partridge Presents, 191
Mr. Pim Passes By, 49, 63, 67, 226
Mr. Pitt, 110
Mitchell, Grant, 105, *252*
Mitchell, Millard, 283
Mitchell, Thomas, 207, 280
Moeller, Philip, 63, 292
Moissi, Alexander, 242
Molnar, Ferenc, 49, 63, 99, 207
Monroe, Lucy, 286
Monterey, Carlotta, *215*
Montgomery, Douglass, 255, 283
Montgomery, Robert, 192, 284
Month in the Country, A, *102*
Moon Is a Gong, The, 216
Moore, Dennie, 283
Moore, Grace, 50, *73*, 96, 138
Moore, Victor, 169, 256, 284, 313

Moran and Mack, 88, 97, 138
Morehouse, Ward, 149, 283
Morgan, Frank, 60, 217, 284
Morgan, Helen, 81, *104*, 159, 256, *271*, 295, 313
Morley, Christopher, 295
Morris, Chester, 216, 284
Morris, Mary, *109*
Morris, McKay, 202
Mortals, 192
Moscow Art Theatre, 71, 58, 99
Mourning Becomes Electra, *289*
Mundin, Herbert, 116
Muni, Paul, 216, 255, *300*
Munro, C. K., 216
Munson, Ona, 241, 284
Murder on the Second Floor, 309
Murray, J. Harold, 24
Murray, Mae, 10, 81
Music Box Revue, *14*, 50, *73*, 74, 88, 96, 105, 138, 157, 159
Music Master, The, 238
My Lady Friends, 21
My Man, 291
My Maryland, 167, 256
My Princess, 256
Myrtil, Odette, 217

Nadzo, Guido, 309
Naldi, Nita, 21, 81
Nash, Mary, 71
Nathan, George Jean, 16, *45*, *139*
National Anthem, The, 71
Nazimova, Alla, *102*, 220, 280
Ned McCobb's Daughter, 212, 223, 230
Newberry, Barbara, 256, 313
New Moon, 167
Nice People, 49
Nichols, Anne, 68, *69*, 192
Nichols, Robert, 280
Nicholson, Kenyon, 242
Nic-Nax of 1926, 217
Night Boat, The, 24
Nightcap, The, 49
Night Duel, 212
Night Watch, 148
Nirvana, 216
Nissen, Greta, *133*
No, No, Nanette, 162, 192, 256, 274, 279
Noose, The, *214*, 216, 278
Not So Long Ago, 21
Now-a-Days, 309
Nugent, J. C. and Elliott, 71, 191

Oakie, Jack, 193
Oakland, Vivienne, *27*
O'Brien, Pat, 71, 212
O'Brien-Moore, Erin, 306, *307*
O'Casey, Sean, 207
O'Connell, Hugh, 207, 242, 283
Of Thee I Sing, 167–169
Oh Boy, 159
Oh, Kay, 161, 168, 270, 272
Oh, Please!, 162, 217
Oklahoma, 162, 229
Old English, 135
Old Soak, The, 71
Oliver, Edna May, 71, 99, 191, 256
Olivier, Laurence, 309
Olsen, George, 256
Once in a Lifetime, 295

About the Author

ALLEN CHURCHILL has been associated with magazines, books and the theatre all his life. Born in New York, he was managing editor of *Stage* and *Theatre Arts*. During World War II he was a writer on the staff of *Yank: The Army Weekly* and since then has devoted full time to writing, contributing to nearly every important magazine, including *Playboy* and *Esquire*. He is also the author of fifteen books, among them *The Improper Bohemians*, *The Literary Decade*, *The Roosevelts*, and *Remember When*.